1927
and the Rise of
Modern America

CultureAmerica

Erika Doss
Philip J. Deloria
Series Editors

Karal Ann Marling
Editor Emerita

1927

and the Rise of Modern America

CHARLES J. SHINDO

UNIVERSITY PRESS OF KANSAS

Published by the
University Press of
Kansas (Lawrence,
Kansas 66045), which
was organized by the
Kansas Board of Regents
and is operated and
funded by Emporia
State University, Fort
Hays State University,
Kansas State University,
Pittsburg State
University, the
University of Kansas,
and Wichita State
University

© 2010 by the University Press of Kansas

Library of Congress Cataloging-in-Publication Data

Shindo, Charles J.
1927 and the rise of modern America / Charles J. Shindo.
p. cm. — (CultureAmerica)
Includes bibliographical references and index.
ISBN 978-0-7006-1715-9 (cloth : alk. paper)
ISBN 978-0-7006-2113-2 (pbk. : alk. paper)
1. United States—History—1919–1933. 2. United States—
Social conditions—1918–1932. 3. United States—Social life
and customs—1918–1945. 4. Popular culture—United
States—History—20th century. I. Title.
E791.S55 2010
973.91—dc22
2009052269

British Library Cataloguing-in-Publication Data is available.

Printed in the United States of America

10 9 8 7 6 5 4 3 2 1

The paper used in this publication is recycled and contains
30 percent postconsumer waste. It is acid free and meets the
minimum requirements of the American National Standard
for Permanence of Paper for Printed Library Materials
Z39.48-1992.

TO THE MEMORY OF MAY SHINDO,

1927–2007,

AND

TO MICHAEL

The America that Columbus discovered was to our ancestors geographically a new world. Today, as a result of the revolutionary changes brought about by modern methods of production, it has again become a new world, and furthermore we have still to rediscover it.

—André Siegfried, *America Comes of Age: A French Analysis* (1927)

Contents

Acknowledgments

In conceiving, researching, and writing this project, I have benefited from the support, advice, encouragement, and friendship of numerous institutions and individuals, without whom this work would not have been possible. Financial support for this project was provided by two sabbaticals from Louisiana State University (LSU), summer stipends from the Council on Research, a research semester from the College of Arts and Sciences, a Manship Summer Research Fellowship, and travel grants from the Office of Sponsored Programs and the College of Arts and Sciences.

The staff at the Getty Research Institute at the Getty Center in Los Angeles provided research support, as did research assistants Joshua Lubin, Kristi Wallace, and Bruce Arnold, who each provided valuable research and comments on drafts. Bruce, along with Michael Higgins, provided many hours of assistance searching and collecting photographs. Kurt Kemper, Court Carney, Matt Reonas, and Jamie Saucier all provided helpful comments and suggestions on an early first draft, and I greatly appreciate the time and effort they put into their critiques. Paul Boyer, Lewis Erenberg, and Erika Doss each provided insightful suggestions and comments that have greatly enhanced this work. The participants in LSU's Works in Progress seminar, at the 2008 Australia and New Zealand American Studies Association Conference, and the 2009 British Association for American Studies Conference all provided helpful suggestions and new avenues of thought for me to explore, and for that I thank them.

The University Press of Kansas has been patient beyond expectations and supportive of every step of the process. Everyone with whom I have had contact has been helpful and enthusiastic, from director Fred Woodward on down. In particular, editors Nancy Scott Jackson, Kalyani Fernando, Ranjit Arab, and Mike Briggs have provided an abundance of enthusiasm and sound advice along with their expertise in publishing. Copyeditor Kathy Delfosse provided suggestions that significantly improved the work, and Jennifer Dropkin and

Susan Schott deftly managed the production and marketing of the book. I owe a deep debt of gratitude to all at the Press.

Throughout this project I have enjoyed the support of many colleagues, past and present, who have added insights, tidbits of information, and anything they found related to 1927 and listened to my endless ramblings about the events of the year. Maribel Dietz, Jordan Kellman, Christine Kooi, John Rodrigue, Tiwanna Simpson, and Charles Royster are but a few of the most helpful. The person most significant to the development and completion of this project has been Ian Gordon, who, as a sounding board for ideas, a source of comments on drafts, a supplier of historiography, career builder, colleague, and friend, has provided more inspiration than I deserve.

Outside of the academic realm, I have numerous people to thank who have kept me from living in the past by enjoying and appreciating the present. Longtime friends Joan Lum, Jeanette Iriarte, Doug Bieber, and their families have kept me smiling for the last thirty years. Though far away and seldom seen, Rex Palmer has been a good friend and conversant. My father, George Shindo; my aunt and uncle, Hazel and Kokki Shindo; my sisters Kathryn Nuss, Carolyn Wills, and Evelyn Okamoto; and my brother Robert Shindo, along with their families, have provided love and support for my entire life. Unfortunately, my mother, May Shindo, has not lived to see this project completed, and it is in her memory that I present this work. For over a decade, Michael Fontenot, as my partner, love, and friend, has provided me with a home, a family, and a sense of peace, and it is to him that this book is dedicated.

Charles A. Lindbergh. (Courtesy of the Library of Congress)

Parade procession for Charles Lindbergh in New York City.
(© Bettmann/Corbis)

The Search for Modern America

THE MEANINGS OF LINDBERGH: *The response to Charles Lindbergh's solo flight from New York to Paris illustrates the ambiguity Americans felt about their nation. As an individual, Lindbergh represented the best nineteenth-century Victorian values of self-sufficiency, courage, and determination, while his achievement represented the pinnacle of modern, cooperative, industrial society. His popularity rested on his ability to represent conflicting visions of America simultaneously. Even though Lindbergh was seen as an extraordinary individual, his achievement brought unity to a diverse America. He stood for the individual as well as for society as a whole.*

In the 1920s Americans faced a perplexing world. While many Americans still believed in the Victorian values of modesty, hard work, and respect for tradition, status, and place, others defiantly broke from convention in their work and personal lives and in their actions and words. Most Americans searched for a compromise between the world they knew and the world they would come to know, not yet ready to fully disengage from the past or to fully embrace the future. While this is true of every historical period, the difference between past and future in 1920s America seems particularly acute, especially for those who lived through it. People sought to reconcile their traditions and values with changes in society, the economy, politics, technology, and culture. This search did not always end successfully. Indeed, although the search to understand one's time never really ends, in most periods there is a chance of finding a comfortable middle ground between past and future. But between the end of the Great War and the start of the Great Depression, Americans found it hard to find an accommodation between tradition and change. No single event, such as a war or depression, focused the nation's attention and presented definitive options for the future (winning the war, ending the depression). As a result, people individually and in small groups sought their own middle ground, their own vision of what America should be, often dependent on what they assumed America had been. They searched for answers in technology, in social justice, in feminism, in migration, in sensationalism, and in such leisure activities as collegiate and professional sports, motion pictures, jazz music, and radio. What they found was modern America, a country not completely new, but one with a very different appearance, sound, and feel.

Some events transcended the differences between past and present and as a result became widely celebrated by all Americans. One single act, flying nonstop from New York to Paris, made Charles Lindbergh the most celebrated man in the country, and indeed, the world. In his single-engine plane the *Spirit of St. Louis,* he traversed the Atlantic Ocean in thirty-three and a half hours, landing at Le Bourget airfield outside Paris on May 21, 1927. Others had attempted or were in the process of attempting the flight. Such well-known aviators as Commander Richard E. Byrd, who had earlier made headlines flying over the North Pole, assembled and trained crews in large multiengine planes in preparation for the crossing. Flight-endurance record-holder Clarence Chamberlin, American Legion–supported Commander Noel Davis, and Great War flying ace René Fonck from France, as well as Byrd, all encountered difficulties in their attempts. Both Byrd's and Chamberlin's teams experienced accidents during test flights and training; Davis and copilot Stanton Wooster were both killed during their final test flight. Two members of Fonck's crew also perished as the tri-engine biplane carrying them crashed and exploded taking off for France from Roosevelt Field in New York. Two other French pilots, Charles Nungesser and François Coli, successfully departed Le Bourget on May 8, 1927, but were never seen again after flying past the French coast out over the Atlantic. Six aviators had died in the attempt to win a $25,000 prize established in 1919 by French-American hotel owner Raymond Orteig for the first nonstop flight between Paris and New York.

Each participant in the race for the Orteig Prize was a veteran flyer and was financially supported by wealthy organizations and airplane manufacturers, except for Lindbergh. Lindbergh was the only contestant to use a single-engine plane, and the only one to forgo both the use of radio communications and a copilot to share flying time during the day-and-a-half-long flight. Lindbergh was also an unknown, not just to the public but to many in the aviation establishment. Younger than the rest of the field, Lindbergh had not flown in the Great War, nor had he established any records or pioneering feats; he was, in fact, a working pilot delivering air mail. His plane, the *Spirit of St. Louis* (named in honor of the group of St. Louis businessmen who backed Lindbergh), was made by Ryan Aircraft, a relatively unknown manufacturer in San Diego, and consisted almost exclusively of a cockpit surrounded by fuel tanks with an engine in front. Because of the need for fuel and the demands of aerodynamics, a tank was placed directly in front of the cockpit, obscuring any forward vision. Lindbergh could not sleep, nor could he contact anyone during his flight. That Lindbergh accomplished the flight is remarkable, especially given the way he accomplished it.

When Lindbergh landed at Le Bourget, he encountered a mob of thousands gathered to witness his historic achievement. Completely underestimating the impact of his undertaking, he flew past the field, which was lit with automobile headlights, since he had expected to see a darkened airfield unaware of his arrival. He carried on his person letters of introduction to guard against French authorities' mistaking him for an antagonist. Indeed, Lindbergh assumed that the French public and administration would be indifferent or even hostile to him for accomplishing a task that had claimed the lives of two of their countrymen. He appeared before the public not as a brash, aggressive American full of bravado, arrogance, and superiority but, rather, as a humble, innocent young man whose naïveté was in part responsible for his success. His diffidence and humility endeared Lindbergh to the French and to the public worldwide, but it was especially important to Lindbergh's own countrymen, who saw in him the best of the American past alongside the best of the American future.

"It is a long flight from New York to Paris," wrote John W. Ward in his seminal 1958 essay "The Meaning of Lindbergh's Flight"; "it is a still longer flight from the fact of Lindbergh's achievement to the burden imposed upon it by the imagination of his time. But it is in that further flight that lies the full meaning of Lindbergh."[1] Ward explored the ambiguity, mainly unnoticed at the time, with which Americans celebrated Lindbergh's flight. Accounts in newspapers, in magazines, and on newsreels, not to mention in poetry, drama, and song, primarily emphasized the singular nature of the Atlantic crossing. These accounts compared Lindbergh to heroes of the past, such as Christopher Columbus and the pioneer settlers of the American West. In many ways, Lindbergh represented for Americans those traits that they treasured as being historically and characteristically American: individuality, courage, and self-sufficiency, all traits associated with the past. But included in these celebrations of the American past were impressive visions of the future hinted at in Lindbergh's success. The potential of air travel, the first major advance in overseas mobility since the steamship and a significant advance over train and automobile travel, sparked the interest of the public and gave a boost to a developing airline industry. But the flight represented more than just potential; it was the culmination of American industry, engineering, and financial investment. Only a highly organized and industrialized society could produce a plane capable of such a feat. Not only the research, both theoretical and practical, but also the way the plane was built and the flight was funded and coordinated all illustrated to Americans and the world the success of the American economy and society. Lindbergh was able to draw on the vision of businessmen who saw his attempt as a way to put St. Louis on the map as an aviation center (both industrially and geographically) for the country, and on the knowledge of engineers and engine mechanics, aircraft designers, flight instructors, and meteorologists. News of the flight spread across the nation and the world via the medium of the day, the radio. Newspaper accounts and photographs were readily accessible within hours of Lindbergh's landing, and once in Paris, Lindbergh was able to telephone across the Atlantic, via London, to talk to his mother and let her know that all was well. The vast network of individuals involved in completing and reporting this event illustrated the success of American industry, organization, and society. While Lindbergh, as a traditional American hero, was exceptional enough to perform such a feat, his exceptionalism, many believed, was a product of a capitalist and democratic America.

Lindbergh, the *Spirit of St. Louis,* and the trans-Atlantic flight were more than a person, a machine, and an event. They were each symbols of the age, as well as important symbols of the past and future. For Americans in 1927, Lindbergh embodied the best American virtues and values, whether individuality, self-reliance, and courage, or cooperation and a belief in progress and technology. Lindbergh could represent each of these values, depending on which part of his story one chose to focus on: the solo flight; the pioneering aspect of being the first to overcome seemingly insurmountable obstacles; the danger involved, as evidenced by earlier failed attempts at the flight; the hundreds of technicians, machinists, engineers, mechanics, pilots, navigators, and so on who played important roles in making Lindbergh's flight possible; or the technology of aerodynamics and navigation that enabled Lindbergh to fly. Lindbergh's flight was the symbolic achievement of the age because it could encompass the conflicting views that Americans held about the world, their nation, and themselves. While Lindbergh's achievement became all things to all people, bringing Americans of all ages, classes, races, and genders together in national celebration, it also highlights the cultural divide between the Protestant work ethic of Victorian America and the therapeutic consumer ethic of modern society. Lindbergh's flight was almost unique in its ability to occupy the comfortable middle ground between past and present. Other events were not so able to unify Americans; rather, they tended to reinforce and even worsen conflicts within society. Many of those events happened in the same year Lindbergh crossed the Atlantic Ocean, 1927.

The events of 1927 illustrate the often awkward ways Americans sought to come to terms with changes in American life, from developments in and increased accessibility to technology, to natural disasters like the Mississippi River flood, to such political and social changes as women's forays into the electorate and African Americans' migration from the rural South to the urban North. Americans also dealt with the development of a mediated culture in the tabloid press, radio, and motion pictures, which in turn created a celebrity culture of not only movie stars, radio personalities, and sports heroes but infamous criminals and other notorious news makers. Those uncomfortable with the changes occurring in American society sought to gain some control over them by incorporating some aspects and rejecting others; those responsible for the changes sought to gain respect and wealth without completely abandoning traditional values. Many Americans found themselves caught in between the two extremes and pulled in both directions. How one reacted to these changes depended on a variety of factors such as age, race and ethnicity, gender, region, occupation, religion, education, and wealth, to name just a few. Americans and American culture were not homogeneous in the 1920s, and the mass appeal enjoyed by such celebrities as Lindbergh, baseball player Babe Ruth, and movie star Clara Bow depended on Americans' ability to interpret those celebrities' achievements according to their own individual values. Not all events and celebrities of 1927 were amenable to conflicting interpretations, and accepting change often meant letting go of the past. How much were Americans willing to give up in order to get the new and modern? There was no single answer for Americans in 1927.

Describing the ways Americans searched for a comfortable middle ground between past and future is not an easy task, since it necessarily relies on an attention to detail and specifics while at the same time requiring discussion of a broad range of topics. Simultaneously keeping a narrow focus and presenting the larger picture is achieved best by looking at many different events of a single year rather than looking at well-known examples from throughout the decade. This narrow focus allows for a deeper analysis of the events, of their meaning and significance, and draws attention to the roles of individuals instead of to larger historical trends, forces, and ideas. While selectively choosing events from throughout the decade would make for a more clearly presented argument about the conflicts, contradictions, and varieties of ideas and events necessary to an understanding of modern America's development, looking at the events of 1927 lets the process of a developing modern America unfold with the same ambiguity and disjuncture that people experienced at the time. An onslaught of events, both positive and negative, overwhelmed Americans in 1927, and they sought to make sense of them much in the same manner as I seek to make sense of the year's events. The focus on a single year allows for a synthesis of historical approaches as political, economic, and social histories illuminate the broader cultural history of the period. Film studies, literary analysis, media studies, sociology, musicology, and cultural theory all help inform this study, emphasizing the description of events, within their context, in order to illustrate their significance in understanding modern American history. Americans in 1927 were particularly focused on cultural issues rather than on specifically political, economic, or foreign policy issues, and therefore the year is ideally suited to describing the development of modern American culture. America did not become modern in 1927; no single year was *the* year

America became modern. The variety of people and events in 1927—from the celebrated, like Lindbergh, Herbert Hoover, and Babe Ruth, to the derided, like convicted and executed murderers Ruth Snyder and Judd Gray; from the disastrous, like the Mississippi River flood and the flawed trial for anarchists Nicola Sacco and Bartolomeo Vanzetti, and the hopeful, like the success of the sound film *The Jazz Singer*—all illustrate the variety of experiences in American life and how Americans tried to make sense of those people and events and to determine what they meant, for better or worse. This is not to say that 1927 is the only year for which this argument could be made, but it is the best year with which to make this argument. While other years may have been better to illuminate an aspect of modern America (immigration reform in 1924, fundamentalism in 1925, or economic instability in 1929), 1927 is the best year to discuss a wider variety of events and ideas. Even though Lindbergh's achievement was the biggest story of the year, it did not influence every other event of the year, as the aftermath of the Great War had dominated the early part of the decade and economic concerns would dominate the final years of the decade.

Earlier studies have also selected 1927 as an important year in the decade, but these works have followed the popular historiographical trend of viewing the 1920s as primarily an age of frivolity and excess. Allen Churchill's *The Year the World Went Mad* (1960) refers to 1927 as the year "the Era of Wonderful Nonsense reached its peak" and focuses each chapter on a big news story from the year, in roughly chronological order and with no analysis of each event. Churchill delights in the extreme and the wacky as he describes divorce and murder trials, Lindbergh's flight, the execution of Sacco and Vanzetti, and the year in sports, without examining the meaning these events held for Americans. Likewise, Gerald Leinwald's *1927: High Tide of the Twenties* (2001) claims that "like a great wine, 1927 was a vintage year," as he focuses on twelve major events of the year, one in each month. Like Churchill, Leinwald refrains from analyzing or explaining the significance of these events beyond labeling something as new, record-breaking, or now obsolete. Both studies fit alongside such broader studies of the 1920s as Frederick Lewis Allen's *Only Yesterday* (1931), the model on which much of 1920s historiography has been based, and Nathan Miller's *New World Coming* (2003), which seeks to build on Allen's narrative and uses the life of F. Scott Fitzgerald as its narrative thread. These works are primarily descriptive and do not seek to explain how these events came to be or what meaning they hold for their readers besides entertainment.[2]

Much closer to my approach are works by such historians as Lynn Dumenil, whose *The Modern Temper* (1995) takes a thematic approach to the decade, arguing that despite the continuities to be found with political, social, economic, and cultural trends from before the Great War, the 1920s still represent a distinctively "modern" age. While I agree with Dumenil, I think the issue is not when the United States became modern but, rather, how the ideas of the modern world came to be accepted, and in part rejected, by various Americans.[3] The focus on a single year allows for a fuller explication of process over description. How Americans dealt with the modern is more telling than when the country became modern. Closer still to my interpretation is Roderick Nash's *The Nervous Generation* (1970), in which he argues that the 1920s were more than the extremes "of resigned cynicism and happy reveling" characterized in such works as Allen's *Only Yesterday* and most 1920s historiography. He describes the post–World War I generation as "nervous," searching for clarity in the changes they were experiencing, but he limits his study to intellectuals and how they expressed their nervousness. Although he does engage popular culture, he does not really view American culture beyond the minds of intellectuals.[4] Paul Carter has also explored the conflicts evident during the decade in his short work *The Twenties in America* (1968), in which he describes these conflicts using three distinct dichotomies, characterized as bohemians versus consumers, Calvin Coolidge versus Ernest Hemingway, and town versus country. In explaining these conflicts, he does suggest that there were not two clearly defined sides to each debate but, rather, multiple shades of gray. In describing the faith many had in progress versus tradition, Carter notes, "the more one probes into attitudes towards progress during the Twenties, the more these attitudes dissolve into ambivalence."[5] It is this ambivalence that I seek to describe and explain. Other short works that have touched on these same ideas in different forms are Lawrence Levine's "Progress and Nostalgia" and Warren Susman's "Culture and Civilization" and "Culture Heroes."[6] All three essays raise the specter of conflict, tension, and ambiguity in the decade; I seek to extend and deepen their work.

Studies looking at a single issue or limiting their scope regionally have also interpreted the Twenties as a transitional period between Victorianism and modernism. Roland Marchand on advertising, Lewis A. Erenberg on New York nightlife, Elaine Tyler May on marriage, Charles L. Ponce de Leon on celebrity, Nathan Irvin Huggins on Harlem, and Lary May on the movie industry are a few of the studies that highlight many of the same ideas about the 1920s that I seek to explicate.[7] Each has provided a necessary aspect to the larger synthesis I present. By looking at the events of a single year, the continuities and conflicts of American society stand out not only because of the events and people themselves, but because of the connections with other events and people as well. This approach allows for an examination of how a wide variety of Americans searched for a comfortable middle ground in modern America. Modern America is not so much a definable historical period as it is a set of ideas and values that emerged to compete with older sets of values (Puritan, Protestant, pioneer, Victorian). And just as Victorian sensibilities in America did not completely replace older Puritan ideas, neither did modern ideas replace Victorian ones; rather, they coexisted, sometimes comfortably, most times not. I use both the phrase "modern America" and the term "modernity" to refer to a combination of industrial modernization (as characterized by a corporate-dominated and consumer-driven economy), urbanization, cultural modernism (as represented by modernist approaches to literature, art, architecture, and music), and the development of a widely accessible popular culture. Each of these factors influenced the others, and none can be understood on its own. Together they brought about the changes that Americans had to deal with, cope with, and understand. The 1920s, and 1927 in particular, illustrate the discomfort that came from the search for understanding. What follows is an attempt to describe and explain the ways various Americans faced their present, based on their understanding of the past and vision of the future.

The goal of understanding how people came to grips with modern America does not lend itself to a chronological approach or to a traditional narrative structure. Instead, I have focused on four separate, but not mutually exclusive, agendas in which Americans engaged: mastery, equality, notoriety, and respectability. In their search for modern America, many people sought mastery over aspects of their lives, whether that meant mastery of industry, as in the case of Henry Ford; the expression of machine-age ideals, as in the case of the precisionist artists; or an understanding of such current events as the Sacco and Vanzetti execution, of the debate over contemporary religion, or of the past sought for by novelists and historians. All in their own ways sought mastery over and comprehension of their world as a way to understand modern America.

Others searched for equality in modern times. Women became the most visible symbol of change during the 1920s, not only in political and economic power but also in appearance and actions. Clara Bow exemplified the "new" woman and was both admired and scorned for it. Theatrical personalities, such as Texas Guinan, and performances, such as the musical *Show Boat*, illustrate the conflicted attitudes many had toward women. Seeking much more basic aspects of equality, African Americans, especially those in the flood-ravaged Mississippi delta, sought equal treatment and a better life. Through organizations such as the National Association for the Advancement of Colored People (NAACP) and the Colored Advisory Commission, created in the wake of mounting criticism of discrimination in the flood-relief efforts, African Americans demanded fair treatment and an end to an economic system that held many in a condition of peonage.

Those less concerned with mastery or equality just wanted to be famous, whether for positive contributions or notorious reasons. Politicians like Herbert Hoover, true-crime figures such as Ruth Snyder and Judd Gray, and even professional and collegiate athletes saw any publicity as a benefit to their careers and lives. Public relations, crime reporting, and sports writing all became industries whose main goals were not to celebrate extraordinary achievement but, rather, to sell a product, be it a politician, newspapers, or footballs.

Those mainly in the newer entertainment professions of motion pictures, jazz music, and radio sought ways for their respective industries to gain respect in a society inundated with leisure pursuits and entertainments but still deeply conflicted about their importance in American culture. Mary Pickford and Douglas Fairbanks epitomized the wholesome Hollywood couple; African American artists and intellectuals capitalized on the popularity of jazz music and black culture to stage the Harlem Renaissance. White entertainers, like Paul Whiteman, sought to legitimize jazz by "elevating" it to the level of classical music, as radio sought to legitimize its role in American society by proclaiming its function as an educational and nationalizing force. Each of these people found ways to find meaning and understanding in the numerous changes occurring around them, and while they did not all succeed in finding success or satisfaction, they all contributed to what we know as modern America and the development of American culture.

Once again, Charles Lindbergh illustrates the way a single event could embody each of these agendas. Lindbergh's flight demonstrated mastery over what many believed was an unobtainable goal. It illustrated the equality—some may say even superiority—of American enterprise and industry, as it made Lindbergh a celebrity both at home and abroad, and the event brought a measure of respectability to aviation, while not necessarily infringing on the traditional values of some Americans or the more modern values of others. The flight celebrated the triumph of both traditional and modern values and emphasized the ambiguity that characterizes modern American culture. But Lindbergh's flight is merely the most famous of events in 1927 that help explain American culture in all of its ambiguity. There are many more.

Charles Sheeler, *Criss-Crossed Conveyors, River Rouge Plant, Ford Motor Company* (1927). (The Metropolitan Museum of Art, Ford Motor Company Collection, Gift of Ford Motor Company and John C. Waddell, 1987 [1987.1100.1]. Copy Photography © The Metropolitan Museum of Art)

Crowd protesting Sacco-Vanzetti verdict. (© Underwood & Underwood/ Corbis)

CHAPTER 1

Seeking Mastery:
The Machine Age and the Idealized Past

MASTERY OVER MACHINE AND MAN: *While the industrial modernization of the United States, represented by Henry Ford's massive River Rouge plant, made possible the consumer culture that characterizes modern America, the loss of individuality brought about by modernization led to the prejudices of the majority sometimes taking precedence over the rights of individuals, as in the flawed trial of executed anarchists Nicola Sacco and Bartolomeo Vanzetti. Ford's success in the automotive industry reflected the overall success of the American economy in the 1920s. The wide availability of consumer goods and higher wages improved most Americans' standard of living, but these gains were made at a cost. Individuality in work as well as in society suffered as labor became mechanized, as at River Rouge, and Americans grew fearful of outsiders and others marked as different, like Sacco and Vanzetti.*

In their attempts to understand the changes occurring around them, Americans sought mastery over their world by controlling, illuminating, utilizing, or limiting the people and things around them. By using new technology and manufacturing practices, Henry Ford and the rest of the automobile industry sought control over both the machines of industry and the consumers buying their products, while advertisers and artists sought to illuminate the ambiguity of the machine age through photography, painting, exhibits, and performance. Even religious leaders utilized modern methods of industry and marketing to make religion pertinent to modern man, best represented by the works of advertising executive and religious writer Bruce Barton. But while some celebrated and adapted modern methods to their work and lives, others sought to limit change or at least to alter the course of modernity by illustrating the dangers of believing in limitless progress. The outcry of support for convicted and executed anarchists Nicola Sacco and Bartolomeo Vanzetti illustrates the divide between those who viewed changes in the demographic makeup of the nation as a benefit for a thriving democracy and those who saw it as a threat. Sinclair Lewis, who supported Sacco and Vanzetti, also warned of religion's commodification in *Elmer Gantry,* while Willa Cather indirectly critiqued modern religion by presenting an idealized past in *Death*

Comes for the Archbishop. Likewise, writers of history and historical fiction, like Charles and Mary Beard and Glenway Wescott, suggested that progress is not inevitable and that not all change is for the better. Each of these people sought mastery over social change by in some way controlling that change through actions and ideas. Their attempts, the conflicts they created, and their successes and failures help explain how modern America developed.

THE MACHINE AS BUSINESS

Just as many Americans celebrated Charles Lindbergh, many also saw Henry Ford as a hero, and for as many different reasons. Yet Ford was more a symbol of modernity and success—in a word, of progress—than he was a role model. Ford backed his celebrity with technological, economic, and cultural substance; the advances he brought to the automobile industry also helped transform American industry in general. Ford's role in the automobile industry's transformation of American life is also significant, but in terms of lasting practical contributions, Ford's industrial philosophy—or Fordism, as it was called—was short-lived. His legacy lies primarily in the imagery of modernity he presented and popularized for the American public.

Ford's achievements in automobile manufacturing—standardized and interchangeable parts, the assembly line, well-paid unskilled labor, rapid production, independence from contractors and other manufacturers, and the production of a single product—all resulted in the affordable Model T, the most successful single car model in history, with over 15 million manufactured. An early Ford production engineer discussed the fact that the automobile industry could be broken down into three distinct endeavors: "the art of buying materials, the art of production, and the art of selling."[1] For years, Ford had perfected the first two endeavors but had neglected the third. As Ford increased production through technological and managerial changes, he paid little attention to advertising, marketing, and sales. Indeed, the Ford Motor Company did not run a promotional campaign for the Model T, but publicity and word-of-mouth sufficed to make it the best-selling automobile, accounting for half of all cars in the world in 1927. Ford spent virtually nothing on advertising the Model T to consumers, since demand for the automobile usually outpaced production, at least until the mid-1920s. Ford considered marketing studies unnecessary because he intended to make a car for everyone, not for a specific market. From 1917 to 1923, the Ford Motor Company had no advertising department at all, relying on individual dealers to promote the product. Customers were made aware of the Model T primarily through news stories about Henry Ford and "the Ford car," as the Model T was widely known, and through an extensive network of Ford dealers.[2] As a result, Model Ts were more readily available than other makes of car, not only in terms of price and production but geographically as well. This availability, coupled with the simplicity of the design, made Ford cars easier to maintain: either the individual owner could do the maintenance, or a nearby dealer or service representative could. Adding to the popularity of the Model T was the tremendous amount of publicity garnered by the vehicle (it was the first to traverse the Grand Canyon in Arizona, the winner of numerous road and country races, and so on), the Ford Motor Company, and Henry Ford himself.

Sales for the Model T declined steadily in 1926. Ford's belief in a universal automobile for the masses had placed the Ford Motor Company at the top of the automobile industry, accounting for more than half of all U.S. auto sales in the early 1920s at roughly 1 million sales per year. But sticking to this belief threatened to lead the company into bankruptcy by 1927. Sales of the Model T made up less than a third of U.S. auto sales in 1926, a drop caused by a number of factors, including market saturation, cost, and Ford's unwillingness to provide credit to consumers. In 1926, 19 million out of 23.4 million U.S. families owned automobiles, making car ownership no longer a novelty and creating a pool of second- and third-time car buyers looking for more accessories and style than the Model T offered. Basic transportation was no longer enough for most consumers. The most desired models were enclosed sedans. Ford's basic and most affordable Model T was an open touring car; his enclosed sedans were priced closer to the competition's and therefore were not a significant bargain. In addition, Ford felt that extending credit was immoral, whereas his competitors supplied easy credit to their customers. When Ford finally agreed to installment purchases, payments needed to be completed before delivery of the automobile. The reliability of the Model T reinforced its own sales decline because its primary market, first-time car buyers, could find many less expensive used Model Ts for sale, in many cases by Ford's competitors, who allowed consumers to trade in their Model Ts on new Chevrolets, Buicks, Pontiacs, and Cadillacs.[3] For all these reasons, Ford's plan of flooding the world with Model Ts fell short of its goal.

Competition, primarily from General Motors and most specifically from its Chevrolet division, pointed out the weaknesses in Ford's methods. Fordism, the idea of mass production of a single product for a mass market, died with the Model T. A 1927 promotional film celebrating the fifteen-millionth Model T as it toured the nation remained unused because the car was no longer in production by the time the film was made. In May 1927 Ford stopped production of the Model T and closed down his factories to retool for a new model. With no advanced plan for such a transition, Ford completely shut down manufacturing while his engineers developed the Model A, and at the same time figured out how to redesign the factory to build it. The retooling process included the replacement of around 15,000 machine tools, the rebuilding of 25,000 others, and the reconfiguring of $5 million in dies and fixtures. In total, the process cost Ford $100 million and lost him market share; in addition, the *New York World* estimated that 500,000 contractors, dealers, and workers suffered financial hardship, and in some cases ruin. Layoffs at Ford's Detroit plants accounted for 45 percent of the city's relief recipients in 1927.[4]

In the process of retooling, Ford completed the development of a single, vertically integrated plant at his River Rouge production facility. The Rouge plant had been the processing site of raw materials from Ford-owned mines, forests, and rubber plantations and the manufacturing locale of automobile parts and components. The final assembly of the Model T took place at the Highland Park assembly plant. Beginning with the Model A, Ford moved the assembly line to River Rouge and created a self-contained manufacturing enterprise in which Ford controlled everything from the raw materials, through processing and manufacturing, to final assembly. The Rouge plant consisted of 23 main buildings, 70 minor buildings and structures, almost 100 miles of railroad tracks, 53,000 machines, docks and slips along the river, and 75,000 employees.[5] The River Rouge plant was a culmination of the ideas of Ford, a visible representation of Fordism.

In the midst of all this turmoil, Ford kept the plans for the Model A concealed from the public. Speculation increased the market for the new model, and by its debut, half a million customers had paid down payments on a car they had never seen. When the Model A was finally unveiled on December 2, 1927, approximately 100,000 curious customers crowded Ford's Detroit showroom. Police had to contain crowds in Cleveland, and in New York the buildup of interested people began at three o'clock in the morning and grew to such great size that Madison Square Garden was enlisted to serve as a temporary showroom. In less than two full days, over 10 million Americans had viewed the Model A, and by the close of a week, 25 million people, or just under 20 percent of the U.S. population, had visited a Ford showroom for a glimpse of the Model A. Many car buyers, knowing Ford would be creating a new model, had postponed their purchases until the Model A's debut, as witnessed by the drop in overall automobile sales in 1927 by nearly 1 million cars. But during Ford's absence from the market (full production at Ford's plants was severely constricted or nonexistent for more than a year), Chevrolet outsold Ford, and for the first time since the introduction of the Model T, Ford did not dominate the automobile industry.[6]

Chevrolet had taken many of the ideas of Fordism (many top executives in competing automobile companies had once been Ford employees and made up a group so large that Keith Sward dubbed them the "Ford Alumni Association") and adapted them to a changing market driven by consumption, not production.[7] In realizing the power of the consumer to choose style over substance, Chevrolet sought to produce an inexpensive car that did not look cheap. As the president and general manager of the Chevrolet division of General Motors, William Knudsen, put it, Chevrolet sought to "modernize its [product's] appearance so as to remove the inevitable stigma which rests on low priced articles that show it."[8] Knudsen, a former Ford employee, helped Chevrolet increase its production by implementing Ford-style organization in Chevy factories, but he developed the use of standardized machines (not single-purpose machines) to create the parts necessary for assembly, which allowed for yearly changes in the manufacturing of various parts, especially body parts. Chevrolet was able to change its automobiles without having to close down its factories and replace and retool its machines. In 1927, Chevrolet began the planning of a six-cylinder production automobile, first by enlarging the bodies of existing models to accept a larger engine (1928 models) and then by adding the larger engine (1929 models). The transition from producing four-cylinder to six-cylinder automobiles was so well thought out that it took only six weeks to accomplish and was accompanied by an increase in production, as opposed to Ford's dramatic shutdown of production. When Ford finally did unveil the Model A, only a few hundred cars existed, many fewer than one for each Ford showroom in the United States.

Not only did Chevrolet integrate changing styles into its production process, but it also differed from Ford in purchasing and contracting practices and in centralization. While Ford was building his ultimate industrial city at River Rouge, Chevrolet was decentralizing the production process, in part by relying on other General Motors divisions for parts, but also by spreading out the manufacturing of parts to four different plants, each specializing in a specific set of components (in Flint, Bay City, and Detroit, Michigan, and in Toledo, Ohio), and the assembly of automobiles to seven different assembly plants strategically located across the country (from Tarrytown, New York, to Oakland, California). This enabled Chevrolet to produce its products closer to where they would be sold and to be independent of any single labor pool. This decentralized model of production, not Ford's River Rouge model, emerged as the industry standard.

For Chevrolet, the look of its cars was as important, if not more important, than their mechanical attributes. Ford had built its reputation on the idea that the Model T was a practical item, a necessity, not a luxury, and that therefore its appearance did not matter. The "black only" color policy of the Ford Motor Company was not an initial feature of the Model T, nor was black the only color choice in the mid-1920s, but the idea that "any customer can have any car painted any color so long as it is black"[9] represented to the public the Ford philosophy of practicality over luxury and function over form. General Motors, on the other hand, sought to appeal to consumer desires by hiring designer Harley Earl in 1927. Earl had made his reputation as a custom designer of automobile bodies for the style-conscious stars of the motion picture industry, and he headed General Motors' newly created Art and Color department.[10]

THE MACHINE AS ART

To increase even further the interest in the Model A, Ford spent around $1.3 million for five days of intensive advertising.[11] Ford had only reentered the advertising field in 1923 when sales of the Model T had reached its peak of 57 percent of the automobile market. This return to advertising was mainly due to Ford's acquisition of Lincoln Motors and Ford's resulting attempt to integrate the more luxurious Lincolns with the more practical Fords in a unified and nationally coordinated campaign. Such marketing also meant targeting segments of the mass market that were most resistant to the pragmatic claims for the Model T, women. Ford also began to develop consciously its corporate image, aiming to "familiarize the public with the Ford industry, its vast facilities for the manufacture of products on a production basis and to point out that by owning and controlling its own sources of raw materials greater value can be passed on to the consumer."[12] Ford's production methods, or Fordism, became a source of advertising itself, since the efficiency and practicality of the production process was ideally represented in the product, the practical Model T.

By 1927, Ford employed the services of the N. W. Ayer advertising agency of Philadelphia to help coordinate this national campaign. Not only did the campaign provide the public with glimpses of the Model A, along with explaining its general concept, its affordability, and its mechanical innovations, but it also continued the practice of associating the products and processes of the Ford Motor Company with Henry Ford himself. It was with the campaign for the Model A that "the company, creator of modern 'cities of industry' at Highland Park and the Rouge, generator of new imagery of modernity almost as a byproduct, began to respond consistently to the new demands of the image."[13] Part of this response to the "demands of the image" was the commissioning of photographer/painter Charles Sheeler as an indirect part of Ford advertising. N. W. Ayer's art director, Vaughn Flannery, often enlisted Sheeler to photograph products for other agency clients, such as Koehler plumbing fixtures and Canada Dry beverages. Sheeler also produced studio portraits for *Vogue* and *Vanity Fair,* in addition to his painting. Sheeler believed that objects, both human and man-made, should be seen for their intrinsic beauty and that, on that criterion, there was no real difference between painting and photography for art's sake or for commercial purposes. Flannery believed that photographs by Sheeler, who was also known in the art world, would result in an artistic rendering of Ford's industrialism, thus making the Ford Motor Company appear more "upscale," aesthetic, and modern. The photographs would not be used in mass-market ads but, rather, would be distributed to more elite publications, such as *Vanity Fair.* These photographs would be not simply documentation or advertisement or art but, rather, a combination of the three. Flannery, like Sheeler, did not categorize photographs into exclusive functions, but in following the lead of the Bauhaus movement, both Flannery and Sheeler sought to combine the applied and fine arts.[14]

Sheeler spent six weeks at Ford's River Rouge plant (during the fall of 1927, when the factory was closed down for the retooling for the Model A), and his photographs not only helped alter the image of the Ford Motor Company but also helped usher in a new image of American modernity.[15] Sheeler believed that artists should attempt to express the concerns of the day, and "since industry predominately concerns the greatest numbers, finding an expression for it concerns the artist."[16] Sheeler admired the accomplishments of Henry Ford, especially as they were embodied in the River Rouge plant. "Even having seen it," Sheeler wrote to his friend Walter Arnesberg, "one doesn't believe it possible that one man could be capable of realizing such a conception."[17] Indeed, it was the realized conception that Sheeler sought to portray in his photographs and in the paintings he created from them. Sheeler's photographs do not document the processes of the River Rouge plant, nor do they portray the workings of the men or machines there; what they do illustrate is the beauty of the created forms, and not the forms of the product (auto bodies, chassis, wheels, and so on), but the forms of the machines and buildings created to make the product (conveyors, smokestacks, cranes, and the like). Sheeler's *Criss-Crossed Conveyors, River Rouge Plant, Ford Motor*

Company (1927) presents two covered conveyor lines crossing in front of smokestacks and water towers. Not a single human figure is visible, nor is there any sense of activity or motion. The scene is completely static. Unlike much industrial photography, especially for advertising, which focuses on the product within the context of its creation, Sheeler emphasized the means of production over the product itself. These means are treated, in his work, as if they were the product, a product that is not only aesthetically pleasing to the eye but functionally pleasing to the intellect as well because of the complexity of its engineering, construction, and function.

In most of the more than forty photographs taken at the plant, Sheeler excluded the human element, most significantly the workers who worked the machines, in favor of showing the machinery itself. This exclusion of the worker presents the idea that the human force behind the machine is not the man who worked at it but the man who created it, who conceptualized it, who built it, and in certain respects, who financed it. The photographs present the idea of the industrialist as artist, or at least artisan, instead of the idea of technology as replacement for the skilled craftsmen. The machine is the new craft, and the engineers and industrialists are the new craftsmen; therefore, technology is not replacing craftsmanship but, rather, creating new forms of it. It is in this presentation that the ambiguities of Henry Ford start to make sense. Ford did not see himself as destroying the nineteenth-century way of life, that of the small farmer, small businessman, and artisan. Rather, Henry Ford believed he was remaking American society by imbuing the mechanistic technology of the twentieth century with the values of the nineteenth century. Ford's desire to give modern technology the stamp of artisanal craftsmanship reinforced his ideas about his workforce and the values they should maintain. He did not view his workers as laborers or consumers but, rather, as yeoman industrialists who should retain the nineteenth-century values of self-sufficiency and gentility.

This concern for craftsmanship and form is also present in Sheeler's earlier paintings of Bucks County, Pennsylvania, barns and New York City skyscrapers, as well as in the work of other painters and photographers who collectively became known as the precisionists. While not a coherently definable artistic movement, precisionists (also known as new classicists, cubist-realists, or immaculates) shared certain traits in their works, mainly precision, objectivity, and simplification in form, along with a preference for machine-age content. They were often viewed as an American variant of an international trend among artists "during and just after the First World War, in which they sought a more orderly and rational art symbolized by, and derived from, machine technology."[18] In this sense, precisionism can be linked to the Dutch De Stijl, French purism, Russian constructivism, and German Bauhaus and Neue Sachlichkeit movements, in that they all view technology, in the words of Reyner Banham, as "the agent of collective discipline and an order that drew nearer to the canons of Classical aesthetics."[19] This classical influence can be seen in the architectonic placement of objects in the works of the precisionists. Cubism also influenced these artists in its attempt to reduce objects to their most basic forms, but the precisionists maintained a greater degree of realism in their representations than did pure cubists, synthesizing French cubism with American realism. In technique, these artists sought to create forms more graphic (or even photographic) than artistic, and therefore they painted smooth surfaces mainly devoid of harsh brushstrokes and variations in paint thickness. It is this immaculate style and precision of form and technique that best characterizes this group of painters.

In addition to Sheeler, painter/photographer Morton Schamberg; painters Charles Demuth, Elsie Driggs, Louis Lozowick, Georgia O'Keeffe, and Joseph Stella; and photographers Alfred Stieglitz and Paul Strand were among the artists working in the precisionist style. Even though industrial subjects (factories, bridges, skyscrapers, machines) dominated the work of these artists, their concern for form and craftsmanship can be seen in works featuring rural structures, as in Sheeler's paintings and photographs of rural Pennsylvanian barns, O'Keeffe's studies of Lake George houses, and Peter Blume's New England winterscapes (*Winter, New Hampshire,* 1927), and even organic forms, such as O'Keeffe's paintings of flowers and Strand's and Edward Weston's photographs of rocks and shells (Strand: "Rock, Georgetown, Maine," 1927; Weston: "Shell," 1927). O'Keeffe saw in these flowers not a symbolic idea but, rather, an aesthetic form rendered closely, forcing the viewer to see its structural beauty (*Red Poppies,* 1927). The same idea holds true for the precisionists' paintings of urban scenes, which primarily focused on buildings and bridges (O'Keeffe: *Radiator Building—Night, New York,* 1927; Driggs: *Queensborough Bridge,* 1927; Lozowick's cities series, including *Butte, Oklahoma, Panama,* and *Seattle,* all 1926–1927) and industrial settings (Driggs: *Pittsburgh,* 1927; Demuth: *My Egypt,* 1927). In all of these works, the structure of the object is the subject of the work. Human figures rarely intrude on the scene, and for the most part the contents of the works are represented as static, more sculptural than mechanical. It was the machine that formed the basic unifying idea behind this artistic movement. These works do not simply celebrate the machine and its prominence in American life; they center their attention on seeing the forms of industry as something created by man, and therefore creative. They also share the idea that since the United States excelled in industry, this emphasis on the art of industry was primarily American, as witnessed by the almost exclusive use of American subjects in these works.

In his essay "The Americanization of Art," published in the catalog for the 1927 art show The Machine-Age Exposition, Lozowick proclaimed the necessity of American art's enriching the "meagre cultural heritage" of America by looking to uniquely American sources of inspiration. And since, according to Lozowick, "the history of America is a history of stubborn and ceaseless effort to harness the forces of nature—a constant perfecting of the tools and processes which make the mastery of these forces possible," then American artists should contemplate the "gigantic engineering feats and colossal mechanical construction" of American industry. But in doing so, "the artist cannot, and should not, therefore attempt a literal soulless transcription of the American scene but rather give a penetrating creative interpretation of it, which while including everything relevant to the subject depicted, would exclude everything irrelevant to the plastic possibilities of that subject." In other words, the artist should seek to represent the essence of the object, not necessarily its function or effect. That essence, according to Lozowick, "is towards an industrialization and standardization which require precise adjustment of structure to function [and] which dictate an economic utilization of processes and materials and thereby foster in man a spirit of objectivity excluding all emotional aberration and accustom his vision to shapes and color not paralleled in nature." This objectivity would then reinforce "the dominant trend in America today . . . towards order and organization which find their outward sign and symbol in the rigid geometry of the American city." The final result of this artistic endeavor to "organize line, plane and volume into a well knit design, arrange color and light into a pattern of contrast and harmony and weave organically into every composition an all pervading rhythm and equilibrium" would be art that is both associative and aesthetic, "clear in its intention, convincing in its reality, inevitable in its logic," thereby creating a "potential audience [that] will be practically universal."[20]

Lozowick's proposition clearly describes the work of the precisionists, who, according to Miles Orvell, fulfilled Walt Whitman's calls for a uniquely American artistic expression and formed the center of "the American contribution to international modernism."[21] The Machine-Age Exposition, which featured works by precisionists, along with "actual machines, parts, apparatuses, photographs and drawings of machines, plants, constructions, etc., in juxtaposition with architecture, paintings, drawings, sculpture, constructions, and inventions by the most vital of the modern artists," sought to bridge the divide created by "museums, dealers, and second-rate artists, [who] have frightened the general public out of any frank appreciation of the arts." The solution to this division between art and the public lay in the union of the practical with the artistic, a union between the engineer and the artist. Indeed, the Machine-Age Exposition had as one of its primary goals the celebration of the engineer as an artist. As Jane Heap, editor of the journal *Little Review,* put it in the exhibit catalog for the exposition:

> There is a great new race of men in America: the Engineer. He has created a new mechanical world, he is segregated from other men in other activities. . . . It is inevitable and important to the civilization of today that he make a union with the architect and artist. This affiliation will benefit each in his own domain, it will end the immense waste in each domain and will become a new creative force.

Central to this idea of combining engineering utility and artistic beauty is the machine. The best artists in this vein "do not copy or imitate the Machine, they do not worship the Machine,—they recognize it as one of the realities. In fact, it is the Engineer who has been forced, in his creation, to use most of the forms once used by the artist. . . . The artist must now discover new forms for himself."[22] The exposition, which ran for three days in May 1927, featured works by American artists, including Sheeler, Demuth, and Lozowick, alongside the work of such American architects as Hugh Ferriss, Raymond Hood, and Eliel Saarinen and the works of artists, architects, and engineers from Austria, Belgium, France, Germany, Poland, and Russia. Products from International Harvester Company, International Business Machines, Studebaker Corporation of America, Boston Gear Works, and Edison Lamp Works of General Electric were also included in the exposition.[23] While not earth-shattering, either in the world of art or in popular consciousness, the Machine-Age Exposition does illustrate an attempt, like those made by the precisionists and even by Henry Ford himself, to adapt the industrial technology of the machine age to the values of modern life without creating a radical division from the past. Ford did not see himself as a completely "modern" man but, rather, as someone who used modern means yet embraced traditional values, at least selectively.

In the automobile industry, 1927 was an important year; it illustrates the transition from one manufacturing philosophy, Fordism—or mass production, as it eventually would be called—to a different one, what historian of technology David Hounshell calls "flexible mass production."[24] This shift primarily entailed the ability to incorporate change (annual model changes) into the production process by keeping the production process open to alteration, making it "flexible." This technological change also involved a change in economic thinking, since this added flexibility meant increased production. Ford's achievement was in reducing the cost of production in order to maximize profits, whereas General Motors, and eventually Ford, the rest of the automobile industry, and all of American industry as well, followed the changing economic landscape by adapting to the growing consumer-driven market, focusing not on production but on consumption and on catering to the consumer. This transition from production to consumption is illustrated in the Model A, the ad campaign supporting it, and the influence that the Ford Motor Company had on Americans' images of modernity. The ambiguity with which Americans approached this modernity is seen in declining sales amid public affection for the

Model T, the complex public image of Henry Ford himself, and the uniquely American combination of traditional subjects and values with the modern style of the precisionist painters. This ambiguity is evident in the public celebration of Charles Lindbergh, a man of science and of technology expressing the very best of traditional American values. In attempting to resolve the conflict between tradition and modernity, Ford, Sheeler, and the public at large elevated the professional and the expert into the noble position once held by the yeoman farmer, the shopkeeper, and the craftsman, and in doing so unintentionally degraded the role of the worker. The nineteenth-century values of the Protestant work ethic and independence were now ensconced in the new technocrats, the very people who made many of those values obsolete.

PROTESTING THE MODERN

Painters and photographers were not the only artists utilizing the products of the machine age as inspiration for their work. Composer George Antheil's piece *Ballet Mécanique* combined percussion instruments, piano, and player pianos with the sounds of machines (propellers, bells, and buzzers) to create a musical impression of the age. First performed in Paris in 1926, *Ballet Mécanique* sought to create a new style of music by mechanizing aspects of the performance, for example, using synchronized player pianos. Originally intended for nine player pianos playing simultaneously, most performances required live musicians, since precisely timing the player pianos proved impossible. The technology, which the performance sought to celebrate, was not up to the task of the performance. While Antheil, with his daring works, made a name for himself in Paris as the "bad boy of music," in the United States his notoriety focused more on the reputation of his music as riot provoking than on the music itself. Book publisher Donald Friede offered to stage the American premier of *Ballet Mécanique* at Carnegie Hall in April 1927, and he reinforced all the most extreme views of Antheil and his music. The performance became less about hearing the music and more about seeing a spectacle. Antheil himself recalled that the publicists for the concert arranged for a real propeller as a prop for the performance in the hopes that the sight of it would frighten the audience. A large painted backdrop added to the spectacle. "This gigantic, rather tasteless curtain (representing a 1927 jazz-mad America!)," Antheil recalled, "single-handedly accomplished two things: it sent me back to Europe broke—and gave an air of complete charlatanism to the whole proceedings."[25] The circus atmosphere of the concert overshadowed the intentions of the music. Antheil wrote the *Ballet Mécanique* with "no idea of *copying* a machine directly down into music, so to speak. My idea, rather, was to warn the age in which I was living of the simultaneous beauty and danger of its own unconscious mechanistic philosophy, aesthetic."[26] Antheil's work was as much a warning against as a celebration of the machine. The precision necessary for a proper performance of the *Ballet Mécanique* dehumanized the performers, turning each into a cog in the machine. Timing needed to be consistent, not flexible; the playing precise, not emotive. It was like looking at an industrial assembly line, beautiful in its function but terrifying in its consequences.[27]

Attending the Carnegie Hall concert was novelist and journalist Josephine Herbst, who excitedly rushed to the theater to be at the premier. "The Antheil performance was," in Herbst's words "a signal for the gathering of the clan." William Carlos Williams, Nathan Asch, and Ezra Pound and his parents were there to celebrate the genius of this modern artist. But in all the excitement of the hour and the backstage hobnobbing, what Herbst remembered most vividly was "Pound's parents, two frail, beautiful old people with white hair, both very slender, with spots of bright color in their cheeks, who stood shaking hands as if they had been parents at the wedding reception of a favorite son."[28] For Herbst, the excitement of the new and modern was eclipsed by the recognition of something much more traditional, and seemingly out of place: family, ceremony, tradition. While others, including Herbst's husband, writer John Herrmann, were enthralled by the performance, Herbst found herself wondering why. "What did the music mean?" she wrote years later.

> I longed to be moved as all our friends seemed to be, including John, but it seemed to me I had heard no more than a hallelujah to the very forces I feared. My longing for a still, small voice, for a spokesman not for the crash of breakers on the rock but for the cur-

rents, down under, that no eye could see, made me feel alone but not an alien, and I looked at John, too, coldly, as one who had joined forces with some mysterious enemy. Was Antheil to be the symbol of an opposition to the Philistine? In a corner of my heart a slow movement of the pulse began to turn my attention elsewhere.[29]

Herbst's attention was turned, along with many others—especially in the intellectual and artistic community—to the death sentence handed down upon avowed anarchists and convicted murderers Nicola Sacco and Bartolomeo Vanzetti on April 9, 1927.

Italian immigrants Sacco and Vanzetti had been convicted in 1921 of murdering a paymaster and guard during the 1920 robbery of a shoe factory in South Braintree, Massachusetts. After six years of unsuccessful appeals, up to the Supreme Judicial Court of Massachusetts, Judge Webster Thayer sentenced Sacco and Vanzetti to death. During their imprisonment, and especially between their sentencing and execution in August 1927, public opinion was conflicted over whether or not they had received a fair trial. Some believed they were innocent and were the victims of the nativist and antiradical hysteria that followed American entry into the Great War in 1917 and the Bolshevik Revolution in Russia that same year. Herbst recalled that the "widening breach in an impassive society had brought many people of assorted temperaments, beliefs, backgrounds, and convictions to the conclusion that the fish peddler and the cobbler were innocent of the crimes of which they had been accused."[30] The public support for the two men was more a cultural phenomenon than a reflection of concerns over criminality and justice. The case did, however, lead to a general questioning of the judicial system. Its legal legacy, according to law professor Edmund M. Morgan, is that "it has revealed defects in our system of administering criminal justice, defects inherent in trial by jury and in the overemphasis upon the adversary features of our process of litigation."[31] The case did lead to changes in judicial procedure in Massachusetts specifically, but for many the case symbolized the larger faults of modern American society, mainly the difficulty of protecting individual rights (and by extension, of maintaining individuality) in a modern industrial society. It was, in particular, the way Sacco and

Vanzetti had exercised their individual rights that challenged the mood of the country. They were agitators in a nation of joiners; they were foreigners who did not speak or write English (until after studying it in prison) in a country fresh from the "100 percent Americanism" campaigns of the Great War; they were draft dodgers, or "slackers" as they were called then, in a nation of volunteers; they were atheists in a nation founded on religious ideals; and they were radicals in a nation deeply fearful of radicals. (Americans supported the Espionage Act of 1917 and the Sedition Act of 1918, designed to rid the country of those who would seek to destroy or change it. Both acts passed in the years following U.S. entry into the Great War.) Each of these characteristics made Sacco and Vanzetti outsiders in American society, and to many, their conviction, sentencing, and execution represented the intolerance of that society. This feeling was especially acute among many who also counted themselves as outsiders: the foreign-born, labor unionists, political leftists, anarchists, intellectuals, and artists. These groups' feelings of being outsiders were based on very different sets of circumstances, but from April to August 1927, they found themselves supporting a common cause: saving the lives of Sacco and Vanzetti.

Widespread support for Sacco and Vanzetti among writers, artists, and intellectuals did not flourish until after the publication of Harvard Law School professor Felix Frankfurter's article "The Case of Sacco and Vanzetti" in the March 1927 issue of the *Atlantic Monthly,* followed closely by the publication of Frankfurter's book *The Case of Sacco and Vanzetti: A Critical Analysis for Lawyers and Laymen.* In both, Frankfurter laid out the case and concluded that Judge Thayer had not ensured the accused a fair trial and in fact had added to the injustice through his actions and statements. Ending with the judge's October 1926 written ruling on the request for a new trial, Frankfurter claimed, "[It] stands unmatched for discrepancies between what the record discloses and what the opinion conveys. His 25,000-word document cannot accurately be described otherwise than as a farrago of misquotations, misrepresentations, suppressions, and mutilations."[32] Frankfurter therefore concluded unreservedly that a new trial should be granted.

Just over a month after the publication of the *Atlantic* article, on April 5, the Supreme Judicial Court denied an appeal to overturn Judge Thayer's ruling, bringing any legal action to an end. Four days later, the two convicted men stood in Judge Thayer's courtroom, and each made a statement. (Sacco, being less fluent in English, did not speak much, but he denied his guilt and accused the judge, while Vanzetti spoke for over forty minutes.) Thayer then sentenced them to die by electrocution. The juxtaposition of the seemingly objective arguments of Frankfurter (and the moderate conclusion asking for a new trial, while more extreme supporters demanded the pair be freed) to the court's denial of their appeal followed quickly by the death sentence shocked many into an impassioned support for the two men. While not all believed Sacco and Vanzetti were innocent, many felt that an execution should not take place with as much doubt as many people had in this case. Support came from religious leaders in the Boston area, as well as from prominent local lawyers, who petitioned for a board of review. They were soon joined by sixty-one members of law faculties from around the United States supporting the idea of establishing a commission to review the case. International concern was expressed in numerous demonstrations worldwide, as well as in a petition sent to Massachusetts governor Alvan Fuller, signed by 472,842 persons from all over the world, requesting Fuller's executive intervention. Yet despite the high-profile support of community, religious, and other leaders, along with the international outcry, support for the two men remained a minority opinion. "Majority public sentiment had reverted to the fearful and angry mood which was characteristic of the Red raid period. It ignored the problem of justice in the issue of life or death, and wildly demanded that the American way of life be protected from the world threat of radicalism."[33]

The concerns of the legal profession, as well as those of many religious leaders and community organizations, dissolved when on June 1 Governor Fuller announced the formation of an advisory committee to examine the situation. The committee consisted of Judge Robert Grant, President Abbott Lawrence Lowell of Harvard University, and President Samuel W. Stratton of the Massachusetts Institute of Technology. The committee conducted private interviews with many of the principal witnesses for the prosecution and persons in the courtroom

(Judge Thayer and members of the jury included), but they did not disclose to the counsel for the defense the substance of the interviews. After receiving the recommendation of the committee, Fuller announced on August 3 his decision not to intervene. The advisory committee report was published on August 7, stating that the committee had found no reason to discredit the decision of the courts. The execution of Sacco and Vanzetti occurred just after midnight on August 22, 1927.

While criticism of the entire ordeal filled the pages of America's, and the world's, newspapers, for most people the event was not life-altering. Only around 20 percent of those in Massachusetts felt an injustice had been done, and the percentage declined the further one got geographically from New England.[34] But percentages alone do not explain the adamancy with which people argued their beliefs. "The conflict within society over the case developed characteristic fears and hatreds. The unfortunate result in this particular situation was that fear for the safety of the established order led to hatred of that order's critics, and finally to a belief that the exercise of mercy would indicate a strategic defeat."[35] Those critics of the established order, who favored either a new trial or an outright pardon, overwhelmingly came from the intellectual and artistic classes. The story of Sacco and Vanzetti sparked the imagination (or ignited the indignation) of artists and writers. Two volumes of poetry, *The Sacco-Vanzetti Anthology of Verse* and *America Arraigned!* appeared within a year of the execution. Upton Sinclair's *Boston* (1928), Nathan Asch's *Pay Day* (1930), Bernard DeVoto's *We Accept with Pleasure* (1934), and John Dos Passos's *The Big Money* (1936) were some of the novels to use the case either as background or as the central theme.

The case did have lasting effects. According to Louis Joughin and Edmund Morgan, "The bequest [of the case] to the law was doubt, and that doubt has grown to such proportions that the case has become a criterion for the study of legal justice. The bequest to society was a revelation of deep cleavage and grave conflict. We have not, unfortunately, seen the end of that struggle."[36] Both these legacies emphasize the failure of the United States to deal with a fundamental problem that arises in a democratic and capitalistic society, namely, how to protect individuals (especially poor individuals who cannot afford to protect themselves) in the face of hostile public opinion. The doubt that the case shed on the law extended further to doubt about modern society as a whole. Herbst realized this when she and her husband walked the foggy streets of Portland, Maine, just after the execution. "All I knew was that a conclusive event had happened. What it meant I couldn't have defined." As they walked, they held hands, and "without saying a word, we both felt it and knew that we felt it: a kind of shuddering premonition of a world to come. But what it was to be we could never have foreseen."[37] What Herbst and her husband feared was the culture that developed out of a highly industrialized and bureaucratic society, a culture in many ways reacting to the forces of modernization through the staunch defense of tradition.

This feeling of doubt about the world to come was shared by many in the 1920s and was expressed in many different ways. Doubts about changes in population and about new and different ideas in religion and politics and science all led to actions designed to curb these doubts. A reinvigorated Ku Klux Klan used modern methods of organization and recruitment to become a national organization with its greatest strength in the Midwest where the primary targets for their aggression were not African Americans but immigrants, Catholics, Jews, and radicals, who threatened the Protestant and American way of life. The passage of the Espionage Act and the Sedition Act enabled the government to suppress dissent not only about World War I but also about the military and about the American form of government. These laws, and their strict enforcement by Attorney General A. Mitchell Palmer, led to the infamous Palmer Raids of 1919–1920, in which thousands of people, mainly immigrants, were arrested and in some cases deported for being "un-American." These pro-American feelings led to the passage of the National Origins Act of 1924, which sharply curtailed immigration from "undesirable" nations, such as those in southern and eastern Europe and Asia. Fearful of the influence of immigrants, especially non-Protestant immigrants, the Ku Klux Klan joined temperance forces in supporting the passage of the Eighteenth Amendment to the Constitution in 1919, enacting Prohibition. The movement to ban the teaching of evolution in public schools also expressed people's doubts about the progress resulting from science and technology.

Walter Lippmann noticed these doubts as he explored the reasons for political indifference in the 1920s. He remarked that average Americans were not concerned about politics, at least in terms of economic issues or foreign and domestic policies; rather, they expressed their concerns through movements against immigration, alcohol, radicalism, and evolution. "These questions are diverse," he wrote, "but they all arise out of the same general circumstances. They arise out of the great migration of the last fifty years, out of the growth of cities, and out of the spread of that rationalism and of the deepening of that breach with tradition which invariably accompany the development of a metropolitan civilization." These social movements, according to Lippmann, express "symbolically the impact of a vast and dreaded social change," namely, "the new urban civilization, with its irresistible economic and scientific and mass power." It is in the cities, "the seat of a vast population, mixed in origins, uncertain of its social status, rather vague about the moral code," that "the patriarchal family, the well-established social hierarchy, the old roots of belief, and the grooves of custom are all obscured by new human relationships based on a certain kind of personal independence, on individual experiment and adventure, which are yet somehow deeply controlled by fads and fashions and great mass movements." And while Lippmann believed these social movements were doomed to fail eventually, they were nonetheless deeply felt and ardently fought. "They are at any rate fighting for the memory of a civilization which in its own heyday, and by its own criteria, was as valid as any other."[38]

In 1927, this revolt against modernity was expressed in less obvious ways than the Klan, the National Origins Act, the Eighteenth Amendment, or the Scopes Monkey Trial of 1925, though each of those had an impact on the lives of Americans during the year. Two areas best illustrate the concern people felt about the modern society they found around them: popular religious literature and popular historical writing. The debates argued in each of these areas illustrate the ambiguity with which Americans faced modernity. In both religion and history, Americans sought for both reassurance and answers to the problems of modern America.

THE VARIETIES OF RELIGIOUS MODERNISM

The most popular religious writer of the 1920s, Bruce Barton, was the son of a Congregationalist minister. Barton's primary vocation was not as a preacher but, rather, as one of the nation's most successful advertising executives. He was founder and partner of Barton, Durstine, and Osborn (which in 1928 merged with the George Batten agency to become the highly successful BBD&O agency), one of the largest advertising agencies in the country with a client list that included General Electric, General Motors, and United States Steel. Barton created ad campaigns that became a part of American culture, such as the slogan for the Salvation Army, "A man may be down but he is never out," and the trademark baker, Betty Crocker, and he helped establish the importance of advertising to an economy no longer dependent on production but, rather, limited only by the demands of consumption. Barton's faith in advertising as the driving force of the economy stemmed from his recognition of the shift from a producerist to a consumerist economy. In 1927, Barton delivered an often reprinted speech, "Creed of an Advertising Man." Barton believed that advertising not only increased sales, allowing for mass production that was efficient in both materials and capital, but also made business better by evolving it beyond the greedy acquisition of wealth to "the best hope of the world. I am in advertising," Barton stated,

> because advertising is the power which keeps business out in the open, which compels it to set up for itself public ideals of quality and service and to measure up to those ideals. Advertising is a creative force that has generated jobs, new ideas, has expanded our economy and has helped give us the highest standard of living in the world. Advertising is the spark plug on the cylinder of mass production, and essential to the continuance of the democratic process. Advertising sustains a system that has made us leaders of the free world: The American Way of Life.[39]

Not only had selling to consumers become more important than the means of production, but Barton proposed the idea that greater efficiency in society meant greater democracy. For Barton, democracy meant that everyone had access to consumer goods, not that everyone had a hand in running society.

While many in the business world knew Barton as a powerful and talented ad man, most Americans knew him as a popular religious writer. His most famous works were produced in the mid-1920s: *The Man Nobody Knows* (1925), a portrait of Jesus Christ as a successful business executive and entrepreneur; *The Book Nobody Knows* (1926), a collection of modernized biblical stories; and *What Can a Man Believe?* (1927), an argument for religious belief in the face of war, prosperity, and science. Much has been written about Barton's characterization of Jesus as the most successful businessman ever and the founder of modern business in *The Man Nobody Knows,* but much less has been made of *What Can a Man Believe?* which was written in response to a letter from a father of two and a "president of the largest business of its kind in the world."[40] The letter writer states that he has seen "certain men, whom I respect, who seem to have faith. It gives satisfaction that I envy. I should like to have such a faith. I should like my son to have it, and the young men in my business. But," he continues, "I shall not be a party to the acceptance and dissemination of bunk." Instead of parables and creeds that induce superstition or fear, this captain of industry asked for a book that would answer five simple questions: "Would the world be better or worse off if it should abolish religion? Has the church done more harm than good? Of the various religions now extant which is best? What few simple things, if any, can a business man believe? If there is to be a 'faith of the future' what kind of a faith will it be?" (6).

In answering these questions, Barton synthesizes his beliefs in the importance of advertising and Christianity to the modern world. He does this by surveying the history of the world's religions and comparing Buddha, Confucius, Mohammed, and Jesus and the religions that have developed from their lives. And even though he admits that their teachings are not always reflected in the institutionalized religions that followed (in fact, he argues that in many ways these men were saying the same thing), he does compare the relative worth of each religion by looking at the effect each has had on the nations that practice it. He concludes that it is "the degree and quality of hope and inspiration which they hold out for the future" that sets these four religions apart. "And each has fixed upon its people the stamp of its own character" (133–134).

> The Chinese neither hoping nor fearing, but patiently enduring; the Buddhist renouncing all active effort as useless; the Mohammedan showing no mercy to his foes, already condemned to eternal punishment, but gladly incurring any risk in exchange for the delights of a fleshy heaven; Christianity teaching that every thought and act has eternal significance, that "God is not mocked; for whatsoever a man soweth that shall he reap."
>
> Few will deny that in the face which it turns toward the future Christianity is markedly superior to the other three faiths. (134)

But religion alone does not determine the worth of a nation, according to Barton. "The United States is Christian and progressive; Mexico is Christian and unprogressive." Differences in "climate, blood, diet, inheritance—help to form national character. We are not made by faith alone" (137). Therefore, the most valuable things a man can believe are those things that not only comfort the soul but also enrich the individual and society; and furthermore, the faith of the future should combine those best elements of Christianity and American business, two institutions that are not antagonistic to one another but, rather, similar in their goals. "Business, in [Jesus's] eyes, was the machinery which God had set up for carrying on the unfinished task of creation." Barton concludes, therefore, that "the salvation of the modern world depends upon the mutual understanding, and reaction upon each other, of business and the church" (187). In this relationship, Barton sees the lessons of business teaching the church how to be more efficient and more attentive to the needs of the community through market research. As Barton sees it, business has already learned from religion, since the goal of business in America is not simply wealth but the betterment of individuals, society, and all of mankind, the same goals as religion has. Churches in the United States, however, need to learn the lessons of business in order to compete in the modern world. According to Barton, the church has in many respects lost its faith. "It sounds almost shocking, yet it is true, that in some respects the church does not have as much faith as business" (192). The difference is, Barton explains, that "business *knows* that to-morrow is going to be different; the church is too often merely *afraid* that it may be. There is a gulf between them. The church trembles at anything that looks like change. It sticks to old methods, believing them sacred because they are old" (193). It is this lack of adaptability that is the root problem for American churches, and by extension, for modern American society. For Barton, as for Henry Ford, embracing the modern did not mean relinquishing the traditional, but it did mean adapting only those aspects of the traditional that fit with the modern. This compromise was a healthy process for both religion and business since, according to Barton, it brought both back to the fundamentals upon which they were based. Modern religion, as Barton saw it, had strayed from the original teachings of Jesus and needed to return to the simple core beliefs. He logically outlines the steps of this argument:

1. I believe in myself.
2. I know that I am intelligent.
3. Because I have intelligence, there must be Intelligence behind the universe. "In other words, because I am, I believe God is" (157).
4. That God is not only more intelligent than man, but since man is ultimately good, God must be better, and God must have a plan for man, because to not have a plan seems unjust (162). And furthermore, there must be a heaven "where life goes on, where injustices are righted and inequalities evened up, where those who have been thwarted and disappointed and cheated are given a fairer field and a better chance. This world as we know it can not be the whole answer, for it does not square with intelligence. And Intelligence is God." (163)

Therefore, for Barton, belief in God was reasonable, and the teachings of Jesus served to instill hope for the future, but the best way to realize those hopes was through business, and doing the job of business was doing the work of God. This divine interpretation of business was more succinctly summarized by Calvin Coolidge when he said, "The man who builds a factory, builds a temple. The man who works there, worships there, and to each is due, not scorn and blame, but reverence and praise."[41] For both Coolidge and Barton, business and religion were mutually beneficial and were beneficial to the nation, especially if religion did not get in the way of business. And indeed, for Barton, religion had much more to learn from business than vice versa, for a religion based on business principles would be a religion that was simple, adaptable, and useful in the pursuit of business success.

Whereas Barton and others saw the opportunities that business and religion offered each other, others saw the dangers of religion's using modern methods. The most widely read critique of religion in 1927 was Sinclair Lewis's *Elmer Gantry,* the best-selling novel of the year, in which Lewis illustrates how modern ideas about psychology and advertising have corrupted religion. The novel's main character, Elmer Gantry, is a small-town midwesterner who rises to fame and fortune by taking advantage of opportunities and of the people he meets along the way. Gantry is not a noble clergyman but, rather, the most hypocritical, pragmatic, dishonest, and successful character in the novel. He manipulates the masses at tent revivals, in sermons, and through his use of the press, and he manipulates individual men for power and wealth and individual women for sex. For Lewis, Elmer Gantry is representative of the kind of danger modern society holds for the country, someone who understands how publicity, advertising, status, and wealth influence the public and who uses them for his own gain. Such earlier Lewis characters as Carol Kennicott in *Main Street* (1920) and George Babbitt in *Babbitt* (1922) eventually accept modernity and conform to modern society; another, Martin Arrowsmith in *Arrowsmith* (1925), rejects modern society altogether.[42] Each of these stories depicts a loss of innocence and simplicity in the wake of modernity. *Elmer Gantry* is not a story of loss; rather, it is a warning about the threats to society unleashed by modernity. Elmer Gantry uses similar means but has different ends than does Bruce Barton's ideal Christian businessman. For Barton, modern business practices will help churches become more successful by making religion more responsive to the public's needs, by providing a spiritual balance to the material ends of business. But for Lewis, modern business practices teach religion to be as ruthless and manipulative as any business and justify these means with the sacred end of saving souls. Elmer Gantry threatens the modern society that created him, and thus he illustrates the modern American dilemma: how is an individual to act in the face of an increasingly mass society; that is, by what standards, values, and motivations should an individual live? For Barton, the answers are to be found in the practice of business and simple religious belief, but for Lewis, placing one's faith in modern business and modern religion as answers to the problems of modern society is like turning to a thief to stop crime. While Barton sees progress in economic modernization and some aspects of modernism, Lewis sees abuse, subterfuge, and loss of individuality.

Yet Lewis really has no answers for the conflict he describes. Moral honesty and a critical eye for the teachings of religion as well as for the modern devices of persuasion are not the answer for Lewis, as is evidenced by the one noble character in *Elmer Gantry,* Frank Shallard, Elmer's college roommate and antagonist. Shallard is neither successful in society's eyes nor content in his own. He is critical of religious dogma, and he does not totally discount the findings of science. He is beaten nearly to death for his convictions after losing his pulpit because of Gantry's machinations. Politically, economically, and socially, Gantry is successful, but Lewis's narrative shows us that the culture has lost. Like all of Sinclair Lewis's novels of the 1920s, *Elmer Gantry* not only warns the reader of the pitfalls masked by prosperity but also describes the shared origins of both, the benefits and dangers of modern society. Lewis criticizes an American culture dominated by a shallow materialism and image consciousness that has seeped into every aspect of American life, even religion.

Barton saw modern religion (informed by a business sense) as the solution to the materialism of the age; Lewis saw in modern religion all the worst aspects of materialism. Under a very different set of circumstances, Willa Cather saw religion as a source of inspiration for individual action, but hers was neither the efficient and pragmatic religion of Barton nor the egocentric and hypocritical religion of Lewis but, rather, a historical religion, one that was, in many ways, lost to the modern world. In 1927 Cather published *Death Comes for the Archbishop,* her semihistorical novel recounting the life of the first archbishop of New Mexico in the mid-nineteenth century. *Death Comes for the Archbishop* is more than simple nostalgia for a time passed, when a religious calling itself could be seen as a full and meaningful life, regardless of worldly success (unlike in Barton's and Lewis's books). The central figure of the novel is Archbishop Jean Marie Latour (the historical Archbishop Jean-Baptiste Lamy), a French-born, Roman Catholic priest sent to the American Southwest to revive what is seen as a dying Catholic church. Latour slowly comes to appreciate not only the landscape of the New Mexican desert but the religious devotion of its people, including many of the native Indian tribes and their practices.

Despite its title, the life-affirming story celebrates the success of Latour's life in Santa Fe. The novel chronicles Latour's life in New Mexico but does not present it in terms of success or failure, either materially or spiritually. Latour does not succeed in amassing wealth for himself or for the church, nor does he succeed in converting many people to Catholicism, since the majority of the population is already Catholic. Latour's success, and that of his close friend and vicar, Father Joseph Vaillant, is measured in the lives they encountered and touched, the lessons they learned in their journeys about the people and places of the Southwest, and the satisfaction they received from performing their sacred duties. They have not changed the world, but they have participated in and encouraged positive change in the world by helping people (themselves included) find contentment in everyday life. Cather's novel illustrates the beauty to be gained in reconciling the worldly and the spiritual, not by ignoring one for the other but by seeing the connections between the two. The harshness of the southwestern desert, as well as the difficulties of the historical circumstances of mid-nineteenth-century America, contrast with the spiritual devotion of the characters, both priests and parishioners. As a result, the religion practiced by the characters in the novel is flexible, not static. The tribal customs of Native Americans as well as the traditional practices of the Mexican American Catholics blend together with the French Catholicism of Latour and Vaillant. This melding of practices is echoed in the building of the cathedral in Santa Fe, the archbishop's physical legacy, with its French architect and native materials combining to create something precious and unique; the cathedral is not just a copy of European architecture and style but, rather, an American creation, and as such it is modern.

According to scholar Nicholas Birns, "Cather's Christianity is not anti-modern and does not conform to the stereotype of Christianity as anti-modern held by Left and Right alike. It is part of modernity, and indeed it underscores the way that the Christian message, with its departure from the given and the normative, has always been laden with modernity."[43] But the modernity expressed in *Death Comes for the Archbishop* differs from that expressed in Bruce Barton's *What Can a Man Believe?* which is more a call for the modernization of religion, as opposed to Cather's view of religious belief as an integral part of the modernization process. For Cather, religion helps people adapt to their circumstances, not by preventing change from occurring, nor by simply accepting the changes that occur, but, rather, by placing those changes within the larger agenda of a sacred life. The result is a presentation of religion that is not opportunistic (as it is in both Barton and Lewis) but that is relevant to the ambiguities of modern America.

A HISTORY OF PROGRESS AND FAILURE

In a larger sense, *Death Comes for the Archbishop* is modern in that it reinforces a progressive view of American history, one that is inclusive and tolerant of some differences (but not all) and that shows the course of American history to be, despite its mistakes, a history of progress. On his deathbed, the archbishop tells his student, "'My son, I have lived to see two great wrongs righted; I have seen the end of black slavery, and I have seen the Navajos restored to their own country.'"[44] The novel then goes on to recount the American government's forced removal of Navajos to the Bosque Redondo, "hundreds of them, men, women, and children, perished from hunger and cold on the way; their sheep and horses died from exhaustion crossing the mountains. None ever went willingly; they were driven by starvation and the bayonet; captured in isolated bands, and brutally deported" (291). But, Cather notes, "At last the government at Washington admitted its mistake—which governments seldom do. After five years of exile, the remnant of the Navajo people were permitted to go back to their sacred places" (294–295). This simplistic recounting of the plight of the Navajos, while not very critical of the American government, is progressive and ahead of its time both in the inclusiveness of its equating racism against African Americans with racism against Native Americans and in its ideology of progress.

By the same token, *Death Comes for the Archbishop* is a bit behind the times, since by 1927 the view of American history as a history of triumph and progress had already been brought under serious scrutiny, by both historians and novelists. This revision of the triumphal course of American history was best presented to a popular audience through Charles and Mary Beard's *The Rise of American Civilization,* which first appeared in two volumes in 1927. The work was proclaimed by Richard Hofstadter as having done "more than any other such book of the twentieth century to define American history for the reading public."[45] Although the Beards' work places American progress firmly in the center of an advancing world civilization, they are nonetheless cautious about the realities of progress. According to Dorothy Ross, in combining ironic prose with romantic rhetoric, "the Beards alternate between—seem deliberately to stretch the reader between—the ironic all-too-human present and the mythic destiny of America." *The Rise of American Civilization,* she notes, "is a story not of America's achievement of a prefigured identity but of American society's struggle for progress."[46] Even though the basic narrative is optimistic and celebratory about the course of American history, it does not take that course for granted or assume that the nation's future is predestined, and since the accomplishments came from the hand of man, they often included unintended consequences and the evils to which man is susceptible. By making the actions of man more important than destiny, the Beards secularized what was once a religious notion of America's predestined role in the world. *The Rise of American Civilization* marks a change in Charles Beard's historical thinking, not a departure from an earlier religious paradigm but, rather, a swing back toward a humanist view and away from a scientific view of history. Before 1927, Beard primarily saw history as the workings of economic laws, an empirical approach to understanding the past, but *The Rise of American Civilization* seeks to "explain writers to themselves, audiences to audiences, actors to actors while disclosing the reciprocal relations of writers, audiences, and actors. The profounder, wider, and more realistic the history, the greater its services presumably to letters and criticism."[47] This means understanding the political, social, and economic implications of the arts, as well as the political, social, and

economic impacts on art. In doing so, ideas become supremely important in understanding creative endeavors as well as political, social,
and economic actions. The central idea in *The Rise of American Civilization* is progress, "the most dynamic social theory ever shaped in
the history of thought" (443). The Beards define progress as "the continual improvement in the lot of mankind on this earth by the attain-
ment of knowledge and the subjugation of the material world to the
requirements of human welfare" (443–444). Including the role of ideas
in understanding the actions of men was "perhaps the most important
turning point in Beard's intellectual development."[48] The ambiguity
that intellectual history brought to *The Rise of American Civilization*
struck a chord with readers: "Judging by their large sales, their audience was indeed still torn, as they themselves were, between ironic
doubts and mythic hopes."[49]

This historical ambiguity can also be seen in historical fiction. Two
novels in 1927 looked to the American pioneer past, but they did not
simply celebrate the accomplishments of the pioneers, nor did they
openly criticize their actions. Both O. E. Rolvaag's *Giants in the Earth*
and Glenway Wescott's *The Grandmothers: A Family Portrait* recount
the struggles of American pioneers and are built around the ideas of
failure, regret, and disappointment, and both have as much to do with
the psychological motivations of the characters as with the physical
environment.

Norwegian-born Ole Edvart Rolvaag gave up the life of a fisherman
when he was twenty years old to come to the United States to farm in
the Dakotas with his uncle. Finding the life of a farmer not to his lik-
ing, Rolvaag went to school and developed his love of literature. As a
professor of Norwegian literature at St. Olaf College in Minnesota,
Rolvaag wrote several Norwegian-language novels about Norwegian
Americans. *Giants in the Earth* was the first of his works to be translated into English (actually the first two, since the novel's two books
originally were published separately in Norway) and was one of the
first novels about the American immigrant experience to be translated
from a foreign language. Rolvaag wrote during a period of debate over
Norwegian American identity resulting from the nativist sentiments
of the Great War, the attack on "hyphenated Americans," and the Red
Scare. In 1925 over 200,000 Norwegian Americans celebrated a hun-

dred years of immigrant history at the Norse-American Immigration Centennial Celebration at the Minnesota State Fairgrounds. The event illustrates the way the Norwegian immigrant community in America utilized cultural products to express its identity. While older expressions of immigrant identity, such as Norwegian immigrants' associations, Norwegian-language newspapers, and language use, continued to decline in the mid-1920s, others "rose to take their place—historical associations; academic departments devoted to Norwegian-American studies; yearly festivals and celebrations; and, a new 'patron saint' who has in many ways replaced Leif Eriksson, the author Ole Rolvaag, whose tragic view of immigration is often at odds with the progressive vision still evident in much Norwegian-American activity."[50]

What puts Rolvaag at odds with a progressive view of history is not his characters' lack of ability to succeed economically, politically, or socially in the United States—indeed, in all these things they are successful. For Rolvaag, the price one pays for success in America is psychological. In *Giants in the Earth,* Per Hansa and his wife Beret, along with their three children, settle in the Dakota territory, and although they succeed in farming the land, building a home, raising a family, and founding a community, theirs is ultimately a tragic tale. Beret, for whom life on the plains has resulted in loneliness, depression, anxiety, and fear, survives Per Hansa, who was perfectly suited to the pioneer life and was the main factor in Beret's survival. As a result, Beret is left at the end of the novel without her basic survival tool, her husband. The novel is not, however, a critique of American values and ideals of success; rather, it is an examination of what is lost in the transition from old country to new world. The creation of an American can only be accomplished through the destruction of what came before.

This theme is seen in all of Rolvaag's works, especially in the two sequels to *Giants in the Earth, Peder Victorious* (1929) and *Their Fathers' God* (1931). Rolvaag was also instrumental in the founding of the Norwegian-American Association, which sponsored the 1925 Centennial Celebration, and with teaching Norwegian language and history, especially the history of Norwegian Americans. While teaching at St. Olaf College, Rolvaag emphasized the need for young Norwegian Americans to know and respect their history. "You must not erase your racial characteristics in order to become better Americans. You must deepen them if possible."[51] For Rolvaag, the country would be served best not by melting immigrant differences in an American pot but, rather, by the creation of a pluralistic society in which difference is respected and celebrated. In this sense, Rolvaag was in line with critics of the U.S. home front's record during the Great War, when difference was automatically suspect and condemned. He was also in line with those who believed that Sacco and Vanzetti had been guilty only of being immigrants and anarchists, not of being criminals. Yet Rolvaag was not opposed to the American values of acquisition and success; indeed, he encouraged Norwegian Americans to be as successful in America as they could. It was of the means of gaining that success that Rolvaag was most critical. Success did not have to come at the expense of ethnic identity, and, Rolvaag suggested, success could be better gained through ethnic self-knowledge and respect, while still buying into the American dream.

Like Charles and Mary Beard, Rolvaag saw the potential of American life but did not believe that progress was predestined. Only through making the right choice of what to lose in order to gain could America prosper. This still optimistic view of American history allowed for the possibility of making the wrong choices, but it is an account of wrong choices that informs Glenway Wescott's *The Grandmothers: A Family Portrait,* which looks back at three generations of Wisconsin ancestors of expatriate American writer Alwyn Tower. The novel has the potential to aggrandize these pioneers and farmers, but Wescott turns this family history into a study of failure, regret, and unfulfilled promise. The purpose of Alwyn Tower's sorting through the past is to exorcize history, to try "to understand, for his own sake, shadowy men, women and children," his family, so that he can rise above the family's characteristics, which seemed always to lead to disappointment.[52] Alwyn (like many nonfictional writers, Wescott among them) went to Europe to understand America, to gain an understanding of America above and beyond what Americans understood. What he discovers is that America has been filled with pioneers, and not just the physical pioneers, the settlers, but spiritual pioneers, "disillusioned but imaginative, these went through the motions of hope, still pioneers" (29). These pioneers never really settle down because they never find what they think they seek, and as a result they doom each future generation to the same failures as theirs. But by understanding the past, Alwyn comes to understand not just his family but his country, and he sees that his understanding of it runs counter to it:

Indeed, it was an instinctive law for Americans, the one he had broken. Never be infatuated with nor try to interpret as an omen the poverty, the depression, of the past; whosoever remembers it will be punished, or punish himself; never remember. Upon pain of loneliness, upon pain of a sort of expatriation though at home. At home in a land of the future where all wish to be young; a land of duties well done, irresponsibly, of evil done without immorality, and good without virtue. Maturity, responsibility, immorality, virtue are offspring of memory; try not to remember. (378)

America, as a young country, "had as yet nothing worth remembering" (378), and it continued on its way believing that the future would be better, that it was destined to be better, and that, therefore, what had been done in the past was necessary for that better future. This justification of pioneer actions—the eradication of Native Americans, the environmental destruction—as well as of more recent actions such as participation in the Great War, was exactly what Wescott sought to understand and explain. Only by critically viewing the past can one hope to make the best decisions for the future.

Wescott, though he dealt with a single family's story, was concerned about larger, more generalized history lessons than was Rolvaag, who sought to teach the history of a specific group, but for both, history, not technology or science, held the key to creating a better future. While neither writer was a modernist, in style or subject, both presented a modern view of history by critically examining the basic assumptions of teaching history in order to create good, "100 percent American" citizens. This debate over the role of historical education found itself in a Chicago courtroom in 1927, led by the town's mayor William "Big Bill" Thompson. On the surface, the debate was an attack against the critical "new histories" of writers such as Charles Beard, who many felt diminished American greatness by being critical of the founding fathers. Patriotic "100 percent Americanism" groups such as the American Legion and the Ku Klux Klan supported Thompson's attack on the new history, as did the Sons of the American

Revolution and the Daughters of the Confederacy. Also joining the attack on the "new history" were ethnic societies eager to have their stories told in the nation's textbooks. Both the patriotic societies and the ethnic societies agreed that there was a pro-British slant to many of these works, but more significantly, they both criticized the move away from a "great man" narrative of history to one more socially and economically descriptive. Yet this alliance was a fragile one. In their struggle to make sure that "each 'race' could have its heroes sung," groups argued over which great men accomplished which great feats; for example, Italian Americans and Norwegian Americans argued over who had discovered America, Christopher Columbus or Leif Eriksson. These debates, however, for the most part only included white heroes, not black, Asian, or Native American ones. As a result, the history textbook debates of the 1920s illustrate that "cultural pluralism could itself reinforce *ideological* conformity. Across the country, racial and ethnic groups successfully inserted a colorful new set of characters into American history textbooks. At the same time, however, they helped block a more critical, sophisticated analysis of the nation's origins."[53] As a result, most Americans' view of history remained one in which great men accomplished great things in the great course of American history, with the implicit understanding that America was therefore a patriarchal, white-dominated society, and that this accounted for its success as a nation.

This basic understanding of American history informed the debates over Sacco and Vanzetti, nativism, religion, and education, as well as the celebration of such cultural heroes as Charles Lindbergh, Henry Ford, and Bruce Barton, who were all seen as great men making history. What they made, according to their celebrants, was a world of opportunity, possibility, and hope. Yet the clamor over the execution of Sacco and Vanzetti, Lewis's *Elmer Gantry,* and the debate over historical teaching suggest that the world made by Lindbergh, Ford, and Barton was not necessarily one with which all Americans were comfortable. Even though Ford could find satisfaction in the engineer as techno-artisan, the precisionists could find beauty in the function and form of industrial objects, and Barton could celebrate the benefits of modernization on business and Christianity, many Americans questioned, were wary of, or even feared the modern. Some questioned those aspects of modernity that fostered the need for standardization and efficiency, creating a desire for a homogeneity that had little tolerance for the likes of Sacco and Vanzetti and other immigrants, radicals, and outsiders. Their voices of protest fell on deaf ears, reinforcing their doubts. Some, like Sinclair Lewis and his readers, were wary of the uses to which modern methods could be put to achieve private gain over the public good. And some, like the Beards, Rolvaag, Wescott, and their readers, feared that the lessons of the past would not be adequately learned. In both celebration and trepidation, diverse Americans sought to master their country through physical, economic, artistic, spiritual, and intellectual means. Greater tensions appeared as women and African Americans sought equality in modern America.

Poster illustration for the movie *It*. (© CinemaPhoto/Corbis)

Three African American women with children. (Courtesy of the Library of Congress)

CHAPTER 2 *Seeking Equality:*
Feminism and Flood Waters

UNEQUAL STRUGGLES FOR EQUALITY: *Clara Bow and Hollywood provided a role model and opportunities for young women raised in the wake of feminist successes, but not all women shared in that success. Not only African American women but African American men as well suffered under segregation, peonage, and the harsh conditions of southern rural life. Bow gained financial success and celebrity as the "It" girl; African Americans in the Mississippi Delta found their situation worsened by the massive river flooding and the discriminatory handling of the relief efforts. In terms of equality, Clara Bow may have signaled how far the nation had come, and African Americans in the South illustrated how far there was yet to go.*

In searching for ways to cope with the changes resulting from a consumer-driven, industrial economy, Americans debated not only what was good and bad about those changes but also the effect they were having on different groups of people. Two groups who highlight the changes of the 1920s are women and African Americans, and in particular young urban women and rural southern African Americans. These groups' attempts to break away from tradition, whether it be the Victorian image of womanhood or the traditional subservience forced upon African Americans, especially in the South, illustrate the conflicts with which Americans dealt. For women, the increased opportunities brought about by the vote, education, and jobs created a minority of American women looking to rebel against the Victorian morals of their mothers. No symbol of modernity was more widespread than the "new woman." By 1927 debates over the "new woman" no longer centered on women's suffrage; rather, the discussion had moved on to cultural issues of morality, marriage, and sex. For African Americans in the rural South, the gradual yet constant encroachment of the federal government and national corporations into the southern economy and culture, through such means as agricultural programs and chain stores, meant a weakening of local white control of the South and an increase in migration northward for African Americans. In 1927 two things illustrate these two processes: the film career and life of Clara Bow and the aftermath of the Mississippi River flood. Both illustrate the divisions within society that were aggravated by the rising expectations of women and African Americans, and both illustrate the ambiguities of American culture apparent in conflicts between women and men, blacks and whites, urban and rural, and North and South.

FLAPPERS AND FEMINISM

Women in the 1920s worked in greater numbers and were less likely than their mothers to devote their lives to finding and serving a husband and having and raising children. The products and services of modern life liberated women from such domestic chores as sewing, hand washing, and baking and also created opportunities for employment both by generating new jobs (from secretarial positions in growing corporations to labor positions in factories) and by making time available for women to work outside the home while still fulfilling what were seen as a woman's domestic responsibilities. Women who took advantage of those products, services, and opportunities constituted the group collectively, and most broadly, known as the "new women." For the most part, these women did not come under public scrutiny because they posed no real threat to the established order; they merely became more a part of it by taking on the economic role of worker along with the social role of wife and mother. But many women, mainly younger ones, saw these new opportunities not as the ends of their movement toward equality but, rather, as the means with which they would express their modernity. From this younger group of women rose the archetypical female character of the 1920s, the flapper.

While other eras also had representative images of the idealized woman—the Gibson Girl of the 1890s was the generational predecessor of the flapper—never before had the representative woman of the time been so young or so independent or so rebellious. This youthful rebellion did entail some fundamental, though not radical, changes in values and ideas concerning gender roles in society, but it was primarily a surface rebellion, one of outward appearance, of style, and fashion. The flapper was most often described not by what she did but by how she looked: short bobbed hair, loose-fitting sleeveless slip gowns

that exposed the leg below the knee, sheer stockings rolled down below the knee, tight-fitting cloche hat, and an abundance of accessories, including necklaces, bracelets, gloves, and handbags. Some of
the change in style was a result of the fact that working women
needed clothes that were less cumbersome than the corseted and tai-
lored outfits worn by their mothers, but it also expressed fundamental
differences in these young women's attitudes toward sex and sexuality. Externally, the flapper was a model consumer, not only because
she bought ready-made clothes, cosmetics, and accessories but also
because she was very concerned about outward appearances as a statement of personality and about consumption as a means of expression.

Yet, at a more substantive level, the flapper could be called, in
Dorothy Dunbar Bromley's words, a "Feminist—New Style." Flappers
were not feminist in the old suffragette sense. Bromley wrote in 1927,
"'Feminism' has become a term of opprobrium to the modern young
woman," because it conjures up images of unfeminine zealots who
"bear a grudge against men, either secretly or openly; they make an issue of little things as well as big; they exploit their sex for the sake of
publicity; they rant about equality when they might better prove
their ability."[1] Feminists in the new style, however, do not protest
their status as women; rather, they work to become complete individuals. "In brief, Feminist—New Style reasons that if she is economically independent, and if she has, to boot, a vital interest in some
work of her own she will have given as few hostages to Fate as it is hu-
manly possible to give" (555). In other words, these young women
sought independence for the possibilities it provided. Bromley made it
very clear, however, that these young women did not want to be just
like men, but remained "purely feminine, as nature intended them to
be" (557). But what particularly sets these new-style feminists apart
from their predecessors is that they "profess no loyalty to women *en
masse,* although she staunchly believes in individual women" (556).
She is "intensely self-conscious whereas the feminists were intensely
sex-conscious. . . . She knows that it is her American, her twentieth-
century birthright to emerge from a creature of instinct into a full-
fledged individual who is capable of molding her own life. And in this
respect she holds that she is becoming man's equal. *If this be treason,
gentlemen, make the most of it*" (560).

Bromley's manifesto attempts to explain the shift in the woman's movement from political issues to cultural concerns by infusing the economic interests of the younger generation, expressed through consumer culture, with political meaning. While not overtly political, the carefree flapper was making a statement about established social values. The flapper was clearly modern in that she rebelled against traditional values, not only concerning proper attire and economic independence but also, much more disturbing to the traditional sensibility, in leisure pursuits and sexuality as well. The flapper was not, however, opposed to such traditional aspects of womanhood as marriage and family. In 1927, psychologist Leta Hollingworth defined the ideal feminist as a happily married woman with children.[2]

The flapper was the feminine expression of the modern consumer who spent what she made, or in many cases spent more than she made with the extension of credit, with pleasure as the goal: pleasure in appearance, pleasure in activity, pleasure in drinking and smoking, and pleasure in sex. This pursuit of pleasure reflected and reinforced America's transition from a producerist to consumerist economy. This economic shift developed alongside a cultural shift favoring personality over character.[3] The Gibson Girl was a model of pure womanhood. She wore her long hair up and neat, and her tight-fitting corseted attire emphasized her curves and therefore her attractiveness to men yet left little flexibility for any work other than that of wife and mother. The ideal nineteenth-century woman was celebrated for her character, with the most valued traits being devotion, chastity, and selflessness. The ideal flapper, by contrast, was more valued for her personality, and especially for her spontaneity, style, and ability to have fun. And while economic changes account for a measure of this transformation in the characteristic feminine type, generational differences reinforced the transformation. As F. Scott Fitzgerald put it in 1927, "They are just girls, all sorts of girls, their one common trait being that they are young things with a splendid talent for living."[4]

Nowhere was the "new woman" more evident than in the motion picture industry. It was the movies more than any other medium that presented the "new woman" to the American public, and no movie star embodied the image, attitude, and lifestyle of the "new woman" more than Clara Bow. "Clara Bow is the quintessence of what the term 'flapper' signifies as a definite description: pretty, impudent, superbly assured, as worldly-wise, briefly-clad and 'hard-berled' as possible," stated Fitzgerald. "There were hundreds of them, her prototypes. Now completing the circle, there are thousands more, patterning themselves after her."[5] In 1927 Clara Bow was the top box office draw, appearing that year in *Wings, Children of Divorce, Rough House Rosie, Get Your Man, Hula,* and the film with which she is most identified, *It.* The film *It* was based loosely on a novel by Elinor Glyn of the same name in which Glyn describes that elusive quality, "it." Glyn defined "it," at various times, as being "largely to do with animal magnetism," but "'it' does not depend upon looks . . . it does not depend upon intelligence or character or—anything—as you say, it is just 'It.'"[6] Serialized by *Cosmopolitan* magazine in 1926 and published as a novel in 1927, *It* became the major marketing tool to sell Clara Bow to the public. Paramount producer Budd Schulberg offered Glyn $50,000 to endorse Bow as "The 'It' Girl." At the first meeting between writer and star, Glyn defined "it" as "an inner magic. . . . Valentino possessed this certain magic. So do John Gilbert and Rex," and Bow wondered what she, two actors, and a horse had in common. Later "Madame" Glyn would make additions to her list of those who had "it" (including the doorman at the Ambassador Hotel) before dropping them all except for Clara Bow and Antonio Moreno, who had been cast as the male lead in *It.* Released in February of 1927, *It* was an instant success, bringing in 50 percent more business in its New York opening than any other film, and in every other city exceeding competing films by 100 percent or more. Although Glyn marketed the idea of "it," it was Clara Bow who made people care about it, and with *It* Bow secured her position as the biggest box office draw of the late silent era.

In *It,* Bow plays Betty Lou Spence, a department store salesgirl who sets her sights on the new owner of the store, Cyrus Waltham (Moreno). Using all of her feminine wiles (flirting, manipulating Waltham's close friend Monty, cutting off the collar and sleeves of her work dress to make an evening dress), she catches Waltham's attention at the Ritz, just after Elinor Glyn (playing herself) has explained to Waltham what "it" is: "'It' is self-confidence and indifference to whether you are pleasing or not, and something in you that gives the impression that you are not all cold." Waltham's dinner companion, his fiancée, asks him if he believes in "it," to which he responds (with an eye toward Betty Lou), "I certainly do!" Having caught his attention, Betty Lou manages to force Cyrus on a date, this time on her turf, Coney Island. As Betty Lou introduces the well-bred Cyrus to the simple pleasures of hot dogs and amusement park rides, the two start to fall in love, but when Cyrus tries to kiss her in his automobile at the end of their date, she slaps his face, saying, "So you're one of them minute men—the minute ya know a girl, ya think ya can kiss her!" Having shown him her fun and carefree side, she has also shown that she is a lady. Things, however, get complicated when Betty Lou must claim that she is the mother of a friend's child to keep welfare authorities from taking the baby. Reported in the newspaper and verified by Monty, Cyrus learns of the child and tries to avoid Betty Lou, but because she has "it," he cannot. Cyrus offers Betty Lou all she desires except marriage, which is the one thing Betty Lou desires most. Betty Lou, hurt and humiliated, quits her job and tries to forget him, but because he has "it," she cannot. When Betty Lou discovers the reason for Waltham's offer, she vows to get revenge for his not having given her the benefit of the doubt. She sneaks aboard Waltham's yacht, breaks up Cyrus's engagement, and forces him to propose marriage to her, to which she responds, "I'd rather marry your office boy!" Though she has gained her revenge, she is still heartbroken. When the boat crashes and she and Cyrus's fiancée fall overboard, Betty saves the struggling socialite by punching her so she stops panicking, and ends up in a wet embrace on the ship's anchor with Cyrus, and they live happily ever after.

What is notable in *It*, and in most of Clara Bow's films, is the aggressiveness of her character. Betty Lou discovers what she wants, and she proceeds to get it, by her own means and by her own rules. She is the master of the situation, and though her ultimate goal is marriage, she is presented as completely self-sufficient and also able to care for a girlfriend and her child. When the welfare ladies inquire about the father of the child by asking Betty Lou whether she has a husband, she replies that it is none of their business and that she has the means to support both herself and the child. And while the film suggests that single-motherhood was distasteful to an elite sensibility, it never condemns the practice. For most moviegoers, the underlying political message of the film was concealed by Bow's energetic performance, in which all of her raw sexuality and ebullient personality are evident. She presented an idealized version of the modern woman, a young, independent, aggressive, stylish, and playful girl who uses her intelligence as well as her femininity to get what she wants. She has the ideal "new woman" occupation, salesgirl in a large department store, emphasizing the consumer ethic, yet her ultimate goal is marriage. Betty Lou, like most of Bow's characters, straddles the line between a completely independent, modern woman and a completely dependent, Victorian woman who finds comfort and security in marriage.

This tension between independence and marriage is evident in the rise in both the number of women attending college and the percentage of women marrying. As Nancy Cott notes, marriage rates increased as working women contributed to a couple's ability to settle down at a younger age than in previous generations. Educated and working women did not jeopardize marriage but, instead, increased its practice. While marriage did increase, so too did the number of young women who engaged in heavy petting and premarital sex. Sex before marriage was generally frowned upon, but it did not exclude a woman from marrying.[7] The seductiveness of Bow's characters expressed not a dissatisfaction with marriage but, rather, a woman's ability to be active in courtship instead of a passive recipient.

In *Get Your Man*, Bow plays Nancy Worthington, an American in Paris who meets and falls in love with Robert, son of the Duc de Bellecontre, as he shops for his betrothed, Simone, daughter of the Marquis de Villeneuve. The long-standing betrothal agreement between the duc and the marquis is attacked by Worthington as she "accidentally" crashes her automobile into a tree outside the Bellecontre estate and is put up at the estate to recuperate. Nancy discovers that neither Robert nor Simone wishes the marriage to take place, but neither is willing to break the agreement between their fathers. Nancy proceeds to seduce the marquis (who is visiting the estate for the pending marriage), and when he proposes marriage, she accepts, with the provision that her newly acquired daughter be allowed to marry for love, not as the result of a childhood promise. Thinking that Nancy loves the marquis, Robert tells her that he will forget her by traveling to Africa, but before he can go, Nancy gets Robert in her room and starts a commotion for the whole house to hear. When the duc and the marquis discover Robert in Nancy's room, Nancy graciously declines the marquis's proposal, saying she understands that he could never marry her now, and the duc insists that under the circumstances, Robert must marry Nancy. In the end, Nancy and Robert are free to marry, Simone can marry her love, and the duc and the marquis are still friends. Once again, Clara Bow's character has used her feminine wiles and intelligence to get what she wants, marriage to the man she loves.

Directed by Dorothy Arzner and adapted from a French play by screenwriter Hope Loring, *Get Your Man* presents not only a powerful female character but a story that pits the Old World traditions of Europe against the modern views of America. Nancy is modern in her thoughts about love and in her willingness to do whatever it takes to satisfy her desire for marriage, but these traits are characterized in the film as not only modern (especially for a woman) but American as well. Not bound by tradition, as evidenced by her lack of historical knowledge at the wax museum where she and Robert fall in love, Nancy bends tradition to suit her needs without damaging the social order. No one loses his or her social standing, even though the traditional bond of betrothal was broken. This balancing act, between opposing tradition without destroying it, is at the center of all Clara Bow's 1927 films. She is the aggressor in courtship, but her ultimate goal is matrimony; she is the embodiment of the modern, yet she seeks a traditional outcome. She does not seek to change the status quo, yet she criticizes it by failing to abide by it.

Yet this balance between modern aggressiveness and traditional submissiveness was a delicate one to maintain. In *Children of Divorce*, Bow plays Kitty Flanders, who seeks marriage, not for love, but for money. This mercenary approach to marriage is due mainly to her mother (played by Hedda Hopper before her career as a professional gossip), whose views on marriage are tainted by her own divorce. As a result of this upbringing, Bow seduces Ted Larrabee (Gary Cooper), also the child of divorced parents. Ted marries Kitty, after a drunken night of immorality, despite the fact that he is in love with Jean Waddington (Esther Ralston). Realizing their mistake in marrying, Ted and Kitty refuse to divorce as both their parents had, leaving little room for a solution to a bad situation. Eventually Kitty does the only thing she feels will correct the situation: she commits suicide, leaving Ted free to marry Jean. Most Bow characters get the marriage they want and the marriage they deserve, but in this movie, an undeserved and loveless marriage is still preferred to a divorce. The traditional double standard comes into play, since divorce is seen as detrimental only to women and not men. This double standard is evident when *Children of Divorce* is compared to Bow's next film, *Hula,* in which Bow plays Hula Calhoun, an heiress in Hawaii who falls in love with a married British engineer, Anthony Haldane (Clive Brook). Haldane arrives on the Calhoun plantation to build a dam, and Hula quickly falls in love with him. In order to get the marriage she wants, Hula dynamites the dam he built. The resulting humiliation is too much for his wife to take, and she divorces him, freeing him to marry Hula.

Audiences preferred a strong, aggressive Clara Bow to a victimized one. *Children of Divorce* was not a big hit, but it did respectable business primarily based on Bow's popularity. Despite the glimpses of her dramatic abilities (director Victor Fleming proclaimed Bow's death scene as the "greatest ever done on the screen"), the public preferred Bow in less dramatic, more lighthearted, and especially more sexual roles. Bow's other 1927 releases, *Hula* and *Rough House Rosie,* followed the formula that proved so successful in *It,* a carefree Clara Bow playing a character just like Clara Bow. To increase profits even more (since making money was the main concern here) producer and studio executive Ben Schulberg decreased costs by cutting back on everything in these films except Clara Bow. Unknown, and therefore less expensive, leading men and budget productions limited costs yet did not diminish the films' appeal at the box office. Their success was due to the fact that Bow was in them. Even when the big-budget war film, *Wings,* opened in limited release in August 1927, Clara Bow, though she played a supporting role to the two lead actors, was the only actor named above the title of the film. She had become the best commodity Hollywood had to offer in 1927. Not only her films but her private life as well made money for Hollywood and the press, since the public eagerly consumed stories containing Bow, whether filmed or printed, true or false. Most stories revolved around Bow's multiple engagements, first to actor Gilbert Roland, then to director Victor Fleming, and then to *Children of Divorce* costar Gary Cooper, none of which resulted in marriage. But it wasn't just her romances that made news; stories of her wild parties circulated around Hollywood, including a false one in which Bow was said to have hosted an orgy with the entire University of Southern California football team at her Hollywood home. Bow both benefited and was victimized by her celebrity, and many of the pitfalls she experienced (exploitation by the studio, for example) became commonplace during the Golden Age of Hollywood in the 1930s and 1940s.

THE "IT" GIRL AND THE JUDGE

In both the content of her films and the nature of her career, Clara Bow epitomized the modern woman in all her ambiguities. Bow's characters, like Bow herself, were carefree, spontaneous, and fun-loving yet sought the stability of marriage. They were assertive in their methods of courtship, yet they never dominated their husbands. They were economically independent, but they used that independence to buy goods with which to attract a husband, or in the case of Clara Bow the actress, an audience. But Clara Bow is not representative of the "new woman"; rather, she is at the extreme of what was accepted by the mainstream. Granted, not everyone in America approved of Bow's characters or real-life actions (indeed, even many in Hollywood saw her exploits as excessive and damaging to the growing respectability of the film industry), but her status as the biggest box office draw of the year suggests a level of acceptance unthinkable a decade earlier.

Even forward-thinkers, such as Judge Ben Lindsey, who was removed from his bench at the Juvenile and Family Court in Denver for expounding his progressive views on sex and marriage in *The Revolt of Modern Youth* (with Wainwright Evans, 1925) and *The Companionate Marriage* (also with Evans, 1927), found Clara Bow too much to take. Lindsey had seen firsthand the rising divorce rate in America through the cases that passed through his courtroom. As a result of his experiences, Lindsey advocated premarital sex to help couples determine their compatibility. Chased out of Colorado, Lindsey sought refuge in Hollywood, where he and his wife became the house guests of Ben Schulberg. The judge would bring liberal respectability to Schulberg's Hollywood table, but he was particularly interested in meeting the person considered the least respectable. As Schulberg's son Budd remembers, "The apostle of unmarried sex wanted to interview one of its most celebrated practitioners," Clara Bow. Reluctantly, the Schulbergs introduced Judge Lindsey and his wife to Bow, who showed up to dinner slightly intoxicated. "Hiya Judge!" Clara shouted, "Ben tells me ya believe people oughta have their fun without havin' t'get married. Ya naughty boy!" She then proceeded to kiss the judge smack on the lips. The judge had expected a lively discussion of Bow's attitudes toward marriage and sex; what he got was an invitation by Bow to dance. As Lindsey tried to keep up with Bow as she danced across the living room, she started to find out if the judge practiced what he preached. As Budd Schulberg recalls, "Beginning with the judge's top jacket button, she said, 'Rich man . . . poor man . . . beggar man . . . thief . . . ,' her busy little fingers unbuttoning with each designation. By the time the childhood game had brought her to 'Indian chief,' Clara Bow was undoing the top button of Judge Lindsey's fly." Shocked, the judge and his wife fled the Schulbergs' house. Afterward, Clara asked, "Well gee whiz, if he believes in all that modern stuff like ya say he does, how come he's such an old stick-in-the-mud?"[8]

Most Americans saw the judge as progressive (or even radical, according to some critics), but in comparison to the "It" girl, he was as traditional as they come. Of course, Schulberg's characterization of Lindsey as "the apostle of unmarried sex" minimizes the judge's ideas. *The Companionate Marriage* is primarily an attack on the unthinking conformity to tradition that causes so many couples to marry unhappily and on the laws that confine them to these marriages. "It is easier to force married persons to go on living together when they don't love each other," he wrote, "than it is to weld love and marriage into an identical thing, two sides of a shield that would be capable of really protecting the 'Home' that we talk so much about and do so much to destroy by our barbarous stupidities and our ignoble fears of overthrowing 'custom.'"[9] Foremost among these "barbarous stupidities" are "the irrational and dangerous sentimentalities which cluster like slimy barnacles about our conception of love." The modern man "should by this time be capable of rationalizing and adapting [those sentimentalities] without recklessly destroying them" (17). Lindsey felt that it was the older generation who needed to do the rationalizing and adapting because the younger generation would act recklessly. Leaving these changes in social values to the younger generation would only invite disaster, whereas directed change, incorporating the ideas of the younger generation, would prove beneficial for society.

Among the changes foremost on Lindsey's mind were changes in divorce laws to make it easier for childless couples to get a divorce without alimony. The idea behind the "companionate marriage" was to allow couples the time to adjust to married life and to their commitment to one another before they started a family. This meant it was necessary not only to allow couples who were not committed to marriage to divorce, but also to allow women the use of birth control to ensure that uncommitted couples did not complicate matters with children. Lindsey's proposed changes to divorce laws and to laws prohibiting the distribution of information on birth control led to his characterization by critics as an advocate of everything from free love to Bolshevism.

In reality, the judge's positions on morals and marriage were both radical and conservative. He believed in the benefits that matrimony held for society, but he felt that bad marriages were detrimental to individuals, and by extension to the rest of society, and therefore should be allowed to end. For Lindsey, morality was not a static list of allowances and prohibitions but, rather, a fluid notion of what was acceptable and what was unacceptable in a society. In an earlier book, *The Revolt of Modern Youth,* Lindsey had discussed the changing attitudes of youth and had argued that many of these attitudes were good examples of adjusting to modern society. In *The Companionate Marriage,* he begins with the idea of "The Revolt of Middle Age," in which older, established couples are adapting to modern society by adopting new values regarding love and marriage. Lindsey provides the example of Mr. and Mrs. Blank (none of the names he uses are real, but the situations, he assures readers, came from his own experience), who have come over time to an agreement in their marriage in which they both have occasional affairs. "We agree on these things," the judge quotes Mrs. Blank. "We love each other, but we enjoy these outside experiences; so why not take them? I think we care more for each other on account of them." "What's the harm," she continued, "aside from the fact that we have always been told that it was wrong? If he has an affair with a girl he takes a fancy to, it really means nothing more to him or to me than if he took her to dinner or the theater. It is all casual and harmless unless one *thinks* harm into it." The result, according to Mrs. Blank, is that she and her husband "are free, and our married life is ideal,—in spite of the whole world saying, 'It can't be done'" (22–23). Mrs. Blank justifies this liberation from custom and repression in clearly Freudian terms: "What I mean is that I do what I want to do, and that I find it increasingly easy to do it without my fears and my old habits of thought tearing me to pieces inside. Save for the restraints contingent on other people's rights, there isn't a repression in my body. I think that is the way one should be in order to be healthy and happy" (28).

Lindsey does not present the Blanks as a model for others to follow, nor does he condemn their situation. He admires the fact that their marriage is one of equals, despite his sense that this is a concession on the part of the husband and not a right won by the wife. "It is particularly extraordinary that a husband should be willing to grant his wife the sort of liberty he feels is permissible for himself. I congratulate you and your husband on having at least gotten onto the same level, regardless of whether it is high or low" (30). What is most important for Lindsey is what the Blanks' situation says about changing ideas and values in American society. "That there are people in the world with your convictions seems to me significant and not necessarily alarming. There are some persons who regard as alarming every aberration of social conduct with which they don't happen to agree; but I am not of their number" (31). Throughout his narrative, Lindsey writes of the Blanks in very respectful and admiring terms, much more so than in the way he writes of those whom he sees as hypocritical or self-righteous.

Despite his claims and admonitions that his ideas and proposals were conservative—that is, that they retained the best of tradition without holding on to it lock, stock, and barrel—Lindsey's work came to represent the new ideas in sex. "*The Companionate Marriage* became the leading literary symbol of the American sexual revolution of the twenties."[10] Lindsey's progressive credentials dated from the pre-

World War I era and his efforts at legal reform, mainly in regards to juvenile law, but they also extended into a very public role supporting isolationism (he had traveled on Henry Ford's "peace ship" in 1915), labor unions, and prohibition (a position he would later reverse after seeing the result of this experiment to legislate morality). His views on a variety of issues basically supported the idea of the "new woman," the availability of birth control, and divorce laws that neither stigmatized women nor assumed that a woman's only means of support was her husband, or ex-husband in the case of alimony. Yet when Lindsey came face to face, and toe to toe, with the most celebrated "new woman," he fled.

Like Clara Bow, most people simplified Lindsey's work from a complex analysis of changing social mores to a justification of promiscuity, and "companionate marriage" became synonymous with everything from "pal marriage," "contract marriage," "jazz marriage," "free love," and most often, "trial marriage."[11] Lindsey was attacked in the press, in letters, and from the pulpit. Popular radio evangelist Sister Aimee Semple McPherson denounced the judge and pronounced, "I believe only in permanent monogamous marriage." Privately, the judge described Sister Aimee as "very human, well-meaning, and one of the most frightfully oversexed women I have ever met."[12] One young female reader wrote to Lindsey to protest his suggestions of more lenient divorce laws and blamed society's obsession with sex as the main cause of the problems Lindsey mentioned. "Why are the young folk so obsessed with sex?" she asked, then answered, "for the simple reason that they get sex at every turn. Everybody's talking sex. Every play or movie they see is 100 percent 'sex appeal.'"[13] Not only the films of Clara Bow, but other films and plays capitalized on the greater acceptability, and marketability, of sex.

The Companionate Marriage inspired a play, *A Companionate Marriage,* which opened in Chicago during the 1927–1928 season. Written by Jean Archibald, the play tells "the story of a liberated daughter who assumes all the responsibilities of matrimony without taking pains to go to the altar, but the youth in the arrangement makes a good woman of her by tricking her into a legal ceremony."[14] As with most entertainments produced for profit, such as films and plays, progressive ideas are incorporated but do not dominate. What results at the

end of *A Companionate Marriage,* as in Clara Bow's films, is a traditional marriage in which both parties pledge their love and devotion
to one another exclusively. Several other plays produced on Broadway
also illustrate this tendency. In *Her First Affaire,* a comedy by Merrill
Rogers,[15] "Ann Hood, eager for the full test of life at 20, is convinced
she must have an affair or two before she will be ready to settle down
to marriage." She sets her sights on Carey Maxon, a "free-thinking
novelist," who does not respond to her advances, which include "a
negligee costume and a provocative manner." Ann is unable to seduce
Carey, but "the adventure serves, however, to excite Brian Cutler to
action, and he elopes with Ann."[16] In *5 O'Clock Girl,*[17] "Patricia
Brown, working in a cleaner's shop, carries on a telephone flirtation
with an unknown young man whom she calls up at 5 o'clock every af-
ternoon." Patricia extends the charade when she finally meets her "5
o'clock boy" by borrowing clothes from the cleaners and pretending
to be someone she is not. But her tactic leads to love, "at which moment her deception is discovered and all seems lost. But is it? You
know very well it isn't."[18] Once again, the aggressive machinations of
the "new woman," attractively packaged in negligee or borrowed
clothes, still results in traditional, patriarchal matrimony.

One of the best examples of the "new woman" on Broadway was not
a character in a play but, rather, the actress and club owner Texas
Guinan. Mary Louise Cecelia Guinan came from Waco, Texas, and had
made a name for herself in rodeos and traveling shows before appearing
in Broadway musicals and eventually silent films. Capitalizing on her
Texas upbringing, Guinan starred in such films as *The Wildcat* (1917),
The Hellcat, The She Wolf, The Gun Woman (all 1918), and *Little Miss
Deputy* (1919). Known as the "female William S. Hart," Guinan became
best known as the hostess of the hottest nightclubs in Prohibition-
era New York. Hired as a singer at the Beaux Arts Hotel, she quickly
rose to mistress of ceremonies with her ability to trade jabs with the
audience and encourage them to buy more drinks. Starting with the El
Fay Club in 1924, Texas became a celebrity for both her talents as a
hostess and her notoriety with the law. As hostess, or more accurately
ringleader, Guinan led the frenzy of nightclub patrons, whom she
greeted with her signature "Hello, suckers!" Her brassy voice and
bawdy humor were as well known as her arrests for operating a

speakeasy. Each time the authorities closed down her club, she simply opened another. Though never convicted, Guinan wore a necklace of golden padlocks, symbolizing the number of times her establishments had been closed down, and she even starred in her own musical revue on Broadway, *Padlocks of 1927*,[19] in which she played herself, a nightclub hostess.

Although Guinan was not a great beauty, nor a great singer or actor, she was very adept at gaining publicity. Each arrest increased attendance at her clubs, and every occasion was a possible media event. In February 1927, in the midst of raids by New York City police on illegal nightclubs, Sister Aimee Semple McPherson visited Texas Guinan's 300 Club. The club had been closed down by the police, and Guinan had spent the evening in police custody, but she could be found the following night presiding over an even larger crowd than before the raid. Sister Aimee, on a national tour to rehabilitate her image after her disappearance/kidnapping incident of the year before, was in New York City to aid in the attempt to clean up the town. Once Guinan discovered her spiritual guest, she promptly announced to the crowd that "a great little lady from the Golden West, a wonderful, brave woman, is going to say a few words." Put on the spot, Sister Aimee admonished the crowd to stop their evil, materialistic ways before it was too late. "With all your getting and playing and good times," she said "don't forget you have a Lord. Take him into your hearts!"[20] Guinan then encouraged the audience to join her and her girls at Sister Aimee's sermon at the Chapel of Glad Tidings the next day. Guinan sat in the front row at the chapel, singing hymns and making sure that the press took pictures of the two women together and that they noted not only her presence but what she was wearing as well. The event proved more beneficial to Texas Guinan than to Sister Aimee. McPherson, long the champion at creating notoriety, had met her match.

Texas Guinan represents the "new woman" in a number of ways. Economically independent, and therefore fully capable of taking advantage of the consumer culture, Guinan did not conform to traditional stereotypes of what a woman should be. She was a successful businesswoman (in addition to her nightclubs, she also briefly ran her own film production company) and a star of stage and screen, but she is most accurately described as a celebrity. People were interested in her whereabouts, and rarely did a week go by without a mention of her in the papers. She was known, primarily, for being famous. She was an embodiment of people's excitement about modern America. Her "ranch-to-riches" story was uniquely American and entailed the particularly modern industry of motion pictures and the modern novelty of a female club owner operating an illicit business. Guinan took advantage of the opportunities available to the modern woman, yet she still embodied some characteristics of traditional womanhood. Her flamboyant dress and anything-but-demure personality combined the urban sophistication of the flapper with the rugged independence of the western cowgirl. Guinan made the most of her western roots, emphasizing her tomboy nature and independent spirit, right in line with pioneer women and such figures as Annie Oakley and Belle Starr. While such western women may have gone against the grain of acceptable female behavior, they were not modern in that they were not urban, sophisticated, or educated. The talents Guinan was known for, likewise, were seen as extensions of traditional women's roles of entertainer and service provider. She was the attraction of her nightclubs, and her fame rested on her "particularly modern talent of getting along with all kinds of people up and down the social hierarchy,"[21] a modern usage of a traditional female role.

TRADITION IN THE SOUTH

Modern notions of women were acceptable in the big cities and in the Wild West, but not in the South. In 1927, portrayals of southern women, as opposed to urban dwellers or westerners, maintained Victorian ideals of womanhood, marriage, and sex. As one reader of Lindsey's *Companionate Marriage* wrote, criticizing his proposal to change existing divorce laws, "Your law may be suitable for the 'wild west,' but not for 'our dear old Georgia' and the South."[22] Southern womanhood seemed to be the last bastion of respectable ladies in an era of flappers, divorcées, and working women. One of the early hits of the 1927–1928 theater season in New York was *Coquette,* written by George Abbott and Ann Preston Bridgers and starring Helen Hayes.[23] Hayes played Norma Besant, the title character and daughter of Dr. Besant, "a gentleman of the old South, dignified and formally courteous" with "an intolerance of things outside his strict code of conduct." Norma, as a well-bred southern belle, has a number of suitors vying for her attentions, but her heart belongs to the one suitor her father deems unacceptable, Michael Jeffery, "a roughneck."[24] Dr. Besant forbids Norma and Michael to see each other, but despite the obstacles, they carry on their romance. When Norma's father discovers her disobedience, he reacts by shooting and killing Michael. Distraught and enraged, Norma must testify in court that Michael's advances were unwanted in order to spare her father's life. The case hinges on whether or not Dr. Besant was defending Norma's honor or killing for revenge. Ultimately, the main issue in question is whether or not Norma's "honor" is intact and therefore worthy of defending. Norma confesses to Stanley (friend, suitor, and son of Dr. Besant's lawyer) not only that she is no longer a virgin but that she is pregnant with Michael's child. With no other way to save both her reputation and her father, Norma kills herself.

Like Bow's *Children of Divorce*, *Coquette* describes the limits of acceptable feminine behavior. In both cases, good but fallen women sacrifice themselves for the happiness of others and at the same time also relieve others and society of their tainted selves. While on the surface these dramas present a traditional morality play, with virtue outlasting pleasure and desire, they also subtly criticize traditional values by showing their rigidity. Both characters, Kitty Flanders and Norma Besant, realize that the existing moral code offers them no alternative but suicide. The audience is not relieved by their decision but, rather, sees the tragic implications of their conclusions. Even though the new order of easy divorce and acceptable promiscuity does not triumph in the end, the old order is portrayed as anachronistic. Set in a small southern town, *Coquette* establishes itself as a drama about traditional values simply by placing the story as far away from modern values as possible. Whereas large cities were the site of modern technology and ideas, small towns were isolated from modernity. Likewise, the South was less "modern" than the North or the West; its conservatism was primarily due to the lack of large urban centers but was also reinforced by the morality of the old South. In the South the gentleman and lady still existed, and the past exerted a greater hold on the popular imagination than elsewhere.

One of the hit musicals of 1927 was also set in the South, *Show Boat*.[25] With lyrics by Oscar Hammerstein and music by Jerome Kern, *Show Boat* was based on the 1926 best-selling novel by Edna Ferber. In the novel, Ferber laments the passing of an era, and the simple entertainment of the showboat reflects that simpler time. She recounts the lives of three generations of the Hawks family, and she not only recounts the workings of a showboat, a unique American institution, but describes the changes that occurred in popular entertainment from the 1870s to the 1920s. The novel also touches on issues of morality, marriage, race, and love. The novel was not a likely source for a Broadway musical in the 1920s, since it was considerably more serious than the variety/review type of musicals descended from vaudeville that were a staple of Broadway. What Hammerstein and Kern developed was a new kind of musical: not just a story sprinkled with songs and dancing, but a work in which the songs and dancing were an integral part of the narrative. In so doing, they also took Ferber's story about three generations of strong women and developed a story about the lasting bonds of marriage.

In both novel and play, Magnolia's life is at the center of the story. The play, however, focuses on Magnolia's married life. It starts with Magnolia's meeting Gaylord Ravenal, the first act ends with their marriage, and the play ends with their reunion. Captain Andy, Magnolia's father, along with Ravenal, are the two main influences on her throughout. Andy helps his daughter succeed in show business after she is deserted by Ravenal, and it is Andy who orchestrates the reunion of the couple at the end of the play (a departure from the novel, where he drowns). One does see a transformation take place in Magnolia (something not usually seen in musical comedy of the time) from innocent to self-sufficient, though never out of love with Ravenal. This focus on Magnolia and Gaylord's marriage is expressed in the repeated use of the song "Can't Help Lovin' That Man," which describes the inability to stop loving someone despite who he is and what he does. The other thematic song in the play also describes something unalterable and everlasting, the Mississippi River: "He don't plant 'taters, He don't plant cotton, An' dem dat plant 'em, Is soon forgotten, But ol' man river, He jes' keeps rollin' along."[26] But against this backdrop of everlasting love and the enduring Mississippi is a story about changing times and changing people. In the musical, everyone is happiest when they find their place, whether it be on the river, in another's arms, or on stage, and for the women in the play, their place is with their man.

Ferber describes Magnolia's life as a dynamic, ever-changing force of nature like the Mississippi River itself. As a child Magnolia states that if she were a river, she'd "want to be the Mississippi." When asked why, she replies, "The Mississippi is always different. It's like a person that you never know what they're going to do next, and that makes them interesting."[27] Magnolia experiences in her life the calms and rapids, the low and high water, and the changes of course experienced by the river. She grows up on the *Cotton Blossom Floating Palace Theatre* under the strict supervision of her New England mother Parthenia Ann and is thrust onto the stage as a last-minute replacement and becomes successful. She falls in love with her leading man, Gaylord Ravenal, a gambler with a shady past, and they elope. Their daughter Kim—named after the fact that she was born at the point where the Kentucky, Illinois, and Missouri rivers all converge—was born during a flood on the river. After the death of Magnolia's father, Captain Andy (drowned in the Mississippi), the Ravenals escape Parthy Ann's control and move to Chicago, where Magnolia lives the life of a gambler's wife—sometimes rich, sometimes poor. Deserted by Ravenal, now unable to make a living after reformers shut down the gaming houses, Magnolia becomes a star on the variety stage to support herself and Kim. Eventually Kim herself becomes an actress on the Broadway stage. The novel ends with the death of Parthy Ann, who has become a legendary showboat operator, and with Magnolia's return to the river life as owner/operator of the *Cotton Blossom*.

Each woman, Parthy Ann, Magnolia, and Kim, illustrates a stage in the changing role of women and the changing values of the society. Parthy Ann is a strong-willed woman whose only outlet for her energy and drive is in dominating her husband, her child, and eventually the workers of the *Cotton Blossom*. As Ferber tells us, "Life had miscast her in the role of wife and mother. She was born to be a Madam Chairman. Committees, Votes, Movements, Drives, Platforms, Gavels, Reports all showed in her stars. Cheated of these, she had to be content with such outlet of her enormous energies as the *Cotton Blossom* afforded." She had the misfortune of being born in an era when one spoke "not of Women's Rights but of Women's Wrongs" (124). But Parthy Ann's steadfast dedication to the *Cotton Blossom* resulted in her leaving a half-million dollar inheritance for Magnolia and Kim upon her death. Parthy Ann represents the force of the Mississippi, which makes earth and man conform to her power. Similar in character, but different in circumstance, is Kim. "Clear headed. Thoughtful. Deliberate" (386). Magnolia never imagined her daughter as an actress, since Magnolia's experience was that acting came naturally and was not a learned skill. Kim, as a twentieth-century woman with options open to her, spent time in stock companies in Chicago before attending the National Theatre School of Acting in New York, where she learned everything from voice to movement to fencing to French. "She was almost the first of this new crop of intelligent, successful, deft, workmanlike, intuitive, vigorous, adaptable young women of the theatre." Kim was urban and sophisticated, married to a theatrical producer, but "there was about her—or them—nothing of genius, of greatness, of the divine fire" (390). For Magnolia, there was something missing in Kim and in modern urban life, something that was rapidly disappearing from the nation. "There was no Mississippi in Kim" (393). The natural rhythm of life along the river and in rural towns was vanishing, and with it a sense of place, of connection to the land, and of history were vanishing as well.

The connection between the nineteenth-century pioneer woman Parthy Ann and the sophisticated modern Kim is of course Magnolia herself. She represents the tumultuous, ever-changing, and powerful force of the Mississippi, adapting to the times, reacting to her surroundings and situations instead of acting upon them. She is often caught between what is seen as proper (defined by her mother) and what is necessary (defined by her situation). Magnolia gains economic independence, yet her ultimate goal is a stable marriage. She is, ultimately, the ideal 1920s woman, who carefully discovers which traditions to maintain and which to discard. While not the ultramodern flapper, like Clara Bow, Magnolia conducts her life in a way that blends the old with the new, leaving her neither a slave to the past nor a slave to modern society. These three women, along with the characters played by Clara Bow, illustrate the variety of roles for the "new woman" in a consumer society where the entertainment industry—while reinforcing many stereotypes of women—allowed women financial freedom from men. For Ferber, Magnolia best reflects the lessons of a life on the river. As Kim leaves her mother standing on the deck of the *Cotton Blossom* at the end of the novel she remarks, "'There's something about her that's eternal and unconquerable—like the River.'" But in the end, "the river, the show boat, the straight silent figure were lost to view" (398). In the novel, as in real life, the values of southern, rural life were disappearing in the 1920s.

The novel and play also touch upon another source of conflict in the South, race. In both works, local southern authorities force Julie and Steve, a husband-and-wife acting team on board the *Cotton Blossom,* to leave the show boat when it is revealed that Julie is a black woman who has been passing as white. The story makes a point of ridiculing the notion that "one drop" of black blood is all it takes to condemn a person to second-class citizenship by having Steve prick Julie's finger and swallow a drop of blood so that he and the rest of the company can truthfully say that he has black blood in him and that therefore his marriage to Julie is not miscegenation. While the novel and play both condemn the racist attitudes of the South, they also reinforce the subservient roles of African Americans and the characterizations of them as primitive and simple. Queenie and Jo are the cook and handyman on the ship, and they teach Magnolia how to sing spirituals. Ferber describes how the couple left the boat each winter with three hundred dollars and new clothes and shoes and returned each spring "penniless, in rags, and slightly liquored." Still, "Captain Andy liked and trusted them. They were as faithful to him as their childlike vagaries would permit" (122). In the musical, Queenie was played by Tess Gardella, a blackface artist who often used the stage name "Aunt Jemima," and Jo was played by Jules Bledsoe. Gardella portrayed Queenie as the stereotypical mammy, and Bledsoe played Jo as the typical lazy, shiftless coon.

It is Jo's song "Ol' Man River" that states the condition of former slaves in the South and provides an ambiguous take on the lives of southern blacks. "You an' me, we sweat an' strain, body all achin' an' racked wid' pain. Tote that barge! Lift that bale! Git a little drunk an' you land in jail." The songs even elicit sympathy for the black workers and their situation. "I git weary an' sick of tryin', I'm tired of livin' and skeered of dyin'; but ol' man river, he jes' keeps rollin' along."[28] In both the casting of a white actor in the role of Queenie and Jo's song, the musical reinforces Ferber's stereotypical images of African Americans. "Ol' Man River" speaks to the enduring quality not only of nature but of black subservience as well. Just as the river rolls along, so too must African Americans suffer the hardships of their lives. Both are natural phenomena, and therefore neither can be changed. *Show Boat* allowed readers and audiences with progressive attitudes toward racial equality to see the story as a critique of southern society, a remnant of former days. But neither the novel nor the musical challenged the attitudes toward African Americans of those who sought to maintain segregation, and indeed, both novel and musical reinforced many of their prejudices.

While *Show Boat* was debuting on Broadway in the recently opened and monumental Ziegfeld Theatre, much of the geographic area where the action of the play occurs was still recovering from the worst flood ever experienced on the Mississippi River. In August 1926, just as Edna Ferber's *Show Boat* was released in bookstores, rain began to fall on the upper Mississippi Valley and the northern Great Plains. By September, rivers in eastern Kansas, northwestern Iowa, and Illinois began to overflow from the abnormal amounts of rain. By January, floodwaters had overtaken rivers in Alabama, Mississippi, and Kentucky. Continued heavy rainfall throughout the spring, especially in the lower Mississippi Valley, added more rain to saturated ground and already overflowing rivers. Levees meant to hold back the waters of the Mississippi and its tributaries began to break; eventually the waters breached the levees in 145 places. The floodwaters spread out over more than 16 million acres (26,000 square miles) reaching from Illinois to the Gulf of Mexico, destroying farms and towns, and killing at least 246 people. Flood waters destroyed over 5 million acres of cropland, and much of this remained uncultivated for months under the slowly receding waters. Estimated crop losses topped $100 million, while livestock and other farm losses reached $23 million. Over 162,000 homes were flooded, and the American Red Cross relief efforts cared for over 600,000 people for fourteen months.[29]

The flood was significant, not only as the worst natural disaster ever experienced by the nation but also as the largest domestic crisis since the Civil War. As such, the flood helped accelerate changes originally brought about by the war. Black migration to the North and West increased following the loss of productive lands and heightened racial tensions caused by the flood, which in turn reinforced the transformation of agriculture from a plantation-based economy dependent on sharecroppers and tenant farmers to agribusiness dependent on wage labor. The flood also brought about an increase in the federal government's role in the economics, politics, and culture of southern society, most notably in the form of the Flood Control Act of 1928, which gave responsibility for the construction, management, and maintenance of levees, reservoirs, and spillways to the Army Corp of Engineers. The flood not only reinforced trends already in place but also marked the beginning of some that would come to full fruition in the 1930s and 1940s, such as the political realignment of African Americans from the Republican to the Democratic Party. Many of the long-terms effects of the flood were not directly the result of high waters but rather arose from the way the relief efforts, and the part played by Herbert Hoover (then secretary of commerce and presidential hopeful) in heading those efforts, focused attention on the race- and class-based distribution of power in the South. The southern aristocracy of planter families had been giving way to the industrialism of the new South, and for many the flood was a fatal final blow. While the flood did not bring about these changes by itself, the consequences of the flood illustrate this transformation and the extent to which people challenged these changes. Like *Show Boat,* the flood highlighted the changes occurring in society and drew attention to racial inequality in the South.

The waters that ran over the levees of the Mississippi and its tributaries did not discriminate based on race or class. Large planters, black tenant farmers, and white sharecroppers all experienced the devastation of the flood. Of course, the wealthier or more politically powerful counties and parishes along the Mississippi were able to build higher levees, which theoretically would make them better protected than their neighbors, but in the end it did not really matter, since the waters flowed through weaker levees and filled in behind the stronger ones. The main exception was the city of New Orleans, the wealthiest and most powerful city on the lower Mississippi and the most cosmopolitan in the South.[30] The "leading citizens" of the city (bankers and businessmen, most of them members of the city's elite men's clubs) devised a plan to spare their city and businesses from the flood by releasing the built-up pressure of the river downstream by flooding St. Bernard and Plaquemines parishes, displacing 10,000 residents and destroying their homes and property.

The result of this blatant show of power by the elite of New Orleans was a political backlash pitting the country against the city. In May 1928, the citizens of Louisiana elected Huey Long governor, marking the end of the hold New Orleans and its "leading citizens" had over state, and even local, politics. The largest banks in New Orleans—including the Canal Bank, the largest in the South—began to fail as a result of the flood and were dealt their final blow with the onset of the Great Depression. Only one New Orleans bank survived the Depression as the same institution. As the social elite of New Orleans isolated themselves from the world around them, their city declined and eventually would be surpassed in size and importance by such new South cities as Atlanta, Dallas, Houston, and Miami.[31] New Orleans had physically survived the flood, but it was devastated in many other ways; the last remnants of the Old South had given way to the new.

AFRICAN AMERICANS AND THE AFTERMATH

Another indication of the passing of the Old South was the destruction of Greenville, Mississippi, a Delta town about halfway between Memphis, Tennessee, and Natchez, Mississippi. Greenville had a population of around 15,000, a lively downtown on the edge of a busy wharf, two train stations, three cotton exchanges, four oil mills, six sawmills, a meat-packing plant, Mississippi's finest hotel, and the Opera House and People's Theater, which presented such nationally known performers as Enrico Caruso and Al Jolson.[32] The area, like much of the Delta, was built on cotton. The rich alluvial land between the Yazoo and Mississippi rivers allowed for abundant cotton production and created vast fortunes for the white planters who owned the land. The work, however, was done primarily by black sharecroppers and tenant farmers, who were generally more successful than black farmers elsewhere in the South but who still remained at the bottom of the economic, not to mention the social, ladder. Former U.S. senator LeRoy Percy lived in Greenville, and it was from him, his family, and his peers that the prosperous Delta society emanated. Percy's political influence ensured the Delta's growth primarily by ensuring protection from the river. This influence and prosperity led to Greenville's being proclaimed "the Queen City of the Delta." Yet the relative prosperity of the region grew from a social system in which whites dominated blacks, not only politically and economically but culturally as well. "The Delta," writes Pete Daniel, "had survived as a tangible link with the antebellum South. Both in Mississippi and across the river in Arkansas the planters jealously guarded their black labor from agents who infiltrated from the North and tempted the black men to desert their agrarian life."[33] Labor was the most important ingredient in the economic success of the white planters in the Delta, and the one most lacking. The plantation society, built on the labor of sharecroppers and tenant farmers, began to die as the continual out-migration of African Americans, begun during Reconstruction, became an exodus. Half of all the African Americans in Greenville's Washington County left the state for points north and west in the wake of the flood.

While the departure of the black population reflects the lack of opportunities in the Delta following the flood, it was also precipitated by the deeply racist society in which black southerners lived, a situation highlighted by the events of the flood. "The treatment of black laborers, the attitude of planters, and the bureaucratic indifference of the federal government and the Red Cross were instructive in understanding how Southern society could contain covert and suppressed customs that appeared only in an emergency."[34] Both during and after the flood, African Americans experienced the worst of racist attitudes and actions, ranging from verbal and physical abuse to being forced at gunpoint to work on the levees, where they faced great danger and in some cases died.

During the flood, all along the lower Mississippi River, gangs of black workers toiled with sandbags, lumber, and shovels reinforcing weak points in the levees and raising the levees above the rising waters. Black workers saw the necessity of preserving the levees, not only to their communities but to their own homes and families, but their work on and off the levees was often not voluntary but forced by white planters. White workers, placed in charge of black workers by local levee boards and governments, forced African Americans to work long hours on the levees, but some planters would not allow the African Americans with whom they had sharecropping and tenant arrangements to assist the flood detail. Local leaders, like Greenville's Percy, repeatedly admonished local planters to release their laborers to help build up the levees.

In Vicksburg, Mississippi, Major John Lee of the Mississippi River Commission coordinated the efforts of 1,500 full-time black levee workers, forming them into gangs and housing them in camps near the levee along the 800 miles of river under his care. Up to 200 African Americans worked under the direction of one or two white supervisors.[35] Guards patrolled the levees, not only to protect them from sabotage (a crevasse on one side of the river eases pressure on the other, as well as up- and downstream) but to keep black workers on the job. At Mounds Landing, just as a crevasse started to develop, black workers brought in to fill the breach began running away in the face of the levee's collapse. "It then became necessary for the civilian foremen and my detachment to force the negroes to the break at the point of guns," reported Lieutenant E. C. Sanders of the National Guard.[36] When the levee broke, the advancing waters swept away hundreds of workers. No accurate count exists of the number of lives lost, but the one official report concerning the crevasse stated, "No lives were lost among the Guardsmen."[37] Observers and local newspapers estimated the figure in the several hundreds.[38]

The abuses of southern racism, as well as the abuses of farm tenancy, became even more pronounced during the relief efforts in the wake of the flood. Since the waters poured out over the land for months and remained for several months more, it became necessary to house, feed, and care for hundreds of thousands of homeless refugees stranded on the levees—virtually the only high and dry land around. The Red Cross took on the task of caring for the flood refugees; no direct federal aid programs existed. According to the official report of the Red Cross, they housed 325,554 people in refugee camps and cared for another 311,922 in public buildings and private homes.[39] The seg-regated refugee camps demonstrated the racism of the region, as evidenced in the situation in Vicksburg, where Camp Hayes sheltered 1,200 white refugees, Camp Juarez housed 400 Mexican workers, and Camp Louisiana and Fort Hill contained 12,000 African Americans.[40] The Red Cross estimated that nearly 70 percent of all refugees housed in the camps were black.[41] To coordinate the efforts of the Red Cross with the War, Treasury, Agriculture, and other cabinet departments, President Calvin Coolidge created the President's Committee on Relief headed by then secretary of commerce Herbert Hoover, whose selection seemed fitting not only for his background in relief efforts during the Great War but for his engineering training as well. Coolidge gave Hoover the authority to direct the various governmental agencies involved, though he was given no separate budget for the effort. Funding for relief came from the Red Cross, which used $100,000 from its own general budget and raised over $17 million in donations from individuals across the country and around the world.[42] Hoover and the Red Cross oversaw the relief effort, but it was primarily administered by local chapters of the Red Cross or by local levee boards or governments. As a result, even though the massive relief effort signaled a trend toward nationally coordinated assistance, it still reflected and reinforced local power structures and prejudices.

Planters, concerned about retaining their workforce until farming could resume, impeded the relief efforts that called for the removal of the refugees from the levees. Dr. Sidney Dillon Redmond wrote to Coolidge about the conditions black refugees faced. "These people are hurdled [sic] in camps of 5000 or more and soldiers from the National Guard are used to let none out of these camps and to keep people on the outside from coming in and talking with them." White refugees, Redmond complained, were removed from the levees and taken to shelters, whereas African Americans were held there by planters "at the point of a gun for fear they would get away and not return." To add insult to injury, rescuing mules took precedence over rescuing black refugees.[43] The NAACP's Walter White reported abuses as well, such as black refugees' inability to leave the camps and the Red Cross's policy of distributing supplies not directly to refugees but to planters. In some cases, planters charged their sharecroppers and tenants for the food and clothing, forcing them deeper into debt and therefore increasing the planters' claim to control the workers.[44]

Complaints to Coolidge and Hoover concerning the treatment of African Americans led Hoover to create the Colored Advisory Commission to investigate the situation. Headed by Tuskegee Institute president Robert R. Moton, the committee did not include anyone from the NAACP, which had become the loudest critic of the relief effort when the press carried stories about White's report on conditions. Hoover countered these stories by denying the poor conditions and announcing the formation of the Colored Advisory Commission. The commission visited camps in Arkansas, Mississippi, and Louisiana in June.[45] Its report to Hoover supported the charges of discrimination in the distribution of supplies, in the forced seclusion of the refugees, and in the general treatment of black refugees as opposed to the treatment of white refugees. The commission's report on the camp at Opelousas, Louisiana, stated that the impression it left was "more of being a prison camp than a refugee camp which probably accounts for the fact that so many of them want to leave." In addition, the commission reported that the guards had "been too free with a few of the colored girls."[46] The commission also reported that of the fourteen camps visited, only the one in Baton Rouge had supplied cots to black refugees.[47] A second report to Hoover by the commission, made in December after a second visit to the flooded area the month before, continued to criticize the conditions created through discrimination. The commission did not blame the National Red Cross for these discriminatory practices, but it did complain about the lack of supplies and services for the black population in the refugee camps. The commission discovered that "supplies were being given out irregularly through landlords and plantation commissaries. The common practices which had grown up in the communities and the local Red Cross officials, adjusted as they were to the plantation system, frequently nullified the intentions and program of the National Red Cross."[48] The commission singled out one local Red Cross administrator in particular, Cordelia Townsend of Melville:

Our investigators were discourteously treated by Miss Townsend and told in a most abrupt manner that they were not needed and were given no consideration. We know of instances where Miss Townsend ordered colored people to give up tents and find some place to live where there was absolutely no place for them to go. We also know that hundreds of homes for white people have been repaired and rebuilt in Melville and these homes furnished with rugs, sewing machines, refrigerators, etc., while only seven Negro homes in Melville have been repaired. Many of the colored people are sleeping on pallets or use mattresses spread upon planks.[49]

In addition to the recommendations that the Colored Advisory Commission made to Hoover and the Red Cross, Moton also suggested to the commission members that they publish a public report to illustrate not only the flood conditions but the situation of black labor in the agricultural South. "They [the refugees] felt that the flood had emancipated them from a condition of peonage," Moton wrote, a condition he referred to as "one of the greatest labor questions of America, which found itself in the relation between the planter and these tenant farmers." These were not circumstances brought about by the flood; rather, they were part of the daily experience of the black citizens of the region, who "lived not only in a state of fear but a state of abject poverty although they work from year to year." Moton hoped that publicizing the refugees' plight would help "relieve the hopeless condition under which these people have lived for all these years" and would give them "a sense of freedom and hope."[50]

The commission did not release a public statement, but Walter White did in an essay he wrote for the *Nation* in June. Under the title "The Negro and the Flood," White described his observations on the conditions of the flood refugees. He relates a conversation he had with General Curtis Green of the Mississippi National Guard in Vicksburg in which Green explained to him "the system by which a plantation-owner or his manager bearing credentials would come to the camp, identify 'his Negroes,' and then take the Negroes back to the plantation from which they came."[51] While White generally applauds the Red Cross relief efforts, he does criticize the way relief administrators allowed, "whether wittingly or not, . . . plantation-owners further to enslave or at least to perpetuate peonage conditions in many parts of the flood area" by restricting the movement of their sharecroppers and tenant farmers. Ultimately, for White, the flood illustrated the basic problem of southern society. "Harrowing as these stories are," he concludes,

> they are the almost inevitable products of a gigantic catastrophe and are part of the normal picture of the industrial and race situation in certain parts of the South. The greatest and most significant injustice is in the denial to Negroes of the right of free movement and of the privilege of selling their services to the highest bidder. That, if persisted in, would recreate and crystallize a new slavery almost as miserable as the old. (689)

The flood and its aftermath highlighted the problems of a tenantry- and race-based economy, but it also hastened the end of that system by introducing federal aid to the agricultural South. While federal intrusion in southern agriculture was not new (federal farm agents had assisted southern cotton farmers in fighting the boll weevil earlier in the century), southern farmers had not been dependent on federal aid. Sharecroppers and tenant farmers were dependent on planters and merchants for supplies, credit, land, and food and on informal local assistance such as that offered by churches, relatives, and neighbors. The suddenness and immensity of the flood overwhelmed local relief organizations, which could not meet the demand for aid, a demand filled by the National Red Cross and coordinated by Hoover's relief committee. Federal assistance, however, did not recede with the flood waters; instead, it became the accepted (though contested) norm, replacing the paternalism of the planter class with the paternalism of the federal government. "The federal government supplanted landlords and merchants with relief and, at the same time, with acreage allotments and benefit payments assumed direction over agriculture that had once belonged to the planter class."[52] This transformation was not exclusively the result of the flood, but the flood did mark the beginnings of large-scale federal aid, which continued with drought relief in the early 1930s and the New Deal in the mid-1930s. Both the drought and New Deal agricultural programs, such as the Agricultural Adjustment Act of 1933, reinforced the shift away from an economy based on plantations and tenants to one based on agribusiness and mechanization. This shift in the agricultural economy from smaller, independent (or semi-independent) farms to large-scale agribusiness organized along manufacturing lines was not exclusive to the South, but the hold of tradition and the sense of southern isolation helped maintain traditional farming practices longer there than in other parts of the nation. With the flood, and the federal aid that followed in its wake, agriculture in the United States became more homogenized, industrialized, and corporate.

But the effect of the flood and federal aid loomed over more than just the agricultural economy. The relief effort, by the Red Cross and by the President's Committee on Relief, illustrates the expanding role of national organizations and the federal government and the importance of the media in raising funds, influencing public opinion, and cultivating political support. The relief-fund campaign by the Red Cross was a highly coordinated, national effort that "built up the greatest Red Cross fund ever raised in the history of the organization, except in time of war, and the largest single disaster relief fund in the history of the world."[53] The total collected by the Red Cross, $17,498,902.16, not only paid for refugees' food, housing, and health care but was also used in rehabilitation programs that rebuilt houses and supplied feed and seed to farmers.

Involving 3,420 Red Cross chapters receiving individual donations, the campaign also relied upon the media to spread information about the disaster and the relief operations. The Red Cross received the cooperation of the Associated Press, United Press International, and the International News Service in publicizing the disaster and relief efforts. Newsreels, radio broadcasts, and newspaper and magazine stories all focused the nation's attention on the flooded region and the need for donations. Radio stations and movie theaters also sponsored fund drives, with many theaters organizing Red Cross benefit showings of films offered free of charge by studios and producers. As a result of

this invaluable cooperation by the press, the radio and the motion pictures, the entire populace of the United States, from coast to coast, was kept informed daily of the progress of the disaster relief work as the crest of the flood crept its way slowly southward along the Mississippi. They knew the amount of money needed to keep the relief job at Red Cross standards, how much had been raised each day, and how much remained to be given before the job was over.[54]

Along with coordinated efforts by churches, the U.S. Chamber of Commerce, local organizations, and fraternal societies, the Red Cross flood-relief program was a national unifying event that marshaled primarily private funds and agencies. Federal agencies did assist the Red Cross relief, but no direct federal funds went to the Red Cross or to the flood refugees. There was government involvement in the relief efforts: the War Department supplied the Red Cross with tents, cots, and blankets for the refugees; the National Guard supplied protection; and other government agencies supplied boats to help rescue and relocate refugees. "But the burden of caring for the homeless," President Coolidge stated, "rests upon the agency designated by Government charter to provide relief in disaster—The American National Red Cross."[55] This reliance on the private sector was the hallmark of Republican politics during the 1920s, but the enormity of the flood-relief effort required national coordination as well as a national sense of unity. It also required the flood victims to accept nonlocal aid, which, although the aid did not come directly from the federal government, meant accepting outside assistance, something rural people, especially southern rural people, did reluctantly. The nature of the flood—an uncontrollable and unforeseen disaster—helped ease flood victims into accepting outside assistance, since their plight was a result not of their own actions but of a natural occurrence. The inability of local agencies to adequately provide relief forced the victims to turn to national sources of relief, and while this was not the first time rural southerners had accepted outside assistance, it was the first major instance of what would become a trend with drought relief, New Deal reform, and home-front mobilization for World War II.

This growing dependence of southerners on the federal government was, in part, a result of federal policy. Indeed, if anyone could be "blamed" for the severity of the flood, it would be the federal government—in the form of the Army Corps of Engineers—which prior to the flood had embarked on a program of only building levees to contain the Mississippi River. Without spillways, cutoffs, and reservoirs, especially along tributaries, the volume of water in the Mississippi had reached unprecedented levels before and during the flood. Southerners along the river accepted the army's plan since it meant the federal government would provide matching funds while states and landowners primarily supplied land. After the flood, with the Flood Control Act of 1928, the government replaced the "levees only" policy with a comprehensive system of flood control, to be built and maintained by the Army Corps of Engineers and funded by the federal government. What had been under the supervision of state and local levee boards was now firmly under the federal government's control.

This increase of outside influences—from the federal government and from northern industrialization and modernization—did not proceed unprotested. In the early 1920s, a group of southern poets at Vanderbilt University, known as the Fugitives, developed a critique of modernization. By 1927, this critique focused on promoting the values of the Old South as a remedy to the dehumanizing effect of the industrialization being promoted by the advocates of the new South. "Our fight," John Crowe Ransom wrote to Allen Tate in 1927, "is for survival; and it's got to be waged not so much against the Yankees as against the exponents of the New South. I see clearly that you are as unreconstructed and unmodernized as any of the rest of us, if not more so. We must think about this business and take some very long calculations ahead."[56] These writers, which included Donald Davidson, Andrew Lytle, and Robert Penn Warren, eventually produced the manifesto of the agrarian movement, *I'll Take My Stand* (1930). Under the collective authorship of "Twelve Southerners," the agrarians promoted the traditions, history, and culture of the Old South as an alternative to the individualistic, and to their minds destructive, values of industrial capitalism. Though their critique does point out some of the flaws in the modern industrial system that had developed in the nineteenth century and come to full fruition in the 1920s, they could not provide solutions that fit the modern circumstances. For example, the agrarians espoused the virtues of the plantation system (in its postslavery incarnation), with its communal workforce and semi-independent and (theoretically) self-sufficient tenants, as compared to the specialization and alienation of industrial labor, which made workers dependent on factory owners. Their vision of the plantation system, however, did not take into account the degree to which sharecroppers and tenant farmers were dependent on planters because of low crop prices and perpetual indebtedness. The failings of the plantation system became obvious in the wake of the flood and the exodus of black farmers out of the Delta and the South.

In addition to bringing greater federal intrusion into the South, the flood and its consequences demonstrated the possibilities created by a national emergency, especially for national politics. Herbert Hoover's role as chairman of the President's Committee on Relief gave him public exposure on an almost daily basis for months during the emergency. Hoover ensured his role would be very visible by creating a press car on the train he used to tour the flood area. As secretary of commerce during two prosperous administrations, Hoover was well regarded by the public, but his reputation primarily stemmed from his humanitarian efforts during the Great War, first in Belgium, then as the director of the successful food administration that not only fed a starving Europe but helped increase production and profits for American farmers as well. But the war had receded in the public's memory, and by early 1927 Hoover was only rarely mentioned as a possible presidential candidate. His very public role in the flood relief not only reinvigorated his image as the "Great Humanitarian" but also reinforced his image as the "Great Engineer," since Hoover publicly took charge of—and credit for—the relief, reconstruction, and flood-control planning operations. Hoover's direction of the flood-relief effort did not, however, immediately signal an increase of federal authority, since Hoover pronounced that his goal was "to coordinate the activities of the War, Navy, Treasury, and Commerce Departments into support of the Red Cross, which it was determined must continue the primary responsibility for the organization and administration of the relief measures to be taken."[57] By doing so, Hoover created no new administration, relying exclusively on existing institutions and organizations to create a comprehensive plan of relief and reconstruction.

This hierarchical structure created by Hoover, with himself at the top of the organizational pyramid followed by public and private organizations and resting firmly on local administrators and volunteers, was the major strength (and weakness) of Hoover's approach to government, the use of bureaucracy to strengthen the individual, what

Bruce Lohof describes as "humane efficiency."[58] Hoover, and the public and private resources he marshaled, enabled local chapters of the Red Cross and other relief agencies to engage in the actual relief operations of building, maintaining, and staffing refugee camps and relief centers without direct federal intrusion, except for the National Guard (the most localized of the armed services), which policed the camps. Information, standards, supplies, equipment, and funding all came from centralized sources to local operations. This was true not only of the immediate relief operations but of the process of reconstruction as well. Once the danger of additional flooding disappeared, the "one great task demanding immediate attention," Hoover declared, was "the replacement on the farms and in industry of this great army of unfortunate people."[59] Much of this reconstruction would be made possible through the extension of credit. Hoover oversaw the creation of statewide credit corporations in Mississippi, Louisiana, and Arkansas whose capital came from banks and commercial interests in each state and from Federal Intermediate Credit Corporations, adjuncts of the Federal Farm Loan Board.[60] While most of the funds eventually issued to borrowers came from local sources, the federal guarantee of the intermediate credit corporations and the "knowledge that their resources were available in case of need not only facilitated the operations of the [state] credit corporations but helped to maintain confidence generally."[61] In addition, Hoover brought together corporate leaders to create the Flood Credits Corporation, an adjunct to the U.S. Chamber of Commerce, which issued bonds to chamber of commerce members and the various state credit corporations. The result was what Lohof describes as "efficient, centralized authority [that] served to sustain an essentially grass-roots effort."[62]

This balance between a central authority and local effort worked well for many of the flood victims by providing them the means necessary to rebuild their lives without the direct intrusion and control of the federal government. It was for many an indication that bureaucracy could work to the benefit, and not the detriment, of the individual. What the agrarians saw as the destructive force of modern life—industrial and bureaucratic values replacing individualism, honor, and duty—Hoover saw as constructive. "For Hoover a bureaucracy was a source of nourishment for grass-roots activity. Properly administered, a bureaucracy would not replace or stifle individual effort or community enterprise; rather, it would vitalize these activities by coordinating and rationalizing the resources upon which they draw."[63] In this way, Hoover resolved the major conflict of modernity, between the bureaucracy and the individual, by not seeing them as adversaries. But this "humane efficiency" did not resolve all the conflicts it addressed. As president, Hoover's direction of relief for the Great Depression relied on the same formula of federal, private, and local effort but could not overcome the immensity of the crisis, primarily because, whereas the flood-relief effort was able to take advantage of sources outside the affected area, the Depression affected the entire nation, indeed the world, leaving no external source of support available.

In the flood relief itself, Hoover's political ideas did resolve the basic and immediate problems—rescuing, housing, and caring for refugees; initiating reconstruction; and implementing flood control—but they failed to address existing problems, such as the economic dependency of tenant farmers and racial discrimination. Hoover contemplated a solution to these problems utilizing the same kind of corporate bureaucracy to implement land reform through the creation of a "land resettlement corporation" that would buy foreclosed plantations, divide and stock them with farm materials and livestock, and make them available to "a great number of buyers amongst both blacks and whites."[64] This resettlement would distribute land more widely than was possible under the plantation system, and it would create a Delta region of small, independent, self-sufficient farmers. "Had the scheme been acted upon, sharecroppers and tenant farmers would ideally have become yeomen, and the valley would come to enjoy, in Hoover's words, those 'infinite values to good citizenship . . . that comes with a population who have a stake in the land.'"[65]

One man who shared Hoover's vision of independent farmers in the Delta was Robert Moton, head of the Colored Advisory Commission. Hoover detailed the plan to Moton, leading him to believe it would be implemented, if not soon after the flood then after Hoover was elected president. As a result, Moton backed down from criticizing Hoover and the relief effort, even after it became clear that nothing would be done about the discriminatory handling of the aid and supplies in the relief and reconstruction efforts. Moton's final report to Hoover from the Colored Advisory Commission was critical of the treatment accorded African Americans by the Red Cross and by planters. When told by Hoover that the report was a "disappointment," Moton relented and revised it to praise the Red Cross and Hoover. Moton also worked to protect Hoover from criticism over the flood relief during the election campaign of 1928. "With Moton's help no scandal had erupted and black Republican delegates had fallen in line."[66] But once nominated, Hoover sought to increase his support by courting white southerners, who would not support Democratic candidate Al Smith, a Catholic. This support would only come at the expense of black Republicans, who saw few benefits in supporting Hoover and the Republicans. As a result, Hoover lost around 15 percent of the black vote, down considerably from Warren G. Harding's 95 percent support from the black community. In the South, the election was significant not only as an early sign of what would become a major defection of African American voters from the Republican to the Democratic Party, but also as the first election since Reconstruction in which southern states voted Republican, a trend that would grow much stronger after World War II.

Political realignment, black migration, the decline of farm tenantry, the decline of New Orleans' old-money power, and the intrusion of federal authority into the South all illustrate how the flood transformed the lower Mississippi Valley and, through dispersion and policy effects, transformed the nation as well. While the "new woman" represented the modern era in this struggle between Victorian and modern cultures, and the Agrarians represented the old southern values, African Americans in the flood-affected South were caught between the two as industrialization and agribusiness, along with federal intervention, replaced the plantation-style system of farm tenantry. But the flood illustrates another characteristic of modern American life in the use of the media and publicity, especially by Hoover, to gain financial and political support. Hoover's use of the available media (newspapers, magazines, newsreels, and radio), as well as his support of a new medium (television), ushered in a new era of political campaigning. Even though this media savvy would be more apparent in Franklin Delano Roosevelt, who was much more adept at using the press to his advantage, Hoover was key in the development of a new political phenomenon, a national media identity. Hoover saw the potential of the media to assist in national efficiency, as he had with bureaucracy, and he used the media accordingly; but also like bureaucracy, the media possessed dangers as well as potential, dangers masked by optimism and the quest for notoriety.

Average net paid circulation of THE NEWS, Dec., 1927: Sunday, 1,357,556 Daily, 1,193,297

DAILY NEWS

NEW YORK'S PICTURE NEWSPAPER

EXTRA EDITION

Vol. 9. No. 173 56 Pages   New York, Friday, January 13, 1928   2 Cents IN CITY LIMITS 4 CENTS Elsewhere

DEAD!

Story on page 3

(Copyright: 1928: by Pacific and Atlantic photos)

RUTH SNYDER'S DEATH PICTURED!—This is perhaps the most remarkable exclusive picture in the history of criminology. It shows the actual scene in the Sing Sing death house as the lethal current surged through Ruth Snyder's body at 11:06 last night. Her helmeted head is stiffened in death, her face masked and an electrode strapped to her bare right leg. The autopsy table on which her body was removed is beside her. Judd Gray, mumbling a prayer, followed her down the narrow corridor at 11:14. "Father, forgive them, for they don't know what they are doing?" were Ruth's last words. The picture is the first Sing Sing execution picture and the first of a woman's electrocution. *Story p. 3; other pics. P. 26 and back page.*

"DEAD!" Ruth Snyder's execution. Front page of the *New York Daily News,* January 13, 1928. (Courtesy of the *New York Daily News*)

Poster illustration for the movie *Babe Comes Home*.

CHAPTER 3 *Seeking Notoriety:*
The Infamous and the Famous

INFAMY AND FAME: *Celebrity came in many guises in the 1920s. Some, such as exe-cuted murderer Ruth Snyder, gained notoriety for criminal behavior symbolic of the era; others, such as athlete Babe Ruth, brought their unique personalities not only to their chosen professions but to vaudeville stages, barnstorming tours, and motion pic-tures. To many Americans, Snyder represented the dangers of such modern values as sexual equality, pleasure-seeking, and lack of respect for authority and traditional val-ues. Ruth also embodied many of those same traits, but his success on the field as a baseball player and off the field as a celebrity grew from his rags-to-riches back-ground, not his demonstration of modern ideas. Both Snyder and Ruth filled the pages of the emerging tabloid press, sold to an eager audience, illustrating the benefits and dangers of celebrity in America.*

Herbert Hoover's faith in publicity and the media as a bureaucratic tool stemmed from his belief in the value of expert management of both business and public affairs. Used wisely, publicity experts could inform the public about the information and services available from the government without being intrusive or obstructive. Publicity had helped Hoover illustrate the benefits of such wartime agencies as the Food Administration and of such peacetime initiatives as the Missis-sippi Valley flood-relief effort, both voluntary efforts and both highly successful. Even though Hoover encouraged the development of the publicity machine into a smoothly running and enormously profitable industry, he did not fully understand its dimensions and limitations. Hoover understood the potential benefits of mass media and publicity, but his own limitations obscured the dangers inherent in a public ser-vice run for profit. Among those dangers was a press dominated not by hard political, economic, or international news but, rather, by soft human interest stories or sensationalistic stories about crime and celebrities. The tabloid press enlarged the newspaper-reading audi-ence as newspapers focused more attention on crowd-pleasing stories. Reinforcing the tendencies of the press, the rise of collegiate and pro-fessional sports provided ample material for soft news. Newspapers became more than a method for informing the public; they became a commodity among many others trying to gain the public's attention. The publicity machine, and the celebrities created by it, were not new to the 1920s, but the dominance of publicity and the sheer number of celebrities during the decade illustrates the central role of image in the modern world.

GENERATING PUBLICITY

As secretary of commerce from 1921 to 1928, Hoover sought to transform the federal government into an efficient and nonintrusive bureaucratic machine. According to biographer Joan Hoff Wilson, Hoover's objective "was the virtual elimination of poverty in the United States," and he planned to accomplish this "through administrative reorganization and mass media dissemination of expert information."[1] By reorganizing the cabinet departments to eliminate duplication and waste, Hoover hoped to make the government function more efficiently, and by making important economic information available to all industries, businesses, and individuals, he hoped to enable businessmen to make informed decisions, which would mean an efficient and smoothly running economy as well. Hoover's reorganization of the executive branch, although not as extensive as he wished, increased the role and importance of the Commerce Department, and of course, its secretary.

To publicize the information gathered by the Commerce Department, as well as to publicize the achievements of the department, Hoover enlisted the aid of public-relations experts as well as of established figures in the press. Such journalists as George Akerson, Frederick M. Feiker, and Arch W. Shaw had worked with Hoover during the Great War and assisted him as secretary of commerce. Other such notable journalists as Ida Tarbell and William Allen White also lent their talents to Hoover's cause. Hoover felt that public relations was a bureaucratic tool for use by experts, and as a result, "his approach reflected his own lack of emotional appeal and human warmth."[2] This impersonal approach can be seen in the over 3,000 conferences and commissions created to bring attention to various problems and solutions managed by the Commerce Department. Hoover tended to trust organizations and groups more than individuals, which gave much of the publicity garnered by the Commerce Department an impersonal air. During the flood crisis in 1927, Hoover's command of the relief effort, while mainly managerial and organizational, had a direct personal impact on individuals in the flooded area, whose stories were relayed by the ever-present press. The flood relief illustrated all the best aspects of Hoover's philosophy—volunteerism and organization—while masking the pitfalls of an impersonal bureaucratic society. The flood-relief effort enhanced Hoover's popular image as the "Great Humanitarian." In the late spring of 1927, near the end of the flood-relief effort, the owner of the *Emporia (Kansas) Daily Gazette,* William Allen White, organized a dinner for Hoover with over fifty newspapermen from Kansas. Another Kansan newsman, and a friend of Hoover's, Arthur Capper, described the dinner in his *Topeka (Kansas) Daily Capital* as "an ovation to Mr. Hoover, the handy-man of America."[3] The media and public celebrated Hoover's seemingly unlimited ability to solve problems. Even though Hoover did not actively promote his own activities, his diverse array of undertakings in the 1920s were a sharp contrast to an otherwise lackluster political decade. "The one political figure," writes Wilson of Hoover, "most out of tune with the flamboyant aspects of the Roaring Twenties became its best known Washington official."[4] He also emerged as a presidential contender when, on August 2, 1927, President Coolidge announced that he would not seek reelection in 1928.

Though Hoover's campaign for president did not officially begin until February 1928, when he entered the Ohio primary, he was quietly lining up supporters much earlier. In 1925 Hoover hired George Akerson as his press secretary, and in 1927 Akerson organized friends in the press, including Will Irwin, George Barr Baker, and Bruce Barton, to develop public support for Hoover. Famed advertising executive Barton wrote a well-publicized rebuttal to H. L. Mencken's dismissal of Hoover as a "fat Coolidge" who was not entertaining enough to be a leader. Mencken labeled Hoover's opponent Al Smith "a cocktail" and called Hoover "a dose of aspirin." Barton responded by arguing that amusing rulers have no place in a modern society, though, he said, Mencken would make an excellent court jester.[5]

Hoover's use of publicity was an integral part of his ideas about how a bureaucracy should function, and in this sense he could be considered the first modern president, in that he recognized the importance of image in a mass-mediated society. His use of radio, the press, and advertising executives in his campaign, especially in the early stages when he was not officially a candidate, proved crucial to his success in the election. But Hoover's use of publicity ultimately proved detrimental. Hoover's public service, from wartime Belgium and the Food Administration to the Commerce Department and the flood-relief effort, created an image of a benevolent bureaucrat, a "Great Humanitarian." Hoover's works justified the label, but to the public the label not only celebrated the accomplishments of a public servant but also implied a warm and caring personality. Whereas Hoover based his life on character, the public saw him as a personality. Hoover seemed unaware of the difference and was incapable of effectively fulfilling the image of a personality. In this sense Hoover was far from a modern president, in that he did not actively cultivate a personality as part of his campaign. It was Hoover's challenger in the 1932 election, Franklin Roosevelt, who combined the publicity methods pioneered by Hoover with an engaging public personality to emerge as the first fully modern president.

As Hoover began his first presidential bid, however, the most-talked-about issue concerning the American presidency was not the question of who would be the next president or anything about the current president, Calvin Coolidge, but, rather, the illegitimate daughter of the late president Warren G. Harding. In the summer of 1927, Nan Britton published *The President's Daughter*, which described her longtime affair with Harding and the product of their affair, her daughter Elizabeth Ann. Of all the scandals arising from Harding's administration, this one was unique in that its revelation was not meant to discredit the president, who was dead, or his administration, which was in the past. The book's intention, according to Britton, was to push for the "legal and social recognition and protection of all children in these United States born out of wedlock."[6] Despite her claim of a "human cause," that "there should be no so-called 'illegitimates' in these United States,"[7] Britton wrote her book after she had made several failed attempts to gain financial support for her daughter from Harding's siblings (Harding died in August 1923 and his wife died in 1924). Britton's call for legal recognition of all children included the requirement that, by law, biological fathers would be named on birth certificates, which would entitle each child to a measure of support during the life of the father and a claim to any inheritance after the father's death.

In order to tell her story, Britton (with the help of Richard Wrightman, head of the Bible Corporation of America) created the Elizabeth Ann Guild, which published the book after the major publishing houses declined to do so. She also founded the Elizabeth Ann League to lobby for state and federal legislation to secure the rights of illegitimate children, though the organization did little more than write encouraging responses to letters from unwed mothers seeking financial assistance.[8] Her main goal, or at least her primary result, seems to have been publicity. She could not conclusively prove her claim that Harding was Elizabeth Ann's father, nor could she even substantiate her claim to have had an affair with Harding. She said that she and Harding had agreed to destroy the love letters they sent to each other and claimed that the fact they had both stuck to their agreement illustrated the depth of their devotion to one another.[9] Whether she sincerely sought the legal recognition of all illegitimate children or just of her own, there was no better way to publicize her cause than to connect her child to the late president. Indeed, Britton had known Harding from his days as a newspaper editor in Marion, Ohio. Proof exists showing her schoolgirl infatuation with Harding, and it is evident that Harding, while he was a U.S. senator, did help Britton find employment in New York. Many analysts, however, dismiss her account, though once again, no solid evidence supports their refutations.

The book was a sensation, selling around 50,000 copies by the end of the year and over 100,000 copies by the early 1930s. Many bookstores would not keep the book out on display but stocked it under the counter instead.[10] Customers could also buy the book directly from the Elizabeth Ann Guild. The book was expensive for the time, at five dollars a copy, but according to Britton,

> its theme has found tender response in the hearts of hundreds of thousands of readers, and may be found in homes from far-off New Zealand to ancient Syria, from the Philippines to Alaska. It has been estimated that a million people in the United States alone have read

The President's Daughter. Lending libraries, even in the most sparsely populated sections of the country, are daily replenishing their supplies of this book, which, it is reported, is all too quickly worn with much reading.[11]

The book also spawned an array of reactions. A lawsuit by Richard Wrightman's wife, Patricia, claimed that he had written the book and should receive credit and compensation. A response titled *The Answer,* written by Dr. Joseph De Barthe, argued in thinly veiled language that Britton's book was the result of her degeneracy and that Harding could not have been Elizabeth Ann's father because he had been sterile. In addition, many articles attempted to prove or disprove the validity of Britton's claims. *The President's Daughter* was one part of a much larger debate over Harding—a debate that included the scandals in Harding's administration under congressional investigation at the time of his death—along with such works as *Revelry* (1926), by Samuel Hopkins Adams, whose Hardingesque protagonist is a deeply troubled president who accidentally poisons himself, and *The Strange Death of President Harding: From the Diaries of Gaston B. Means, a Department of Justice Investigator* (1930), by Gaston Means, which suggested that Florence Harding had poisoned her husband. These criticisms of Harding and his administration were fought by Harding's siblings and the supporters of the Harding Memorial in Marion, Ohio, dedicated in 1927 when the bodies of the president and his wife were interred at the site. This debate, which continues in biographies and histories concerning Harding, has created the perception that Harding was the worst president in the nation's history.[12]

The importance of *The President's Daughter,* however, is not in its accuracy or its effect on Harding's reputation; rather, the book illustrates the modern tendency to seek publicity as an end in itself rather than to champion a cause. Even though Britton claimed to be crusading on behalf of illegitimate children, she did not force any change in the legal standing of such children. She did make a significant amount of money from the sale of the book, as well as being on the payroll of the Elizabeth Ann Guild, but more importantly, she became known as Harding's mistress and the mother of his child, even though she was unable to prove the claim. The notoriety of the book and the publicity it generated made Nan Britton famous. She became newsworthy and notable for writing a book that had no significant impact on policy or on the presidency but that fed the public's prurient interests in illicit affairs and sex. Britton sold the one thing she had that could be commodified, her story.

The media circus surrounding the 1927 arrest, trial, and conviction (and eventual execution in 1928) of Ruth Snyder and Henry Judd Gray for murdering Snyder's husband, Albert, also reveals the public's interest in illicit affairs and sex. Authorities arrested and indicted Gray, a corset salesman, and Snyder in March after the couple planned and implemented a plot to eliminate Albert Snyder and collect $96,000 from a life insurance policy that Ruth had tricked her husband into buying. Exactly who devised the plot is unclear, but in the end both received the death sentence for first-degree murder. The episode contained all the elements of a good media story: clearly definable characters (indeed, stock characters), illicit sex, mystery, murder, betrayal, and a lengthy trial attended by the curious and the celebrated.

The facts of the case are few but significantly damaging. Snyder and Gray began their affair in the summer of 1925, she a thirty-year-old housewife and mother from Queens, and he a thirty-three-year-old salesman employed by the Bien Jolie Corset Company and living in East Orange, New Jersey, with his wife and daughter. Over the next year and a half, they met in hotel rooms (once when Ruth could not find a sitter for her daughter Lorraine, she sat her in the hotel lobby and told her to wait) and at Snyder's home in Queens Village, New York. Over the course of the affair, Snyder told Gray about several of her failed attempts to kill her husband, including by poisoning and by leaving the gas on while he slept (Snyder claimed she had merely related stories about accidents involving her husband), and, according to Gray, Snyder enlisted his assistance in buying chloroform, a sash weight (a 5-pound weight used in window sashes), and other murderous implements.

On Saturday, March 19, Judd Gray entered the home of Ruth and Albert Snyder while all the residents were out (Ruth, Albert, and Lorraine were at a party, and Ruth's mother, who also lived there, was working as a nurse), and, following Ruth's instructions, he hid in her mother's room, where he found waiting for him the sash weight and other items. When the Snyders returned home after the party at around 2:00 a.m. Sunday, Gray was already quite drunk, having started drinking earlier in the day. Once Albert fell asleep, Ruth and Judd entered the bedroom, and Judd struck Albert on the head with the sash weight, but not hard enough to knock him out. A struggle ensued between Judd and Albert until Judd was able to hit Albert again and then strangle him. In order to ensure that he was dead, Judd and Ruth placed cloths soaked in chloroform in Albert's mouth and tightened a wire around his neck. They also placed Albert's own gun near his hand and messed up the house to look like a burglar had entered and fought with Albert. Judd then loosely tied and gagged Ruth and conspicuously placed an Italian-language newspaper in the house before leaving.

On his journey from Queens Village to Syracuse, New York (where he was supposed to be making a sales call as his alibi), Gray talked to and was remembered by a man at the bus stop, a policeman, a cab driver, and the train conductor. Ruth, meanwhile, crawled to her daughter's bedroom door (two rooms away from where the murder took place), woke Lorraine, and told her to go get help. When neighbors arrived to assist Ruth, they found Albert in his room dead. As police and press descended on the house, Ruth told her story of a dark and mustached man who had knocked her unconscious, leaving her bound and gagged until she was able to wake Lorraine for help. While she was recounting her ordeal and answering questions from the police, investigators found evidence that contradicted her story. A doctor examined her and found no evidence of a struggle or any contusion that could have caused her to lose consciousness. Police found the sash weight, hidden in a toolbox and covered with dried blood, but no evidence of a forced entry. The only items missing from the house were the contents of Albert's wallet (which Ruth had given to Gray); her fur coat was hanging in the closet, and no other valuables were missing. Police also found Ruth's jewelry hidden under her mattress. The most damaging evidence was a stickpin with the letters *JG* on it; Ruth's hidden address book containing the names of twenty-eight men, including Judd Gray; and a canceled check for $200 made out to Judd Gray and signed by Ruth.

For over twelve hours, police questioned Ruth Snyder before finally telling her that Judd Gray had confessed to the crime and had related the entire story to the authorities. With this, Snyder admitted to having been involved, but she insisted that she had tried to stop Gray at the last minute and that she had had no actual hand in the killing. Meanwhile, authorities had yet to apprehend Gray, but when they did arrest him at his hotel in Syracuse, he confessed to having had an affair with Ruth and to having been in the Snyders' house at the time of the murder, but he said that he was hiding in a closet while the whole incident of the Italian burglar took place. While on the train back to New York City, police informed Gray of Snyder's confession (producing a newspaper with headlines announcing her confession), and he too confessed to the crime. Once indicted, both Snyder and Gray tried to place the blame on the other. Despite a motion for separate trials, Snyder and Gray were tried together, but they had separate legal defenses. Snyder's defense argued that she had taken no part in the crime—indeed, had tried to stop it—and that Gray was an evil influence on a vulnerable woman caught in a bad marriage. Gray's defense did not try in the least to acquit Gray of the charges; rather, by his own testimony Gray condemned not only himself but Snyder as well.[13] The trial lasted eighteen days, and fifty-eight witnesses were called. The jury deliberated for only one hour and thirty-seven minutes before returning a guilty verdict, for which state law mandated a punishment of death by electrocution.

Throughout the trial, both Snyder and Gray aired their feelings to the press. Snyder sought to gain public sympathy by appealing to "mothers and wives" like herself and by denouncing Gray as a manipulator who betrayed her. "He turned on me like a traitor and a liar. He made me a murderer condemned to die. He came into my home to steal another man's wife and take another man's life. He drank himself into a delirium of murderous mania and killed Albert Snyder with his own hands. . . . I shielded him. But the cowardly fear came up in him; when he saw he couldn't save his own precious skin he turned on me."[14] Even after the verdict was in, Snyder tried to save herself by converting to Catholicism, not for the salvation it might provide but in an attempt to win the sympathy of New York governor Al Smith, a

Catholic. Smith, while inclined to spare the life of a woman, could not stay her execution once she converted because, like Hoover, he was preparing for a presidential bid, and pardoning a Catholic would reinforce nativist fears of a papist conspiracy. Snyder's serialized story in the press became a twenty-five-cent newsstand pamphlet entitled *My Own True Story—So Help Me God!* which John Kobler describes as "a fantastic stewpot of self-pity, hypocrisy, purple phrases and occasionally surprising flashes of self-revelation and frankness."[15]

Gray wrote his thoughts in a book, *Doomed Ship: The Autobiography of Judd Gray,* published after his death. He claimed not to be writing for absolution or "as an excuse for my sins and misdeeds. I am not writing it even for understanding—I have in my mind one purpose only—that of showing how possible it is to fall into anything—how impossible it is to hurdle life's conventions—that the only way to salvage life after practicing duplicity is to confess our sins."[16] The book sought to tell the truth, as Gray saw it, in order to refute the testimony of Snyder, dispel the stories presented by the press, and ponder the frenzy and publicity generated by the event. "The reporters in droves had made prisoners of all my family," Gray wrote, referring to the barrage of media that descended on his wife, mother, sister, and even daughter after his arrest. "One reporter going so far as to go to my little daughter's schoolroom and demand that the child be delivered into his custody." Other reporters claimed to be investigators with the police department or "long lost friends or relatives," or they simply stole items from the yards of Gray's family members, including their mail. His family was, Gray wrote, "quite unaware, however, that this was the beginning of the war maneuvers of the great American Press" (219–220). The approaching trial increased the number of reporters and, according to Gray, the falsity of the reports. "The public had tried the case before it ever came to court, fed by stories, mythical of course;—the products of reporters' brains—tales entirely inconsistent with not alone ethics, but good sense." And Gray confessed that "these lies and falsities were one of the hardest things I had to bear" (228–229). All this attention led Gray to reflect:

> And I could but wonder, though I do not wish to seem cynical nor
> arrogant, how people could clamor and fight to reach the inside of

the courtroom—to listen to the sordid details of the sins of others. All I could think of was the side show of a circus—and Ruth and I the freaks to be viewed. At the minimum cost of a pass. And these people—high and low—well-known stage and screen celebrities—sat day after day being entertained by the review of a crime and the sad, illicit sins of others—fed on the misfortunes of those that loved wrongly—and they tried to pick into the crannies of two souls to see if there was not a little dirt left in overlooked corners—I hope and pray that there were many who took a lesson home from the sordid calamity. (229–230)

The trial was a media event involving the press, especially the relatively new tabloid picture papers like the *New York Illustrated Daily News,* the *New York Daily Mirror,* and the *New York Evening Graphic,* which by 1926 had a combined circulation of more than 1.3 million. The often-married Peggy Hopkins Joyce was hired by the William Randolph Hearst–owned *Daily Mirror* to share her thoughts on the case, and the well-known Reverend John Roach Stratton denounced the couple in another paper for violating each of the ten commandments in their crime. Sister Aimee Semple McPherson wrote in the pages of the *Evening Graphic* (owned by *True Story* and *True Confessions* publisher Bernard McFadden) that men should desire "a wife like mother—not a Red-Hot Cutie."[17] Other celebrities in attendance and sharing their views included playwright David Belasco, film director D. W. Griffith, evangelist Billy Sunday, and contemporary best-selling author of *The Story of Philosophy,* Will Durant. *Chicago* playwright Maurine Watkins, along with lead actress Francine Larrimore, took time out from their current Broadway run to observe the proceedings as research, and publicity, for their own work. In *Chicago,* Roxy Hart (played by Larrimore) proclaims, after committing homicide, "I really have the tenderest heart in the world—wouldn't hurt a worm."[18] According to John Kobler, "Ruth precipitated a near riot by announcing, 'Kill my husband? Why, I wouldn't hurt a fly.'"[19]

The trial itself was high theater, as evidenced by the crowds of people present at the courthouse. Microphones and loudspeakers enabled the overflow crowd in the corridors to hear the proceedings, and some spectators paid as much as fifty dollars for what turned out to be counterfeit admission tickets to the courtroom. Hundreds of stickpins, adorned with a miniature sash weight, were sold for ten cents apiece. The general atmosphere was controlled by the presiding judge, Townsend Scudder, who ordered, "No photographers in the court-room. No minors or picnic baskets."[20]

Snyder was not able to win over public sentiment, as evidenced during the appeals process when the Queens County Court of Appeals received a postcard signed by "The Public" warning, "We will shoot you if you let that woman Snyder go free. She must be electrocuted. The public demands it. If she is not done away with, other women will do the same thing. She must be made an example of. We are watching out."[21] But not everyone was against her. She wrote a poem criticizing the press for spreading lies about her that included the lines "You have blackened and besmeared a mother, Once a man's plaything—A Toy— What have you gained by all you've said, And has it—brought you Joy?" After it was published, she received 164 offers of marriage should she be released.[22] Snyder and Gray, and especially Snyder, re-mained subjects of media attention until their electrocution and be-yond. Even though no photographers were allowed to witness the exe-cution, Thomas Howard, posing as a reporter, strapped a camera to his ankle and took a photograph of Ruth Snyder as she was being electro-cuted. The photo ran on the front page of the *New York Daily News* and became a matter of controversy itself. It also led to changes in the lighting of death chambers to make it impossible to photograph them. Even after the death of Snyder and Gray, within minutes of each other on January 12, 1928, Snyder's appeal lawyer, Joseph Lonardo, at-tempted to block an autopsy of her body. The *New York Times* later revealed that this attempt was part of a scheme to resurrect her with a shot of adrenalin to her heart.[23]

Columnist Damon Runyon characterized the crime as "dumb." "It was stupid beyond imagination," he wrote, "and so brutal that the thought of it probably makes many a peaceful, home-loving Long Is-lander of the Albert Snyder type shiver in his pajamas as he prepares for bed."[24] But the public interest in this trial and others like it was more than just a momentary interest in something unusual. As Charles Merz observed, "A nationally famous trial for homicide is no longer a startling interruption of a more lethargic train of thought. It has become an institution, as periodic in its public appearances and reappearances as the cycle of the seasons."[25] As John R. Brazil pointed out, much of this public fascination with murder trials was the result of aggressive promotion by the tabloid press, which accelerated in 1919 when the *New York Illustrated Daily News* became the first "tabloid picture paper." These tabloids emphasized photographs and illustrations rather than detailed text in covering sensational stories. The tabloids did not, and were not meant to, replace standard daily newspapers in presenting the news; rather, they created a larger newspaper-reading public by attracting people who had not read the standard papers but were attracted by magazines like *True Story* and *True Confessions*.[26] Bernard McFadden, who owned both magazines, also published the *Evening Graphic,* which sought, according to McFadden, to "dramatize the news and features . . . to appeal to the masses in their own language."[27]

The tabloids often did more than report the news; in some cases they created a story, as in the case of the *New York Daily Mirror,* which "uncovered" new evidence in a murder trial from 1922 and forced a new trial in 1926. The case had involved a minister, Edward Hall, and a choir member, Eleanor Mills, found dead together. The evidence brought forth by the *Mirror* led to the arrest and trial of the minister's widow, though it failed to gain a conviction.[28] Murder trials sold newspapers, and since trials lasted for days, they did not sell just a single issue but kept readers coming back for more. "With the single exception of the Lindbergh flight, virtually every sizable paper had its largest average circulation during intensive murder trial coverage: its single best days were when verdicts were announced or when executions were carried out." When Ruth Snyder and Judd Gray were executed, the issue of the *Daily News* featuring the bootleg photograph of Snyder's electrocution "sold 250,000 extra copies and had to run off 750,000 additional pages later."[29]

MURDER TRIALS AND DEMOCRACY

Not only murder trials, but crime in general was more prevalent in the nation's press. A survey of over sixty major American newspapers from 1899 to 1923 found that by 1923, the average paper devoted 77 percent less space to editorials, 180 percent less space to letters to the editor, and 275 percent less space to social news. During the same period, while general, political, business, and foreign news increased slightly, sports news received 47 percent more space, and crime news increased by 53 percent.[30] Most observers believed that the increase in crime reporting was directly related to an increase in the crime rate, though no reliable statistics support the connection. Even an increase in the crime rate does not explain people's interest in crime stories, both real and fictional. John R. Brazil sees a connection between the intense press coverage of murder trials, like Snyder and Gray's, and the development of the "hard-boiled" school of detective novels characterized by such writers as Dashiell Hammett and Raymond Chandler. Unlike such traditional detectives as Sherlock Holmes and Charlie Chan, the hard-boiled detective did not rely on intellect and logic alone. "Working frequently outside the law and occasionally against it, his primary characteristics were toughness and self-control (this control usually contained a passionate, violent nature, which could be released to serve his moral or professional ends)." And while Holmes and Chan sought to restore order to their worlds by solving crimes, the hard-boiled detective sought merely to survive in a chaotic world "while often adding to the general store of brutality and chaos."[31] In other words, the hard-boiled detective was a response to modernity, a reaction to the idea that the world was no longer rationally ordered and was therefore beyond anyone's ability to rationally control it with intellect and logic.

This same reaction to modernity can be seen in the popularity of murder trials as well. It was not the bizarre, unique, or exceptional that made for a highly publicized murder trial or a good hard-boiled detective novel but, rather, the ordinary: domestic disputes, infidelity, greed, and jealousy. Alexander Woolcott claimed that what made Ruth Snyder extraordinary was that she was not exceptional. The most intense interest surrounded the most ordinary of murders.[32] Likewise, most hard-boiled detective fiction centered on ordinary characters and ordinary crimes. Brazil argues that what made both the sensational murder trial and the hard-boiled detective story popular in the 1920s was their relationship to "traditionally accepted but increasingly less secure assumptions about human nature, about the efficacy of the individual, and about the adequacy of post-Enlightenment causal thinking."[33] Brazil also sees this theme of declining tradition at work in other popular fiction of the period, such as the western novels of Zane Grey, F. Scott Fitzgerald's *The Great Gatsby* (1925), and Theodore Dreiser's *An American Tragedy* (1925). The dramatic tension in all these works develops out of a conflict arising from modern ideas that have displaced traditional values and mores. This tension is seen clearly in the play *Chicago* by first-time playwright Maurine Watkins. Watkins worked as a journalist for the *Chicago Tribune* and made a name for herself covering "Murderess' Row," as she called the wing of the Cook County Jail that held women arrested for violent crimes. Her articles, published from March to June 1924, focused on two murderesses in particular, Belva Gaertner, "'the most stylish' of Murderess' Row,"[34] and Beulah Annan, "the prettiest murderess Cook county has ever known."[35] The two women were not the ordinary type of gangsters, bootleggers, and criminals prominent in Chicago newspapers. Rather, they were white, middle- and upper-middle-class women who were not after money or revenge; they had both killed their respective partners rather than lose them. Adding to these stories of extramarital affairs and of women reacting in the most extreme manner were two of the favorite vices of the 1920s, gin and jazz. When asked how her date, Walter Law, had been shot in her automobile with her gun, Gaertner replied, "I don't know. I was drunk."[36] Annan was reported to have sat listening to a jazz record, *Hula Lou,* while the man she shot, Harry Kalstedt, slowly died in her bedroom.[37] Both women had their day in court, and both were proclaimed by a jury to be not guilty of their alleged crimes.

In both cases, the modernism of women unashamedly conducting extramarital affairs, engaging in Prohibition-era drinking, conspicuously consuming the latest fashions and music, and murdering their male partners conflicted with socially held notions of subservient, docile, and weak women in need of the protection of men. This conflict is seen in Watkins's articles and in her play. After Elizabeth Unkafer, one of the seven inmates of "Murderess' Row," received a sentence of life in prison for the murder of her lover, Watkins wrote a *Chicago Tribune* article about what the remaining inmates thought counted most with a jury. Watkins revealed the inmates' beliefs that what mattered was gender ("'A woman never swung in Illinois,' said one triumphantly."), looks ("Elizabeth Unkafer was not cursed with fatal beauty!" and "'A jury isn't blind,' said another, 'and a pretty woman's never been convicted in Cook county!' Gallant old Cook county!"), and youth ("Elizabeth was 43.")[38] Watkins's articles criticize and capitalize on the notion that pretty women, with the right publicity, could indeed get away with murder.

This critique of illegality became the basis for the play *Chicago*, which recasts the story of Beulah Annan into the tale of Roxy Hart and includes a thinly veiled Belva Gaertner as Velma, the "stylish divorcee." *Chicago* was touted, especially during its New York run, which opened on December 30, 1926, as a satire on Chicago politics and the unsophisticated nature of the Midwest. But when *Chicago* opened in the Windy City in September 1927, boosters of the city used publicity about the play to further their own agendas, with Mayor William Hale Thompson suggesting that Watkins act as publicity agent for the city as someone well suited to informing the world about Chicago.[39] Beulah Annan's defense attorney, W. W. O'Brien (characterized in the play as Billy Flynn), came out in support of the play, stating, "It is the finest piece of stage satire ever written by an American."[40] O'Brien hoped the favorable publicity generated by the play would help revive his declining reputation. Belva Gaertner came to the opening and validated the accuracy of the characters: she recognized Velma as herself—"Sure that's me"—and added, "Roxie Hart's supposed to be Beulah Annan."[41]

For Watkins herself, the success of *Chicago* created more demand for her services as a journalist than as a playwright. She was sought after by New York newspapers to cover such court cases involving women as the "Peaches" and "Daddy" Browning divorce case and the Snyder-Gray trial. Her second attempt at drama came with the offer to adapt for the stage the Samuel Hopkins Adams novel *Revelry*, based on the corruption and scandals of the Harding administration. After the play had only a modest run and little success, Watkins ended her career as a playwright and journalist. What is remarkable about Watkins's career and *Chicago* is the way they benefit from and criticize the modernity of American society by entertaining people with their own weaknesses and shallowness. The modern press, especially the tabloid press, created an audience for the type of articles Watkins wrote, while the conflict between traditional values about gender roles, marriage, sex, and immorality, on the one hand, and the more modern assumptions of the "new woman," on the other, gave both her articles and her play the dramatic tension necessary to satirize the criminal justice system, the press, and American society. Watkins herself benefited from the greater opportunities created by the feminist movement as she also capitalized on the increased interest in crime and court cases, especially involving women, and the growing publicity apparatus surrounding any big event. It is her portrayal of this publicity machine—with the press at the center—that puts Watkins in an expanding group of writers and social critics who see publicity as more and more central to the way American society works.

Walter Lippmann, in a 1927 essay for *Vanity Fair,* discussed the publicity machine: "This engine has an important peculiarity. It does not flood the world with light. On the contrary it is like the beam of a powerful lantern which plays somewhat capriciously upon the course of events, throwing now this and now that into brilliant relief, leaving the rest in comparative darkness." The primary problem with the publicity machine, according to Lippmann, is the fact that it is a machine. "It does not have and could not have an automatic governor to regulate its use according to accepted standards, or any standards, of good taste and good policy." In fact, he continues, "The machine itself is without morals or taste of any kind, without prejudice or purpose, without conviction or ulterior motive." It is, says Lippmann, newspapermen who "scan the horizon," looking for the next big event in the hopes of hitting upon something that will catch the public's fascination. Lippmann admits that there is little rhyme or reason in the selection of which events will engage the public but argues that the "best sensations involve some mystery, as well as love and death." But foremost in determining which events will be reported in the modern sense (that is, covered completely down to the merest detail) is timing. "We know that sensations have to be timed properly for the public cannot concentrate on two sensations at the same time. It is no use trying to tell the public about the Mississippi flood when Ruth Snyder is on the witness stand." Also key to these media events is "the personal narrative which gives the illusion of intimacy and inwardness."[42]

The dangers in the publicity machine are more specific and threatening than simply a mass public distracted by frivolity. One specific danger involves the courts, according to Lippmann, especially in heavily reported cases like the Snyder-Gray trial. "No doubt the pair were guilty as Satan. It was nevertheless a scandal to have the trial conducted to an accompaniment of comments by celebrities seated in the bleachers who took the case out of the hands of the judge and the jury, and rendered a daily verdict at so much per column on the precise guilt of the two defendants." But there is a larger, more sinister danger as well. "There is no way of imagining where it will take us. We do not, for example, know how to imagine what the consequences will be of attempting to conduct popular government with an electorate which is subjected to a series of disconnected, but all in their moments absolutely absorbing, hullabaloos." The publicity machine will continue to develop and to create better and faster ways to entertain the public, diverting attention away from public affairs and important public questions. For Lippmann, this is not necessarily a bad thing, since the amount of effort needed to understand important public affairs is so great. "I am inclined to ask myself whether in view of the technical complexity of almost all great public questions, it is really possible any longer for the mass of voters to form significant public opinions."[43] Thus, the management of public affairs rests upon those expert enough and willing to manage, namely a nonhereditary, untitled, governing class.

Whereas Hoover believed that publicity could expand democracy by presenting citizens with the information necessary to participate responsibly in a democratic society, Lippmann saw publicity as responsible for a decline in democratic participation by the masses. These divergent views outline a crucial debate in modern America between individual rights governed by a free market or individual rights limited by civic responsibility. The press often claimed that they were merely presenting "what the public wanted" and that as a business they were bound by the whims of the public. The public, as free individuals, decided what was and was not newsworthy. This conflicts, however, with the idea that the media and publicity machine inform people about things of which they should be aware and knowledgeable. Stories for which people will pay are not, in most cases, stories that are necessary to the smooth and efficient running of a democracy. The attention in the press accorded to Nan Britton, Ruth Snyder, and Judd Gray far outweighed the attention given to the upcoming presidential election, or other political news, and, more often than not, served the interests and bank accounts of the few instead of the many.

While the turn away from democratic participation on the part of the public was partially a consequence of media coverage of sensational events rather than political issues, Lippmann, in his 1927 collection of essays *Men of Destiny,* noted that there were many other factors as well. The lack of strong national political figures and national agendas for the two political parties "bewilder the electorate and make the voters feel that politics is an elaborate game which has no serious and immediate consequences."[44] The main reason for this political floundering was the growing irrelevance of Progressivism. As the economy strengthened, revolt against economic change lessened. "The interested motives which are the driving forces of political agitation were diverted to direct profit making" (23). Not only were people more interested in making money than in fighting for reforms, but the Progressives' targets had disappeared with "the rise of what may be called the New Capitalism" (24). Industrialists and corporate leaders in the 1920s had adapted to the new circumstances of the market, realizing that in a consumer-driven economy, great care needs to be taken to please the consumer. When production controlled profit, reformers could focus their anger at greedy corporate taskmasters squeezing every possible ounce of productivity out of workers; but in a consumer-driven economy, the public image of the corporation is key to a successful business. According to Lippmann, the new executive is a contrast from the robber barons and industrialists of the late nineteenth century. "His attitude toward labor, toward the public, toward his customers and his stockholders, is different. His behavior is different. His manner is different. His press agents are different." And though he is far from perfect, and "no doubt as powerful as he ever was, . . . his bearing is less autocratic." As a result, he does not stir in the populace the same antagonisms as did earlier corporate leaders (24). Without visible enemies, the Progressive movement lost focus.

While economic prosperity and the decline of progressive motivation both increased political indifference, so too did the actions of

Calvin Coolidge. "He has devoted himself to encouraging the people to turn their eyes away from the government," Lippmann wrote. "Public spirit is at best a fragile thing when it comes into competition with the urgent demands of our private lives for money, for power, and for pleasure. So it has not been difficult for Mr. Coolidge to persuade the country that it need not take a vivid interest in public affairs" (21).

The press aided Coolidge in this task by focusing on sensational news, like murder trials, celebrity gossip, and sports reporting. While Hoover touted a responsibly managed information system as the key to modernization and economic prosperity, Coolidge left information management primarily in the hands of the market. This conflict between a market-driven publicity machine and a responsibly managed information system was compounded by another ambiguity of American culture, the tendency to create celebrities who are both extraordinary in abilities and accomplishments and at the same time common in origin. Twentieth-century celebrities, both the famous and the infamous, tended to be alternately worshipped as unique and special and yet described as not much different from the average American. The all-American character of Lindbergh, the everyman quality of Henry Ford, the humble origins of Clara Bow, the rags-to-riches-to-service story of Herbert Hoover, and the ordinariness of Ruth Snyder and Judd Gray made each of those celebrities seem common. This characterization reinforced the notion that in America anything was possible, that hard work, dedication, good luck, and perseverance, and/or circumstances and bad luck, could lead to extraordinary events. Yet, although the publicity that surrounded such events as Lindbergh's flight, the Mississippi flood, or the Snyder-Gray trial was extraordinary, it occurred within an overall increase in publicity that encompassed other types of celebrities as well. Nowhere was this characteristically American celebrity more evident than in the world of spectator sports.

THE GOLDEN AGE OF SPORTSWRITING

Sportswriters and historians of sport in America have characterized the period from the end of World War I to the start of the Great Depression as the "Golden Age of Sport." Sportswriter Grantland Rice felt the designation apt "because this postwar period gave the game the greatest collection of stars, involving both skill and color, that sport has ever known since the first cave man tackled the mammoth and the aurochs bull."[45] For Rice it was not only the achievements of such athletes as baseball player Babe Ruth, boxer Jack Dempsey, golfer Bobby Jones, tennis players Bill Tilden and Helen Wills, sprinter Charlie Paddock, and even thoroughbred racehorse Man o' War that made this a golden age, but also the popular appeal that these athletes fostered with their personalities, or in Rice's word, "color." While the emergence of the United States internationally as both a military and an economic power may account for the higher quality of athleticism that appeared in the 1920s, this does not explain the uniqueness of the era. According to Rice, "Skill and ability were not the major factors in this Golden Age. They were, of course, important factors, but they were, after all, only a minor part of the story. It was their color and their crowd appeal, their vivid splash against the skyline, their remembered deeds, that write their story."[46] But Rice believed that the qualities of personality that made these "Golden Age" athletes into celebrities were inherent in each of them, rather than being the result of media attention and focus in which sportswriting, radio announcing, newsreels, and motion pictures created personalities. What made the period unique was the way the media presented sports figures to the public, from the actual staging of boxing matches, football games, and baseball series to media reporting and celebrity appearances.

Sportswriting in the vein of Grantland Rice was one of the most important factors in the creation of the "Golden Age." "The so-called Golden Age of Sports, the twenties and early thirties, was really the Golden Age of Sportswriting," claims journalist and sports critic Robert Lipsyte, who sees Rice as a transformative figure in sportswriting.[47] According to Lipsyte, "Rice was a True Believer" who loved sports and truly saw its practitioners as heroic figures. Rice wrote "the most famous lead in sports journalism history" when he described the 1924 Notre Dame backfield as the Four Horsemen of the Apocalypse, which "liberated sportswriters from the traditional humdrum recitation of points scored. They were free to exercise their imaginations and flash their often prodigious stores of book-learning."[48] Rice turned sports reporting into sportswriting, a form of entertainment it-self rather than an account of an entertainment. "He was reporting a staged spectacle in a mock-heroic manner, extending the entertain-ment from the field to the page."[49] But Rice, and the many imitators of his style, "dehumanized the contests and made objects of the ath-letes," according to Lipsyte.[50] By taking athletes out of the context of sportsmanlike competition and placing them into a mythical context of heroic figures, sportswriters helped transform athletes into cele-brated beings, or more cynically, commodities for the public market.

Sportswriters were not the only ones commodifying sports figures. The staging and promoting of sporting events, the media hype before, during, and after the event, and the crossover of athletes into such other fields of entertainment as the variety stage and motion pictures all reinforced the image of sports celebrities created by the sportswrit-ers. As sportswriter Paul Gallico put it, "Sports were suddenly inun-dated with money and publicity and blossomed into social accep-tance."[51] In 1927 three sports illustrate best this phenomenon: professional boxing, college football, and professional baseball.

By 1927, professional boxing reached new heights of respectability. What had once been a sport mainly for working-class participants and audiences had become an acceptable, and indeed highly sought after, entertainment for all classes. People not only accepted boxing and box-ers but were intensely interested in them, primarily due to the amount and duration of the press coverage given to championship bouts. Like a sensational murder trial, a boxing championship built up in the pub-lic's attention over time, from the announcement of the fight, to the de-tails of the time, place, and guarantees of profits, to the training of each opponent, to the weighing in, and eventually to the fight itself. Each story would try to present more than just the facts of training programs and financial details and to present to the public a more per-sonal view of the fighters. People knew what these fighters ate and read and how they entertained themselves, and as a result the public developed very personalized opinions of each. As writer Paul Gallico observed, "The human being whom we either loved or detested, ad-mired or despised, was entering a kind of public ordeal and we simply had to be there, either in person or by proxy of our newspapers or radio."[52]

Much of this transformation in the world of boxing was due to one man, boxing promoter Tex Rickard. Bringing respectability and economic authority to the world of sports, especially boxing, was no easy task. Nineteenth-century bare-knuckle fighting was populated by the underworld and the criminal element and was at best attended to by the working classes. Many states banned or severely limited boxing. In New York boxing exhibitions could be held, but there could be no official decision in the fight in order to limit gambling. In 1908 Tex Rickard began his promoting career out West, where fewer restrictions existed, by staging a lightweight championship bout in Goldfield, Nevada. He sold the idea of the fight to the town's leaders as a way to promote their growing city, and he promoted the fight by creating a $32,000 purse for the fighters and displaying it in gold coins in the window of his saloon. Rickard capitalized on the idea that people might want to see a great fight, but, more than that, they wanted to see exorbitant wealth won and lost. As Paul Gallico recalled, "Rickard never forgot the compulsion exercised by large sums of cash, or the lure of the yellow metal. Twenty years later, he remembered to emboss the backs of his tickets for his outdoor fights with gold. They were large, heavy, imposing-looking, and felt like money."[53]

Rickard used guarantees of large purses and predictions of grand gate receipts to lure people to his fights. By 1920 he had staged some of the largest boxing events ever experienced, but he had still not made the ring a respectable entertainment. In 1920 he acquired the old Madison Square Garden and began promoting fights in New York, which had recently legalized boxing. In 1921 he staged a fight at the Garden as a charity event for Anne (sister of J. P.) Morgan's American Committee for Devastated France. This event attracted not only the well-to-do but women as well. Rickard employed a large staff of uniformed ushers and security guards to make the environment safe and accommodating to women. "It became as safe for a woman and her escort to attend a Rickard fight as it was to go to the theater."[54] In the decade of the 1920s Rickard (who died in 1929) sold $15 million worth of tickets to boxing matches, more than enough to build an all-new Madison Square Garden in 1925. He was responsible for the largest crowd for a bout (Dempsey-Tunney; Philadelphia, 1926; 120,757), the largest gate (Tunney-Dempsey; Chicago, 1927; $2.6 million), and the largest purse for a champion (Tunney; Chicago, 1927; $990,445) until late into the twentieth century. His skill as a promoter was reinforced by the fact that he enjoyed the talents of charismatic boxers like Jack Dempsey. Together, they created the spectacle of modern prizefighting. "As a team," wrote *New York Times* boxing editor James P. Dawson, "they were the greatest boxing ever knew, probably ever will know."[55]

In 1927, the biggest boxing event was the rematch title fight between defending champion Gene Tunney, the "Fighting Marine," and former champion Jack Dempsey, the "Manassa Mauler." Dempsey had lost his title to Tunney in a ten-round decision in September 1926 before a record crowd in Philadelphia, which grossed gate receipts of over $1.8 million and garnered Dempsey the sum of $711,868. Despite his loss, Dempsey remained a crowd favorite, attracting over a million dollars in gate receipts in his next fight against Jack Sharkey before his rematch with Tunney. The second Tunney versus Dempsey fight, at Chicago's Soldier Field, grossed over $2.6 million and was heard by an estimated 50 million radio listeners. While some of the attraction was the excitement of a World Championship title, much of boxing's appeal had to do with Dempsey's appealing personality. When Tunney fought to retain his title in 1928, the gate gross was less than $700,000.

According to sportswriter Paul Gallico, Jack Dempsey "created the dramatic image of the perfect pugilist and more than this, he was Jack the Giant Killer who tumbled into the dust men who outsized and outweighed him."[56] Dempsey became the heavyweight champion on the Fourth of July, 1919, when he defeated the gigantic Jess Willard. He successfully defended his title five times between 1920 and 1923, including in two bouts that were the first sporting events to gross over a million dollars, and he fought in over twenty exhibitions before losing the title to Tunney in 1926. Much of Dempsey's appeal was not just in his winning fights but in the way he fought and won them. Dempsey was known for his wild abandon when he fought; he was not a great technician but an emotional boxer. In four of his five successful title-defense fights, Dempsey knocked out his opponent, including seven knockdowns in one round against Luis Angel Firpo, "the Wild Bull of the Pampas." Firpo had knocked Dempsey down in the opening seconds of the fight, and Dempsey sent Firpo to the mat seven times before Firpo knocked Dempsey clear out of the ring and into the press row. Dempsey returned to knock down Firpo twice before knocking him out in the second round. The Dempsey-Firpo fight lasted less than four minutes but included twelve knockdowns in what the *Chicago Tribune*'s James Crusinberry called "the greatest round of battling since the Silurian Age."[57] Dempsey's style of unbridled fighting in this bout drew criticism from the boxing establishment and led to rule changes that included prohibiting contestants who were knocked out of the ring from getting any assistance in regaining the ring (Dempsey, it was claimed, was helped by a reporter to get back into the ring) and mandating that if a combatant is knocked down, the opponent must retire to the farthest neutral corner before the count begins (Dempsey's ten knockdowns of Firpo were the result of his standing over Firpo waiting for him to get up and then knocking him down again).

Tunney's path to the championship title was quite different from Dempsey's. Tunney studied boxing and fought according to well-laid plans based on his opponent's style of fighting, weaknesses, and strengths. He had boxed as part of his service with the U.S. Marines in the Great War. Tunney became the American Expeditionary Forces (AEF) light-heavyweight champion during the course of the war and took up professional boxing afterwards. His style was the opposite of Dempsey's emotional, hard-hitting, offensive fighting. Tunney admitted to being "more interested in dodging a blow than in striking one."[58] He first observed Dempsey's style during the 1921 championship fight between Dempsey and challenger Georges Carpentier in which Dempsey retained his title by knocking out his opponent in the fourth round. Tunney estimated that fast feet and a good defense could defeat Dempsey's battering assault. This feeling grew as Tunney observed more of Dempsey's bouts, both in person and on film, and was nearly confirmed when Dempsey failed to knock out challenger Tommy Gibbons in 1923. Dempsey won a fifteen-round decision, but Gibbons's defensive fighting convinced Tunney that "good boxing could thwart the murder in the Dempsey fists" (155). While training for his first match with Dempsey, a reporter visited Tunney's training camp and noticed that Tunney was in the midst of reading *The Way of All Flesh* by Samuel Butler. The reporter, Brian Bell, began to question

Tunney on books instead of training or fighting, and when Tunney stated that he liked to read Shakespeare, Bell knew he had a story. The Associated Press "flashed the story far and wide—the challenger, training for Jack Dempsey, read books, literature—Shakespeare. It was a sensation. The Shakespeare-Tunney legend was born" (159). This characterization of Tunney—studious, serious, and intellectual—reinforced most sportswriters' belief that he was no match for the powerful Dempsey.

As the brawling champion met the intellectual challenger, "things went so much according to plan that they were almost unexciting to me," recalled Tunney (162). The 1926 match validated Tunney's belief that a good boxer could beat a good fighter; that training, study, and planning could defeat strength, natural ability, and a killer instinct. But while the result of the fight was in Tunney's favor—both in victory and in validation—the public favored Dempsey. Sportswriters and fans alike criticized Tunney for being "sneaky" and suggested that there must have been a fix on the match for Dempsey to lose to Tunney. In victory, Tunney confidently asserted that he had known all along that he would win; in defeat, Dempsey simply told his wife that he lost because he "just forgot to duck." In his press statement he simply said, "I have no alibis to offer. I lost to a good man."[59] The simplicity of Dempsey's remarks contrasted with the perceived arrogance of Tunney's aloofness and reinforced the popular appeal of a working-class Dempsey over a middle-class Tunney, and many people were convinced that, had Dempsey not taken so much time off since his last championship defense (three years), he would have beaten Tunney. Less than a month after their fight, both Tunney and Dempsey attended a fight as spectators. Dempsey was greeted by loud cheering that lasted for minutes, while Tunney received "scattered cheers mingled with boos."[60]

What Dempsey had, and Tunney did not, was charisma, an attractive personality, or what Hollywood called "it." Dempsey was admired by fans not just because he won fights but because of his celebrity, a celebrity based on accomplishment and personality. While Tunney was the more accomplished, in terms of boxing knowledge and skill, and the victorious head-to-head in the ring, Dempsey was the bigger celebrity, the bigger draw, and the crowd favorite. Realizing the attraction Dempsey held for fans, promoter Tex Rickard devised a plan in which Dempsey would have to earn a rematch with Tunney by defeating the lead challenger for the title, which meant holding several elimination bouts to see who would fight Dempsey. The interest in the road to a rematch built as Jack Sharkey won the right to face Dempsey in the summer of 1927. Their fight, the first nontitle fight to earn gross gate receipts over a million dollars, was as big an event as the 1926 Dempsey-Tunney title fight. When Dempsey knocked out Sharkey in the seventh round, a rematch was assured.

Rickard planned the rematch for Chicago instead of New York because New York had no stadiums large enough to hold the anticipated crowd and because the New York boxing commission limited the prices charged for tickets to boxing matches in the state at $27.50, even though spectators paid black marketeers up to $200 for a seat. Rickard selected Chicago's recently constructed Soldier Field as the site of the rematch. Dempsey had earlier drawn criticism for not participating in the AEF during the Great War, even though it was the machinations of his manager—unwilling to lose his chief championship prospect to the trenches of Europe—who obtained a deferment for Dempsey to work in a war industry instead of enlisting. Denouncing Dempsey as a slacker, four of Chicago's aldermen protested the staging of the fight at Soldier Field, built as a memorial to the men who had fought and died in the war, but these protests did not deter the promoters or the spectators. Rickard brushed off these protests by saying, "That war-record business is old stuff. The war is a long way behind us."[61] And ticket sales did not lag either, with total sales of over $2.5 million—the largest amount paid for a sporting event, and perhaps any event, up to that time.[62]

Politicians, film stars, athletes, industrialists, and royalty packed the stadium around the ring, and the hundreds of members of the press corps covered the fight. Radios across the nation tuned in to the fight, as did those who could receive strong broadcast signals as far away as England. Even convicted murderer Ruth Snyder, in Sing Sing prison, listened through an open door between the women's and men's cell blocks. What they witnessed and heard was a former champion better trained and prepared to meet his opponent, but Tunney's boxing skills still frustrated the powerful Dempsey. By the end of the sixth round, Dempsey had not landed enough punches to win many rounds, and most observers understood that he would have to knock out Tunney if he were to regain his title. In the seventh round Dempsey let loose a barrage of right-left combinations that left Tunney stunned and fallen on the canvas. Dempsey, in his usual manner, stood close to his victim, hoping to hit him as soon as he rose, forgetting the change of rules brought about by those actions. Referee Dave Barry directed Dempsey to move to the far corner, but Dempsey did not move. "I couldn't move." he later said "I just couldn't. I wanted him to get up. I wanted to kill the sonofabitch."[63] Barry then took Dempsey by the arm and escorted him to the neutral corner. By the time the referee got back to where Tunney sat, four seconds had elapsed, but instead of picking up the count at five, Barry began at one. Tunney, listening to Barry, waited until he reached nine before standing, as any intelligent boxer would, in order to rest. As a result, Tunney was able to recover for thirteen seconds before regaining his feet and resuming the fight. For the remainder of the round, Tunney fought a defensive retreat, forcing Dempsey to use what strength was left in his legs. Dempsey motioned Tunney to stop running and fight, but by the end of the round Tunney had regained his bearings and energy and was able to take the offensive in the next round and command the fight for the remainder of the ten rounds and win the decision.

The end of the fight, however, did not mean an end to the speculation over the fairness of the fight and over who was the better man. Debate filled the pages of newspapers and countless discussions. Columnist John Kieran wrote in the *New York Times*, "There was hardly as much arguing over the recent result of the late World War as there is over the more recent Tunney-Dempsey quarrel in Chicago. Most of it is quite interesting, but practically all of it is useless."[64] And while the fight may not have revealed who was the better athlete, it does give us some insight into the era and the nation. The *New York Times* felt it was noteworthy "that people will contribute about three million dollars to see two men fight for something less than forty-five minutes" and stated further: "[The fight] will not only be an index of the prosperity of the period, but it will reveal to the historian how much the twentieth century American was willing to pay for a thrill."[65]

The Tunney-Dempsey fights, especially in the media characterizations of the fighters and the descriptions of the bouts, reinforced the conflicts of the era. According to historian Elliott J. Gorn, "Each boxer came to represent key values in American life, and the two men together in the ring symbolized central tensions and contradictions of the 1920s."[66] For Gorn, Tunney represented both the Victorian values of a self-made man—perfecting himself through education, perseverance, and self-restraint—and the ideals of the modern corporate order: a scientific approach to problem-solving, the use of experts and the techniques of psychology, and a sense of being a part of a larger endeavor, primarily a result of Tunney's Marine Corp background. "As a symbol, the Fighting Marine affirmed that America's past and future were of a piece, that virtue and self-reliance could still thrive in a technocratic environment."[67] Much like Charles Lindbergh, Tunney represented the best of the past and of what the future had to offer. But Tunney was popular not primarily for what he represented but, rather, as a foil to all that Dempsey represented. His celebrity "came largely as a result of his being matched against Dempsey."[68]

Whereas Tunney represented an urban Victorian past, Dempsey represented a rugged pioneer past, reinforced by his western birth and work as a miner. As such, Dempsey was seen as a bit of an outlaw, someone who, by virtue of his abilities and temperament, was dangerous. He "made no effort to hide his connections with a loose-moraled, thrill-hungry, big-spending crowd."[69] His fighting style reinforced this image as he fought with an animalistic power and drive, especially in comparison to Tunney's studied approach in the ring. But Dempsey's image and style did not express just a frontier past; it also contained valuable insights for the present. Dempsey fought from the heart, not the head. He fought because he loved the ring, unlike Tunney, who fought as a way to earn big money so he could unashamedly ask for the hand of his sweetheart, an heiress. That difference is why Tunney was able to give up the ring as champion—he defended his title once more in 1928 in one of the few bouts that cost Rickard money—while Dempsey continued to fight over a hundred exhibitions in 1931 and 1932. Audiences stayed away from a championship fight when the champion was seen as a cold, calculating machine. These were the aspects of modern life people feared, while they reveled in the midst of raw natural ability and power exhibited in a man who loved what he did, things that could not be quantified, learned, or re-created by science. Dempsey and Tunney illustrated this conflict in modern America. According to Gorn, "bringing Dempsey and Tunney together in a single ring transformed abstract norms into emotionally satisfying drama, converted a conflict of values into a palpable physical struggle, fused symbols, metaphors, and blood into messages mere words could not convey."[70] This drama, Gorn notes, is in itself simply one of many diversions that people used to cope with the increasing rationalization of modern society, and while it may contain positive elements of modernity, it is in its entirety a means of escaping modernity through entertainment.

Another sporting diversion that developed into a multimillion dollar industry was college football. "More than any other sport," writes historian Michael Oriard, "football embraced the competing values of the modern and the antimodern," as illustrated in the portrayal of college football in the popular media as something different from professional sports like boxing and baseball.[71] In the 1920s, football was predominately a college game. The newly formed National Football League did little to remove the impression that professional football was a disreputable activity. Unlike baseball, which began as a club sport in cities, football began as an extracurricular activity in the Ivy League, primarily at Harvard, Yale, and Princeton. The connection of football with elite institutions (even after its spread to state universities and religious schools) and with young men in a transitional period of their lives reinforced ideas about the amateur nature of the sport. Sportswriters portrayed football as an educational experience, like college itself, teaching young men cooperation, courage, camaraderie, and competition while fostering pride in one's alma mater, all characteristics associated with traditional values. This focus on the team aspect of the sport meant more attention was paid to the coaches than to individual players and had to do both with the philosophical belief that the team was more important than any individual and with the practical realities of a somewhat more permanent coach and transitory players. In addition, the youth of the players encouraged sportswriters and audiences alike to view them as boys being led by an adult coach, students being taught, boys learning to become men. Not only did sportswriters view the coach as the adult spokesman for the team, but they also developed personal relationships with coaches, who through interviews, press passes, transportation to games, and other perks, made the sportswriter's job much easier.

College football benefited from the idea that what the audience was seeing was not something strictly created as an entertainment for paying customers but, rather, a battle between two schools and all that those schools represented. As a result, college football was seen as a traditional activity with traditional ends, the education of boys in how to be men. Much of what reporters wrote about college football reinforced this theme by taking much of what occurred on the field out of its immediate context of a big-time, money-making entertainment and placing it in a context of mythic proportions. Grantland Rice pioneered this tendency to see college football in a mythic context. Under the headline, "Notre Dame's Cyclone Beats Army" in the October 19, 1924, edition of the *New York Herald Tribune,* Rice wrote:

> Outlined against a blue-grey October sky, the Four Horsemen rode again. In dramatic lore they are known as Famine, Pestilence, Destruction and Death. These are only aliases. Their real names are Stuhldreher, Miller, Crowley and Layden. They formed the crest of the South Bend cyclone before which another fighting Army football team was swept over the precipice at the Polo Grounds yesterday afternoon as 55,000 spectators peered down on the bewildering panorama spread on the green plain below.[72]

This is more than a report of an entertainment, or even a gentlemanly match between rivals; it describes a struggle between life and death. This is melodrama at its most extreme, and while it is entertaining in itself and effective in conveying the drama that took place on the field, it is not the most effective way of describing what actually occurred and what it all means. Many people and institutions profited from this melodramatic rendering of college football. Sportswriters became celebrities as they flexed their literary muscle, the subjects of the sportswriters' melodramatic prose gained significance far beyond their achievements, and the demand for college football games and coverage grew, as did the receipts taken in by coaches, schools, and such ancillary industries as sporting goods and newspapers and newsreels.

Though presented publicly as young scholars testing themselves on the field, in reality college football was becoming an industry. Players were a raw material, packaged and sold by the coach and the university, using all the techniques of modern industry, such as marketing, publicity, research, and development. As football spread out of the Ivy League across the country, it still retained many of its elite characteristics, though becoming more a middle-class entertainment than an upper-class one. By the 1920s many universities had made a name for themselves in the world of academia through the promotion of their football teams, most notably the University of Notre Dame, but also Southern Methodist University, the Georgia Institute of Technology, and the University of Southern California. The popularity and spectacle of college football led to the erection of massive stadiums on and off college campuses to house the crowds and pageantry of the sport. Fifty-five concrete stadiums were built in the 1920s, with some seating more than 70,000 spectators. Cities (Los Angeles, with its Memorial Coliseum; Pasadena, with its Rose Bowl; and Chicago, with its Soldier Field) as well as universities (University of Illinois, with its Memorial Stadium, and University of Michigan, with its Michigan Stadium) created vast grounds for the staging of football games and all the incumbent pageantry. Michigan Stadium was built in 1927, funded by bonds sold to alumni who, as bondholders, could buy season tickets to seats located between the 30-yard lines until the bonds retired. Chicago's Soldier Field was the scene of two of 1927's biggest sporting events, hosting not only the Tunney-Dempsey rematch but also the second annual meeting between the football teams of the University of Notre Dame and the University of Southern California, attended by what some claim to be the largest crowd for a college football game ever, approximately 120,000 persons.[73]

Knute Rockne of Notre Dame was one of the best-known college football coaches in the 1920s, partly because of Notre Dame's national Catholic following and partly because of Rockne's use of the press to promote himself, his team, and Notre Dame. From the early 1920s on, not only was Rockne the football coach and athletic director for the University of Notre Dame, but he also wrote articles and columns for

Christy Walsh's syndicate (Walsh pioneered the profession of sports agent), ran several different summer coaching schools for other college coaches as well as high school coaches, wrote an instructional manual that he sold to students in the coaching school, and organized and ran Camp Rockne for boys. In 1927 he signed an endorsement deal with the Wilson Athletic Equipment Company for "exclusive rights and license to manufacture, sell, and advertise footballs, football helmets, football shoulder pads, football kidney pads, football pants, football shoes, football knit goods, and any other items of football equipment identified by the name, facsimile, signature, initials and/or portrait of said Rockne and/or any nickname which hereafter may be popularly applied to said Rockne."[74] The deal netted him, by the end of the decade, about $10,000 a year beyond the proceeds of his writings, coaching schools, and personal appearances. Rockne also made sure that publicity and press about him that he did not himself generate would be positive by cultivating contacts with sportswriters and publishers, usually through such favors as complimentary tickets to games and offers of jobs as game officials. In the early days of college football, it was common for the coaches of each team to select the officials, and since there was not a consistent supply of trained officials, many sportswriters (who would be at the games to cover them) made extra money as game officials. Rockne was able to hire those sportswriters who were in a position to give Notre Dame positive publicity. As a result, Notre Dame was often held up as the model of a successful athletic program, not just because the team won games but also because the university benefited from the athletic program, as did the young men who participated in it and went on to become successful coaches themselves. While Notre Dame's football proceeds did substantially aid the academic agenda of the university, providing the funding for academic construction projects, that benefit was primarily due to the administration's tight control over the proceeds and the frequent rejection of Rockne's plans for a large concrete stadium on the Notre Dame campus (a plan he was finally able to push through after a winning and financially successful 1927 season). Most athletic programs did not contribute to the academic mission of their schools, and in many cases cost the universities money. Sportswriters reinforced the belief that college athletics benefited the universities by dramatizing the success of these programs. Rockne became known as a molder of men—particularly ethnic, working-class men with few opportunities but with potential—who profited by Rockne's mentoring.

Rockne had the unique situation, and its attendant problems and perks, of coaching at a private, religious university not connected to any established intercollegiate league. As such, Rockne and his program were able to weather the forceful criticisms of reformers actively trying to de-emphasize collegiate athletics, primarily through the Western League (what would later officially become the Big Ten Conference). The main thrust of the critique was the commercialism of big-time college football, whose vast profits led to a win-at-all-costs mentality, which benefited the pocketbooks of coaches and athletic departments but did little good for the universities and the students. Most people believed that financial support should be given only to those college students who had earned it through academics, not athletics. And while this was the goal in theory, in practice, most football players received financial support of some kind, whether in the form of a scholarship, a job, or a scam.

The reformers were led by the Carnegie Foundation for the Advancement of Teaching, which in 1924 issued a short report denouncing the "commercialism," "excessive expenditure of money," and "too great an insistence on turning out a winning team" evidenced in college sports. Much of the blame, the report stated, should be placed on the coach, who "sets the standards of the whole system of intercollegiate sports and is responsible for many of its most demoralizing features."[75] They followed up this report with a five-year study of the problems of big-time college sports. Yet while the Carnegie investigation sought to uncover the seedy side of college football, its final report did little to reform college football; rather, it served as an observation on an emerging system of subsidized college athletes and on college football as an industry. Much of the failure of the Carnegie report had to do with the timing of its release in October 1929, just as the stock market crashed, marking the beginning of the Great Depression. But the failure of the reformers also had to do with the declining ideal of amateur athletics in a society that increasingly celebrated professionalism, expertise, and specialization. While college football was packaged for the public, by the press, universities, and even Hollywood, as an integral part of college life, it in fact dominated the academic mission of many universities.

Knute Rockne best exemplifies the college coach as CEO of an entrepreneurial enterprise: he cultivated relationships with powerful sportswriters, developed a network of recruiters among former players and influential alumni, and scheduled opponents that helped Notre Dame's exposure. Rockne's early teams traveled so much that they were generally called the "Ramblers" or the "Nomads," before the Notre Dame administration gave official sanction to the name "Fighting Irish." Rockne established one of the most profitable intersectional rivalries when, in 1926, the Fighting Irish traveled to Los Angeles to play the University of Southern California (USC). This series proved beneficial to both schools financially and in terms of publicity. USC developed into a national football powerhouse as a result of the series, and Notre Dame profited from USC's close ties with the Hollywood publicity machine. Studios located in Hollywood found USC football an easy and appealing subject for newsreel coverage because of its proximity, the weather in southern California, and the star-studded sidelines. USC football players often found employment in the studios, as stagehands or extras, and one member of the 1927 squad, Marion Morrison, made his career in Hollywood after changing his name to John Wayne. Knute Rockne also attempted to capitalize on the connection between Hollywood and college football by acting in films, but he died in a plane crash in 1931 while en route to Hollywood to sign a $50,000 contract to star in a film version of the popular play *Good News*. But no star athlete made more of the media, both news and entertainment media, than New York Yankee baseball player Babe Ruth.

THE BABE AND MODERN CELEBRITY

In the 1920s, while professional boxing gained respectability and college football gained a national audience, professional baseball attempted to regain the respectability and audience it had lost after the 1919 "Black Sox scandal," in which baseball commissioner Judge Kenesaw Mountain Landis banned from professional baseball eight members of the Chicago White Sox for participating in a scheme to fix the

World Series. Not only did professional baseball come under the iron fist of the baseball commissioner, but it also changed from a game focused on pitching and defense to one that highlighted the crowd-pleasing attraction of hitters, especially home-run hitters. Owners increased the possibility of hits by, among other things, eliminating trick pitches, such as spitballs, and using cleaner, more frequently replaced balls during the game. These changes allowed more players to hit the ball, making the game more exciting for spectators and much more profitable for owners. In addition, owners increased their profits by enlarging the capacity of their fields by building stands in the outfield, thus making in-the-stands home runs much more possible and likely. As a result, overall batting averages increased in the 1920s, as did the number of home runs, hits, and runs batted in and pitchers' earned-run averages. Baseball won back its audience and their respect by making the game more entertaining and dynamic.[76]

Much of that lost respectability returned in 1927 with the incredible run of the New York Yankees, who won 110 games that season and swept the World Series against the Pittsburgh Pirates. H. I. Phillips, writing in the "gee whiz" style popularized by Grantland Rice, claimed the 1927 Yankees to be "a team out of folklore and mythology." He described the roster as having "magicians, miracle men, jinns, a Beowulf and a couple of Thors on it."[77] The press dubbed the team "Murderers' Row" for its punishment of the baseball and its opponents. In strictly statistical terms (another popular method of judgment in the 1920s) the team lived up to much of its praise. The American League's top four pitchers in winning percentages were all on the Yankee roster (Waite Hoyt, Urban Shocker, Wilcy Moore, and Herb Pennock), as were the league's top hitters. Earl Combs led the league in base hits (231) and triples (23). Tony Lazzeri amassed the third-most home runs in the league (18) and the third-most stolen bases (22). Lou Gehrig led the league in runs batted in (175), total bases (447), and doubles (52) and was second in base hits (218), triples (18), bases on balls (109), and home runs (47). Babe Ruth was second in runs batted in (164) and total bases (417) and led the league in slugging percentage (with a slugging average of .772), runs scored (158), and home runs (60, breaking his previous record of 59, set in 1921). Many still consider the 1927 New

York Yankees the best team in baseball history, but as impressive as the players were as a team, no member of the "Row," or of professional baseball, was as well known and popular as Babe Ruth.

Born in 1895 to Kate and George Ruth in Baltimore, George Herman Ruth was one of eight children, only two of whom survived to adulthood. Growing up around his father's saloon, Ruth, as he put it in his autobiography, "was a bad kid." In 1902 he was declared "incorrigible" and sent to St. Mary's Industrial School for Boys, where he would stay, for the most part, for the next twelve years. In early 1914 Jack Dunn, the owner of the minor league Baltimore Orioles, offered Ruth a $600-a-season contract and also agreed to be Ruth's legal guardian (both his parents had died while he was at St. Mary's). As Dunn's "son," Ruth's teammates called him "Dunn's Baby," which eventually turned into "Babe." Ruth made a name for himself as a pitcher, but the minor league team was strapped for cash, so Dunn sold Ruth to the Boston Red Sox, along with two other players, for $25,000. In Boston, Ruth gradually transformed himself from a pitcher to a slugger, as well as living the unrestricted and hedonistic life that made him infamous.[78]

At the end of the 1919 season, Harry Frazee, owner of the Red Sox and a Broadway play investor, needed funds to finance a musical, *No No Nanette!* so in January 1920 he sold Ruth (by now the biggest star in baseball) to the New York Yankees for $125,000. Once with the Yankees, his days as a pitcher coming to an end, Ruth began a number of record-breaking home-run years that turned baseball from a game of pitching and strategy to one highlighted by strength and home runs. His best year was 1921, when he hit 59 home runs (nine more than any other team's total), had a batting average of .378, and led the league in runs (177), runs batted in (171), and walks (144, many of them intentional). After the 1921 season, Ruth embarked on a barnstorming tour, as had become customary among big-name ballplayers, who would travel mainly the South and the West playing exhibition games for those who would not normally get a chance to see a major league game. The baseball commissioner, Judge Kenesaw Mountain Landis, hired by club owners to clean up baseball after the Black Sox scandal, banned barnstorming as an activity detrimental to baseball and demeaning to professionalism. As a result, Ruth was sidelined for part of the 1922 season, and subsequent seasons were sometimes marred by illness (mainly as the result of too much drinking and sex with prostitutes) and personal troubles (a bookie filed a lawsuit against Ruth for gambling debts owed, and Ruth's wife, Helen, suffered a breakdown in 1924). Still, he managed to perform in grand fashion until he collapsed during a preseason exhibition tour in 1925. While newspapers proclaimed Ruth's illness to be "the stomach ache heard around the world," it is more likely to have been a case of a venereal disease. After a dismal 1925 season, Ruth performed well in 1926, as illustrated by his three World Series home runs in a single game, but many felt his best years were behind him. What was not behind him was his popularity. Ruth had become a fixture in daily American life.

Babe Ruth was, according to historian David Voigt, the most photographed man in the country during the 1920s.[79] Newspapers across the country carried stories about him almost daily, even in the off-season, when Ruth would perform on the vaudeville circuit, on radio shows, in newsreels, and in theatrical films. Ruth was able to translate his success on the baseball diamond into mainstream celebrity status rivaling that of Charles Lindbergh, Henry Ford, and Clara Bow. His widespread popularity was the result not only of his celebrated talent as a slugger but also of his charisma as a showman and the media's need for exciting and titillating copy. As newspapers reduced the space devoted to national and world issues of politics and economy and increased their coverage of crime, entertainment, and sports, they also shifted away from their nineteenth-century role of local political advocate and mouthpiece and became nationwide commodities searching for a mass audience through syndication. Ruth provided this journalistic shift with "the perfect content for the dailies. Ruth, despite his often questionable behavior, was never politically or culturally controversial. He presented a safe ideology that antagonized few, and, most importantly, he gave New Yorkers and Americans everywhere a sense of national pride."[80] The ideology that Ruth presented to the public was an archetypical rags-to-riches story.

Though it was Ruth's record in 1927 that brought him acclaim, it was his actions (both on and off the field) that brought him notoriety. He embarked on an approved barnstorming tour with Lou Gehrig and other members of the World Series–winning New York Yankees and released his second film, *Babe Comes Home,* in 1927. Both events illustrate the role Ruth played in Americans' adjustment to the modern world. Ruth began filming *Babe Comes Home* in the winter of 1927 after a post–1926 season barnstorming tour ended in Los Angeles. The film, like his first, *Headin' Home* in 1920, featured Ruth as a baseball player; but instead of being a semiautobiographical coming-of-age story like his film debut, *Babe Comes Home* touched on Ruth's less-than-heroic actions off the field. Ruth plays Babe Dugan, a star player with a nasty habit of chewing tobacco, much of which ended up on his uniform. His laundress, Vernie (Anna Q. Nilsson), concerned about his untidiness, attends a game and is struck by a ball hit by Dugan. This incident brings the two together, and after a date to an amusement park, Babe and Vernie fall in love and become engaged. Vernie plans to reform the ball player, especially after a flood of tobacco cubes and spittoons arrive as wedding gifts, but the resulting cleaner Babe is ineffective on the ball field and is benched by the manager. At a crucial moment in a game and in the season, Babe comes to bat after Vernie, realizing her misguided attempt to change her man, tosses him a plug of tobacco; as a result, he hits a home run.[81] The film basically forgives Ruth's off-the-field indulgences because of his on-the-field abilities. Unlike *Headin' Home,* in which Ruth plays George Ruth, a sincere but not too intelligent young ballplayer who wins both the girl of his dreams and a big-league career primarily by being a good guy, *Babe Comes Home* implies that performance on the field is more important than values and behavior.

In these two films (the only two in which he had a starring role), Ruth illustrates the tension present in American society between nineteenth-century Victorian values and twentieth-century modern values. Whereas George Ruth succeeds because he maintains his good character, saving the girl of his dreams from moral disgrace, Babe Dugan succeeds regardless of (and in fact because of) his uncouth manners. George Ruth is good on the field as a result of being good in life, while Babe Dugan is so good on the field that he is allowed transgressions in life, a basic conflict over means and ends and over which one should be the basis for American celebrity. Both films were, at various times, the same stories told about Babe Ruth in newspaper and magazine articles, celebrating his humble origins while forgiving his hedonism, both in explanation of his tremendous talent. For some, Ruth's talent outweighed any character flaws he exhibited, while for others, his background was what accounted for his baseball success.

As much as Ruth's actions reflected the carefree lifestyle of the Roaring Twenties, he was, for the most part, a celebrity of the nineteenth century. Ruth's movies did not do well, primarily because he had no acting ability, and even when he was playing himself, his natural charisma did not translate to film. Neither did it translate well on radio. His manager, Christy Walsh, tried to keep Ruth off the radio as much as possible, never being sure what might come out of the player's mouth. Grantland Rice recalled an incident on his radio show in which a coached Ruth was to refer to the Duke of Wellington's famous statement that the Battle of Waterloo had been won on the playing fields of Eton: "Babe managed to come out with this gem: 'As Duke Ellington once said, the Battle of Waterloo was won on the playing fields of Elkton.'" When asked how he had messed up the line so completely, Ruth explained that he did not know Wellington, but he did know Ellington, and that he had been married in Elkton, Maryland, and that was what had confused him (in reality Ruth had been married in Ellicott City, Maryland).[82] Ruth was at his best when face-to-face with an audience or crowd. He was best seen unmediated by technology, since what people wanted most was to be in his presence. Still, whether on film or not, Ruth was never an entertainer. Having been suspended for the start of the 1922 season for his violation of the barnstorming prohibition, Ruth toured in the off-season in vaudeville theaters. Vaudeville shows, made up of multiple acts, would often use sports stars as a way to attract audiences to the theater. Ruth's twenty-week, $60,000 contract was one of the longest and most profitable for an athlete, made possible by Ruth's suspension until late May 1922, but Ruth's performance in skits and comic banter did not take the stage by storm. While crowds did appear, many preferred to see Ruth in uniform, not on stage. Ruth's vaudeville tour ended weeks early by mutual consent.

Aside from actual major league games, barnstorming events were the preferred way to see Babe Ruth. Following the Yankee's victorious 1927 season, Ruth and Lou Gehrig embarked on a sanctioned barnstorming tour from New York to Los Angeles, covering over 8,000 miles, visiting eighteen states, and reaching more than 200,000 spectators. While Gehrig—always the quiet, shy type—shied away from attention and publicity, Ruth devoured it. The tour consisted of ceremonies with local dignitaries, visits to children's hospitals, photo opportunities at local newspapers, and exhibition games. Most of the games featured Ruth and Gehrig forming opposing teams with local players. The Bustin' Babes and Larrupin' Lous would battle it out in front of packed crowds. On many occasions the games could not be completed because of the number of young boys who would inundate the field after a Babe Ruth home run. In some cases, the boys were coaxed onto the field by Christy Walsh as a way to bring the event to an end. Ruth never failed to make an impression on the locals, shaking hands and backslapping all the right people. In fewer than three weeks, Ruth and Gehrig played twenty-one games in nineteen different cities. Ruth signed 5,000 autographs (slightly more than Gehrig) and earned $30,000 (compared to Gehrig's $10,000). In total, Ruth's official income for 1927 was $180,500 ($70,000 salary from the Yankees, $30,000 for the barnstorming tour, $5,500 as his share of the World's Series pot, $25,000 from newspaper columns and other publishing projects—none of which were actually written by Ruth but simply used his name—and $50,000 for starring in *Babe Comes Home*). Unofficially, Ruth may have made almost twice that amount, if one includes public appearance fees, endorsements, investments, his 10 percent cut from Yankees exhibition games, and other undisclosed sources.

Like Jack Dempsey and college football, Babe Ruth benefited from the changing cultural values in 1920s America. While being celebrated for individual achievement within a group context, Ruth utilized the modern media to present to the public a rather traditional tale of humble beginnings transformed to lofty status through talent and perseverance. At the same time that audiences thrilled to the achievements of a self-made man, they were also entertained by the thoroughly modern way in which Ruth lived his life. Ruth was ambiguously modern in that he was still being celebrated for his abilities, which were remarkable, and not just for being a celebrity, but his abilities on the playing field made it possible for him to star in films, on the vaudeville stage, and in print and photographs, for which he had little talent. Dempsey was a much more successful stage act, not only because fewer people had a chance to see him fight than to see Babe Ruth play, making Dempsey a greater novelty, but also because the fighter's ability to exude his charm on stage and in film was greater than Ruth's. Though both took advantage of what the modern media made possible, neither was a bona fide crossover success. Other, lesser-known athletes did make successful crossovers—such as swimmer Johnny Weissmuller, who became famous as Tarzan—and are therefore much more representative of the modern era.

Ruth, Dempsey, and college football all benefited from the modern media and from Americans' desire for and ability to support spectator sports, yet all relied very heavily on traditional elements (Ruth's wayward youth, Dempsey's raw power and emotion, and college football's adherence in name to amateur athletics) for their popularity. In this sense, they each utilized the media much as Herbert Hoover did, promoting his self-reliant volunteerism and using publicity to become celebrated. They each in their own way allowed Americans to celebrate the traditional while engaging in the modern. The flip side of fame was the infamy garnered by Nan Britton, Ruth Snyder, and Judd Gray, as well as by other momentary celebrities who also used the media to gain notoriety but found that their modern stories of extramarital affairs, illegitimate children, and murder positioned them as warnings against modernity. Since everything about their stories was modern, they did not possess the ambiguity found in Hoover and the sports figures, and they therefore did not resonate with the public as positively or powerfully. In the end, Britton, Snyder, and Gray did not have the respectability that a connection to traditional values imparted to the public. Celebrities in the newly emerging industries of motion pictures, jazz music, and radio sought out the kind of respectability that came from a connection to traditional values.

Douglas Fairbanks and Mary Pickford canoeing at Pickfair. (© Bettmann/ Corbis)

"Amos 'n' Andy" talking on the phone. (© Bettmann/Corbis)

CHAPTER 4

Seeking Respectability:
Modern Media and Traditional Values

RESPECT AND DISRESPECT: *The new industries of motion pictures and radio sought to gain public recognition and respectability. In Hollywood, the wholesome image of Douglas Fairbanks and Mary Pickford, as well as their leadership in the industry through their participation in the newly created Academy of Motion Picture Arts and Sciences, helped accelerate the development of film technology and artistry, as well as the audience for movies. Radio too boomed as a business by promoting its benefits to education, industry, and democracy. Both industries, however, gained their respectability at the cost of disrespecting African Americans. Hollywood's big hit of 1927,* The Jazz Singer, *perpetuated the stereotypes of blackface entertainment, and radio's expansion and regulation by the federal government drove ethnic- and race-based stations off the radio dial. Like Hollywood, radio capitalized on blackface comedy with shows like* Amos 'n' Andy, *performed by white actors Freeman Gosden and Charles Correll. The success of these industries resulted from the exploitation of and discrimination against African Americans.*

Just as Babe Ruth and Jack Dempsey each brought a measure of respectability to professional sports, as well as earning large fortunes for themselves and the industry, other industries also sought respectability as a means of self-promotion. Douglas Fairbanks and Mary Pickford brought respectability to the film industry and to Hollywood through the cultivation of a wholesome lifestyle. The creation of the Academy of Motion Picture Arts and Sciences also added to the respectability of the industry, as did films with such serious subjects as the Great War and religion. As with Ruth and Dempsey, it was the ability to take advantage of modern opportunities while maintaining traditional values (or at least the air of traditional values) that raised the image of the movie business. Jazz musicians used record sales and radio airplay to bring respectability to what many deemed distasteful music, though much of the respectability would be won by white musicians instead of the African Americans from whose culture the music developed. Respected African American artists sought to distance themselves from the jazz culture by seeking to bring the African American experience to the same level of cultural expression as existed in mainstream American culture. Much of the motivation for the

Harlem Renaissance derived from this desire to be respected as artists. Likewise, the developing radio industry touted its potential to enlighten and educate the masses by bringing informative and culturally sophisticated entertainment to Americans' living rooms. Each of these cultural industries sought respectability as a means of economic success, but each received more than financial wealth.

Each industry became central to the way Americans viewed themselves and to the way others viewed Americans. Indeed, Fairbanks and Pickford generated more wealth than any sports figure of the decade, and it was their vision of America that was sold worldwide to an eager audience. In the film industry—more than in professional sports or even for journalistically created celebrities like Ruth Snyder and Judd Gray—fame could rest on perception and image more than on ability or actions. Yet Hollywood, as industry, image, and ideal, was perhaps more evocative and representative of what people thought of America in the 1920s than any other idea. In Hollywood an unknown could become a star, with all the fame and fortune that stars received, simply by being in the right place at the right time. The randomness of the process reinforced ideas about the role destiny played in the creation of a motion picture celebrity, even though in reality the process was, even in its formative years, a coldly calculated business venture.

RESPECTABILITY AND RELIGION IN HOLLYWOOD

The modernity of the medium found respectability in its most traditional stars, Fairbanks and Pickford. While the "new woman" antics of Clara Bow (both on- and off-screen) demonstrated the limited revolutionary aspects of the Hollywood film industry, the family atmosphere of Pickfair (the Beverly Hills home of Fairbanks and Pickford), along with the squeaky-clean characters played by both actors, brought elements of traditional values to Hollywood. The public viewed Fairbanks and Pickford as Hollywood royalty, and in return, the couple dutifully accepted the responsibility of promoting the film industry. Writer Allene Talmey acknowledged this duty when she wrote in her 1927 book *Doug and Mary and Others* that "Doug and Mary are, of course, the King and Queen of Hollywood, providing the necessary air of dignity, sobriety, and aristocracy." The air of dignity came from Fairbanks and Pickford's upholding of traditional family values (despite the fact that they had divorced their respective spouses to be with each other) and was illustrated by the close ties they maintained with family members, especially their parents and siblings. The sobriety was apparent in Fairbanks's teetotaling ways (supposedly as the result of a boyhood pledge to his mother). A dinner at Pickfair, without wine, usually ended with a movie screening at which guests were served Ovaltine and peanut brittle. And the air of aristocracy came from the couple's hobnobbing with the Duke and Duchess of Alba, Lord and Lady Mountbatten, and the King and Queen of Siam, all of whom were guests at Pickfair, and from several grand tours of Europe where Fairbanks and Pickford were hosted by royalty and the rich and famous. But ultimately, the responsibility they held most dear was to the industry that made them famous. "Gravely they attend movie openings, cornerstone layings, gravely sit at the head of the table at the long dinners in honor of the cinema great, Douglas making graceful speeches, Mary conducting herself with the self-abnegation of Queen Mary of Britain. Cornerstone layings, dinners, openings are duties; they understand thoroughly their obligation to be present, in the best interests of the motion picture industry."[1] Indeed, Fairbanks and Pickford perfectly illustrate the duplicitous nature of Hollywood, in that they were more than the characters they played, more even than actors playing specific roles. They both were business forces creating economic empires, first separately, then together as business partners (with Charlie Chaplin and D. W. Griffith in the creation of United Artists), and later as husband and wife. Yet it was Fairbanks's boundless optimism and Pickford's virginal sweetness, not their business acumen or even their acting ability, that made them the "most popular couple in the world."[2]

The characters they portrayed reinforced the image they presented of their private lives. Pickford fluctuated between her child roles (*Pollyanna*, 1920; *Little Lord Fauntleroy*, 1921; *Tess of the Storm Country*, 1922; *Little Annie Rooney*, 1925; and *Sparrows*, 1926) and her attempts to break out of the little girl persona and portray someone her own age or close to it (*The Love Light*, 1921, in which she plays a woman caught in the tragedy of the Great War; *Rosita*, 1923, in which she plays a Spanish dancing girl; and *Dorothy Vernon of Haddon Hall*,

1924, a historical drama set in England). The child roles did considerably better than the adult roles, and when she went directly to her fans and asked readers of *Photoplay* to suggest roles she should play, they overwhelmingly suggested such child roles as Cinderella, Anne of Green Gables, Alice in Wonderland, Heidi, the Little Colonel, and Sara Crewe. The magazine selected one prize-winning letter for publication; it pleaded with "My Dear Little Mary" to stick to characters between ten to fourteen years old. "These particular roles are your greatest opportunities for showing us what a wonderful actress you really are by your ability to create and preserve an almost perfect illusion."[3] The "perfect illusion" was not only that of a woman in her thirties playing an adolescent but also the illusion of a perfect child who always made the right decisions and always held fast to traditional moral values. It did not matter if the character was rich or poor, white Anglo-Saxon or immigrant, or even male or female; all these characters shared a strong moral fiber and triumphant virtue.

In *My Best Girl* (1927), Pickford plays Maggie Johnson, a stock girl at Merrill's five-and-dime. Maggie also cares for her father, who works as a postal carrier and comes home tired each night, and her mother, who spends her days going to the funerals of people she does not know. She also has to watch out for her sister, who, unlike hard-working Maggie, spends her nights going out on the town with Nick Powell, a man of questionable reputation. At work Maggie trains Joe Grant (played by future Pickford husband Charles "Buddy" Rogers), who she thinks is from a working-class family like her own when in reality he is the son of the store's owner and thus heir to the Merrill fortune. Joe is proving himself in business by starting at the bottom and working his way up on his own merits rather than on his name. From the start we know that Maggie and Joe are the bearers of morality in the film. Maggie and Joe fall in love, but the combination of the Merrill family's expectations and Maggie's sister's careless lifestyle leads to a courtroom brawl that lands on the front page, forcing Mr. Merrill to send Joe off to Hawaii "until this scandal blows over" and to offer Maggie $10,000 to never see Joe again. Not wanting to ruin Joe's career, Maggie tries to convince him that she was after the money all along and that she never loved him, but Joe sees through her act, and with both families' changes of heart, Joe and Maggie rush to catch the boat to Honolulu and live happily ever after.

In the film, Pickford was not a child, but she nevertheless maintained the same innocence and virtue as in her child roles by being poor and virtuous. Maggie exhibits none of the extravagance of her sister, whose stylish clothes contrast with Maggie's modest outfits, nor does her family display the kind of lavish life that is seen in the Merrill household, especially on the part of Joe's mother and fiancée. Joe, too, engages in hard, decent work and treats Maggie with the utmost respect. The film as a whole upholds the traditional values of family, respect for parents, and romantic love and of work as superior to unearned profit. These values were present in all of Pickford's films and are part of what made her "America's Sweetheart." Audiences and fans believed that Pickford's private life also reflected these values, and in many ways it did. Both Pickford and Fairbanks were very aware of the image they portrayed both on-screen and off, and both did their best not to deceive their fans. Pickford did often place the needs of her family over Fairbanks's wants. She canceled or postponed several European trips because of her ailing mother, Charlotte, or her frequently scandal-laden siblings Lottie and Jack. The couple even moved into Charlotte's house near the end of 1927 and cared for her during her last four months of life. Even Pickford's and Fairbanks's divorces and quick marriage barely diminished fans' beliefs about the virtue and wholesomeness of the couple. In fact, most fans interpreted the events as illustrating the obstacles Fairbanks and Pickford had overcome to be with the true love of their lives. While America loved Pickford and Fairbanks separately as movie stars, they loved them even more together as the king and queen of Hollywood. *My Best Girl* was not Pickford's only screen appearance of 1927; she also had a very small cameo role in *The Gaucho*, starring her husband.

Fairbanks had, by 1927, solidified his position as the swashbuckling hero of such period epics as *The Mark of Zorro* (1920), *The Three Musketeers* (1921), *Robin Hood* (1922), *The Thief of Bagdad* (1924), *Don Q, Son of Zorro* (1925), and *The Black Pirate* (1926). In *The Gaucho* (1927), he added a sense of religious importance to his steal-from-the-rich, give-to-the-poor characters. Playing the most wanted man on the

Argentine pampas, "the Gaucho," he displayed a much darker character than in most of his films. Not only is the Gaucho a criminal for his own gain (unlike Robin Hood), but he also drinks heavily, smokes constantly, and tries to seduce the virginal "Girl of the Shrine." Yet, as always, Fairbanks's character is moral, even though he is an outlaw. The villain, the usurper Ruiz, is immoral, as evidenced by his willingness to take the wealth of the shrine (wealth meant to help the poor) for himself. Yet the Gaucho has to pay for his transgressions against the higher morality of religion. As a result of banishing a leper, telling him to "find someplace to kill yourself," the Gaucho is himself infected and runs off to kill himself. Rescued by the Girl of the Shrine and the healing waters she protects, the Gaucho is visited by an image of the Virgin Mary (played by an uncredited Mary Pickford) and vows to rescue the holy city from the clutches of the evil usurper Ruiz. Once he recaptures the city in the name of the church, he settles down with his gypsy woman (played by Lupe Velez). The outlaw Gaucho has been converted to wholesome morality.

While in *The Gaucho* Fairbanks is cast as a much darker character than in his other films, what is especially telling is the inclusion of religion as the ultimate moral arbitrator. Film actors and makers were not considered religious moralists, and the greatest criticism of the film industry came from religious groups, especially the Catholic Church. Not only were such groups concerned about the content of movies, but they were also concerned about the actions of those in the industry. The early 1920s had been plagued by scandals, including Mary Pickford's 1920 Nevada divorce, which was challenged by the state's attorney general after Pickford had already married Fairbanks, and the 1921 Fatty Arbuckle scandal, in which the rotund film comic was acquitted of causing the death of Virginia Rappe, a guest at a party he hosted, but which stirred widely circulated rumors about casual sex and drug use in Hollywood. These rumors were reinforced by the sudden death of actor Wallace Reid in 1922, caused by drug addiction, following the death of director William Desmond Taylor amid allegations of drug use, sex, and murder that ruined the careers of movie comedienne Mabel Normand and Mary Pickford look-alike Mary Miles Minter. These scandals attracted the attention of the U.S. Congress and raised the specter of federal censorship. Following the lead of professional baseball, which had undergone its own scandal with the 1919 "Black Sox" fixing of the World Series, industry leaders hired William H. Hays, postmaster general of the United States, President Harding's campaign manager, a Presbyterian elder, and a Republican, to head the Motion Picture Producers and Distributors of America (MPPDA, also known as the Hays Office). Hays did not institute censorship, but he did assist filmmakers by reviewing projects and suggesting cuts that would help a film stay clear of local censors across the country, as well as acting as a promoter of good values in Hollywood.

Including religion was one way to promote good values in film, as evidenced by Fairbanks's use of it in *The Gaucho,* but one of the biggest films of 1927 was more overt in its religiosity, Cecil B. DeMille's *King of Kings.* DeMille had earlier established himself as a leading director of biblical epic films with *The Ten Commandments* (1923), and religion had also been the focus of 1925's big film *Ben-Hur: A Tale of the Christ.* But with *The King of Kings,* DeMille saw himself as creating more than another film based on a biblical story. "To give the peoples of the modern world the same opportunity to see the wondrous life-drama of Jesus as was given to the citizens of Judea nineteen hundred years ago has been the object of my endeavors in making *The King of Kings.*" DeMille continued by admitting that "my purpose is, of course, dramatic entertainment," not just any run-of-the-mill leisure-time entertainment but, rather, "drama in its highest sense as defined in the immortal apothegm of Aristotle." To achieve this lofty goal, DeMille consulted religious leaders during the preproduction phase of the project and imbued the production with an air of religious significance by assembling "representatives of more than thirty religious sects and beliefs" to open production with "a service and a prayer." In addition to claiming that this religious gathering was the first time in history that representatives of the "Buddhist and Mohammedan faiths . . . had ever appeared together in public," he also asserted that all these leaders had a firm belief "that the motion picture medium possessed the power to carry the story of Jesus to millions who might not otherwise be sympathetic to it, or who would find difficulty in grasping it because of racial or linguistic reasons."[4]

For DeMille, film was perfectly suited to bringing the story of Christ's crucifixion and resurrection to the masses because of its ability to convey a story plainly and simply. The film is presented primarily in images, without an overwhelming number of titles or a lot of dialogue. DeMille felt that what earlier generations had learned through reading, the younger generation would need to learn from the movies. "The story will present to the coming generation who now fill our schools and colleges a picturization of the life and particularly the ideals of this Man of Galilee," DeMille told the cast and crew at the first reading of the script. DeMille's concern for reaching younger generations emanated from a study he had read describing the lack of biblical knowledge among college students. In the discussion following the script reading, DeMille suggested addressing the theory that the disciples had removed the body of Christ from the tomb, and his brother W. C. DeMille commented that audiences would believe what they had always believed and that this film would not change anyone's mind. "They are not going to believe in it anyway just because they see it on the screen." To which the director responded, "Yes, they are. . . . Their idea of the life of Christ is going to be formed by what we give them. This next generation will get its idea of Jesus Christ from this picture."[5] DeMille's boast was not primarily a personal one but, rather, an indication of his belief in the importance of the subject and the power of motion pictures. "I am only the humble and thankful instrument," he told a radio audience, "through which the screen . . . is carrying the greatest of all messages to hundreds of thousands of fellow human beings."[6] DeMille felt that the Roaring Twenties were the ideal time to bring this message to the screen, since a decade earlier the movie industry had not established itself as an artistic medium "embodying the thoughts of many of the world's greatest thinkers." Also, a pre–World War I audience would not have needed to be told the story of Christ because "religion was a thing conventionally accepted by the great majority of people." The Great War had changed all that and sent man on a search for understanding. "The ideals of the Man of Nazareth have persisted throughout all the centuries, and there is an almost universal demand for the return to greater knowledge of Him and the influence of His mission." For DeMille, *The King of Kings* would fill a void in the spiritual education of the nation. "At no time in the world's history has humanity so hungered for the truth. Science has declared there is a God. And a groping, eager world cries,

'How may we find Him?'"[7] DeMille, through Hollywood and the motion picture industry, would lead the way.

A film with as much importance as DeMille placed on *The King of Kings* deserved a premiere equally impressive. DeMille teamed up with theater owner and showman Sid Grauman to coincide the premiere of the film with the grand opening of Grauman's newest movie palace, the Chinese Cinema Temple on Hollywood Boulevard. Advertised as "The World's Most Magnificent Playhouse," Grauman's Chinese Theater promised moviegoers a spectacle for its opening night. Not only did the theater host the premiere of *The King of Kings,* but Grauman staged a lavish show both inside and outside the theater. He convinced the city of Los Angeles to declare May 18, 1927, a "holiday in honor of the Chinese Government," and he proclaimed, "Every patron at the opening will be presented with a magnificent Mandarin coat to be worn throughout the performance." He also promised "miles of Chinese lanterns . . . , one thousand Chinese Cavalry soldiers as honorary guards—two hours of spectacular fireworks and illuminated arches, the courtesy of the Chinese Government, which will make the heavens jealous—one thousand Chinese beauties—one hundred floats!" All to celebrate "TWO GREAT EVENTS Crystallized Into the One Night of Nights in Motion Picture History."[8] An estimated 25,000 people came to witness the event, and a riot broke out as crowds tried to catch a glimpse of the stars attending the premiere, some of whom claimed to have left their cars "several blocks away" and to have fought their way to the theater. Headlines proclaimed, "Hundreds of Police Battle to Keep Crowds in Check."[9] The *Los Angeles Times* declared the evening's affair to be "the most important event in recent Western theatrical history."[10]

With 2,258 seats, Grauman's Chinese Theater is not the grandest of the movie palaces, but it does hold the distinction of its famous courtyard, in which movie stars' foot- and handprints are preserved in concrete. One story claims the idea came from Fairbanks and Pickford, who, after inspecting a newly installed irrigation dam at their Rancho Zorro outside of San Diego, had pressed their hands and written their names in the wet cement. Their friend Sid Grauman, who happened to be looking for a gimmick for his new theater, embraced the couple's idea. Indeed, Pickford and Fairbanks were the first to imprint the courtyard, on April 30. Another story claims that actress Norma

Talmadge accidentally slipped into the wet cement during construction, thereby inspiring Grauman, but Talmadge's official prints do not appear until May 18, after Pickford and Fairbanks made their prints, making it more likely that the idea was the couple's. By January 1928, ten stars had placed their mark in the courtyard, including comic actor Harold Lloyd, western star William S. Hart, actresses Colleen Moore and Gloria Swanson, Charlie Chaplin, film cowboy Tom Mix, and his horse Tony. The courtyard of Grauman's, with its ever-growing number of foot- and handprints, turned the theater into a Hollywood landmark that attracted visitors as well as audiences, allowing audiences to be transported to far-off places (even before the program started) and, at the same time, allowing visitors to compare their foot and hand sizes with those of their favorite stars. Grauman's theater enabled people to escape their lives and enter an exotic world, where their film stars were larger than life in the theater and ordinary humans, with life-size feet, outside. Like sports figures, movie stars needed to be both extraordinary and ordinary.

The combination of religious spectacle and Hollywood ballyhoo in Chinese garb illustrates the ambiguous nature of Hollywood. In the 1920s, the industry realized its potential impact as a positive contributor to society, and at the same time it exploited the public's thirst for the latest fads and sensationalism. While *The King of Kings* sought to enrich and enhance the lives of the audience, the events surrounding the opening of Grauman's Chinese Theater were meant to entertain visitors through the exploitation of the exotic and the extreme. The day after the premiere, Grauman's ads in local papers declared that "30,000 persons sought to gain admittance to the opening of the showplace of the world. . . . Never before has any box office turned away so many people."[11] Even the film itself was a calculated business venture that prolonged the life of DeMille's studio. DeMille and his financier and partner Jeremiah Milbank used an inflated budget of over $2.6 million for *The King of Kings* to cover a million dollars' worth of studio improvements and paychecks. Later, when they sold the studio, they retained the rights to *The King of Kings,* since on the books it looked like an unsuccessful film, while in reality it did make money. The film broke box office records, running at New York's Gaiety Theater longer than any previous film.

For the motion picture industry, respectability came not only from the approval of churches and local boards of censorship (those concerned about content) but also from the industry's ability to make money. By 1927, the motion picture industry had become the fourth-largest industry in the nation. While studios competed for talent and film projects, they were united in keeping government censors at bay and in promoting the industry as a whole. The MPPDA dealt with promoting a positive image for the industry, but it did little to promote film as an art form or to coordinate the various segments of the motion picture industry and the various studios. To this end, the Hollywood elite joined together to form the Academy of Motion Picture Arts and Sciences. Initially conceived, in part, as a response to the Studio Basic Agreement of November 1926, which provided for the unionization of carpenters, painters, electricians, stagehands, and musicians at nine major film studios, the academy sought to bring standardization to the industry in both business practices and motion picture technology. The idea for the academy arose from a dinner conversation at the home of producer Louis B. Mayer among Mayer, producer and director Fred Niblo, and actor Conrad Nagel. They all agreed that the industry needed a single organization to represent the industry against attacks from outside groups, such as reform organizations and censorship groups. They also agreed that the organization should represent all aspects of motion picture production within the five categories of actors, directors, producers, technicians, and writers. Unlike the MPPDA, this organization would be primarily concerned not with the exhibition of films (that is, neither making suggestions to steer clear of censorship boards nor promoting wholesome films and activities) but with the production of films. Mayer hosted a dinner of thirty-six invited guests representing all facets of motion picture production at the Ambassador Hotel on January 11, 1927, to propose the idea of the academy. Among those in attendance were producers Irving Thalberg and Jesse Lasky (Lasky's Feature Play company had merged with Adolph Zuckor's Famous Players to form the Famous Players–Lasky Corporation in 1916, which became Paramount Studios in 1927), producer and theater owner Sid Grauman, directors Raoul Walsh (*What Price Glory?* 1926) and Cecil B. DeMille, writers Jeanie Macpherson (*The King of Kings*) and Frank Woods (*Birth of a Nation,* 1915), set designer Cecil

Gibbons (who designed the "Oscar," the Award of Merit statuette), special-effects artist Roy Pomeroy (*Wings,* 1927), and actors Harold Lloyd, Mary Pickford (who is often listed as a producer), and Douglas Fairbanks. The group of thirty-six became the founding members of the academy and went about the task of organizing the academy and its five branches representing the five categories of film production. By mid-March, the founders selected a board of directors (later changed to a board of governors) and officers, with Fairbanks as the first president of the academy. By May, the state of California had granted the organization a charter for incorporation, and the founders planned an organizational banquet for May 11, 1927.

The invitation-only banquet brought together 300 film professionals; Cecil B. DeMille, reinforcing his belief in the power of film, stated that the attendees "constituted the most powerful group ever assembled in the world, a group that influences the mental processes of all mankind."[12] The founders invited the attendees to "join unselfishly into one big concerted movement, . . . to effectually accomplish those essential things which we have hitherto neglected," such as to take "aggressive action in meeting outside attacks that are unjust," "promote harmony and solidarity among our membership and among our different branches," "reconcile any internal differences that may exist or arise," "protect the honor and good repute of our profession," "encourage the improvement and advancement of the arts and sciences of our profession by the interchange of constructive ideas and by awards of merit for distinctive achievements," and in general "develop the greater power and influence of the screen."[13] The admission fee was $100, and 231 people paid it to participate in the organizational banquet and become charter members of the academy, whose first official act was the granting of an Honorary Membership to Thomas Edison for his pioneering role in the development of motion picture technology and the motion picture industry. While the creation of the academy did help bring more standardization to the industry, publicly it announced to the world the status of the industry by selecting distinguished practitioners for membership in an organization based along the lines of scholarly academies.

The public's main interest lay in the "awards of merit," which were first presented in May 1929 for films released in the Los Angeles area between August 1, 1927, and July 31, 1928. While the ceremony did not have the suspense or prestige that later years would bring (winners were selected by committee and announced months before the awards banquet), it did serve to distinguish films that were considered of artistic merit from the hundreds of films released each year. By singling out a few selected examples of the best of the industry, the academy, in a sense, educated the public about superior film art. The awards were meant not to reflect public tastes but, to some degree, to shape them. While Pickford, Fairbanks, Chaplin, and Bow were the top movie stars in terms of box office appeal, only Chaplin was nominated for an acting award, and he lost out to German actor Emil Jannings (for his work in *The Command* and *The Way of All Flesh*). Chaplin did receive a special award of merit "for versatility and genius in writing, acting, directing, and producing *The Circus.*" Fairbanks and *The Gaucho* were not mentioned, and only Pickford's cinematographer on *My Best Girl* was given a nomination. Out of the six films Clara Bow released in 1927, only *Wings* (which was not really a Clara Bow vehicle even though, as the biggest box office draw in the cast, she received top billing) was selected, winning awards for its engineering effects and as Best Picture. *Seventh Heaven* was the most-mentioned film (nominees not winning an award received honorable mention awards), with three awards (for actress Janet Gaynor, director Frank Borzage, and adaptation writer Benjamin Glazer) and two honorable mentions (for art direction and best picture). *Sunrise* also won three awards (for actress Gaynor, who received the award for three performances: *Seventh Heaven, Sunrise,* and *Street Angel;* for cinematographers Charles Rosher and Karl Struss; and for "Artistic Quality of Production," a category used only in the academy's first awards), and an honorable mention (for art direction). The films recognized by the academy as superior achievements shared another aspect of respectable art: serious subjects. In the case of *Seventh Heaven* and *Wings,* that subject was the Great War. *Seventh Heaven* is the story of two lowly Parisians, Chico (Charles Farrell), a sewer worker, and Diane (Janet Gaynor), a slum-dwelling waif living with an abusive sister. The two find happiness in their seventh floor apartment until Chico is called to war. Diane's love endures through the absence and his presumed death, and is rewarded with his eventual return on Armistice Day.

The use of the war in *Seventh Heaven* was secondary to the love story, but it gave the film an emotional resonance for an audience not a decade away from the war. In *Wings,* the war was the central element in a story of four people affected by the war. Jack Powell (Charles "Buddy" Rogers, from *My Best Girl*) is the all-American boy who tinkers with cars and has a crush on the wealthy and refined Sylvia Lewis (Jobyna Ralston). Mary Preston (Clara Bow) lives next door to Jack and has loved him all her life, but she is seen by Jack as one of the guys and a friend. Sylvia is in love with the wealthy David Armstrong (Richard Arlen), who becomes best friends with Jack when they both sign up to become fighter pilots. As the boys leave for the war, Jack expresses his love for Sylvia, and, not wanting him to leave for Europe brokenhearted, she lets him believe that she feels the same. Meanwhile, a brokenhearted Mary decides to escape town by joining the Red Cross and serving in Europe. While the film does glorify the war, especially in the dynamic aerial sequences filmed from a plane, it does not ignore the costs of war. Mary, having run into a drunken Jack in Paris, is caught in his room with him passed out on the bed and is sent home in disgrace. David discovers that his best friend is in love with his girl, after which he is shot down during a dogfight, but he manages to return to friendly terrain by stealing a German plane. Flying to safety, David is shot down again, this time by Jack, who realizes his mistake as David lays dying. Receiving a hero's welcome back home, an aged Jack visits David's parents and witnesses the real toll of the war. He also realizes that his love belongs with the one who loves him, Mary, the girl next door. Although the film questions the cost of the war, by not emphasizing the end of the war but instead focusing on David's death, it does not question the reasons for the war, something left primarily to such novelists as Ernest Hemingway and John Dos Passos. King Vidor's *The Big Parade* (1925) was another war film released generally in 1927 (after two years of road-show engagements), and like Dos Passos's *1919* (1932), it seeks to uncover the shallowness of American patriotism in the Great War. In covering the same critical terrain as the "Lost Generation" writers, Vidor brought an artistic respectability to motion pictures in a manner more contemporary than the historical and biblical dramas of D. W. Griffth and Cecil B. DeMille.

HOLLYWOOD, *THE JAZZ SINGER,* AND JAZZ

The 1929 Academy Awards ceremony was unique not only because the awards were new, but also because it was the only time the ceremony was not in some way broadcast to an audience, the only time there was an award category for title writing, and the only year the academy recognized silent films. The reason for these anomalies was, of course, the widespread acceptance and demand for sound films after the release of *The Jazz Singer* (October 6, 1927). While *The Jazz Singer* was not the first film to employ synchronized sound, nor a fully "talking" picture (the majority of the film is silent, with a musical score and only a few lines of dialogue and synchronized singing by Al Jolson), its success did force studios to abandon silent films and make the transition to sound. It was in the field of sound that the academy did some of its most productive industry work. Early attempts to use the academy as an industry-wide arbiter for labor conditions met with only limited success and created more controversy than results, forcing the academy to withdraw completely from labor issues when its constitution was revised in the 1930s. Nor did the academy provide much leadership in the fight against censorship; that fight was mainly taken up by the MPPDA with the formal writing of a production code in 1930 and its strict enforcement by Joseph Breen starting in 1934. What the academy did succeed in was encouraging and sponsoring education and research in film technology.

In 1929, the academy created the Producers-Technicians Joint Committee to direct "the handling of specific problems that would benefit from cooperative research, investigation, and experimentation."[14] The committee recommended concentrated effort on three main problems: "(1) silencing the camera, (2) developing special set construction materials for sound pictures, and (3) silencing the arc."[15] Most of the early technical bulletins issued by the academy dealt with sound technology. Issued by the academy's Research Council, such titles as "Theatre Acoustics for Reproduced Sound, also Reproduction in the Theatre," "Camera Silencing Devices," "Architectural Acoustics," and "Methods of Silencing Arcs" helped spread technical knowledge around an industry in which, previously, individual studios had closely guarded their technical secrets. This emphasis on sound technology reflected the studios' urgent need for skilled sound technicians. By sharing this information throughout the industry, the transition to sound occurred at a faster rate, allowing the technology to keep pace with artistry. This rapid transition was especially important after the start of the Great Depression, when film revenue was lost just at the moment greater capital outlay emerged as a necessity. The academy pooled the resources of the studios to train qualified sound technicians by establishing a school for studio personnel to learn the elements of sound recording and reproduction and by establishing a collection of film periodicals from around the world that would form the basis of the most extensive research library on motion pictures. By emphasizing research and education, the academy brought to the industry not only standardization but respectability, as an industry concerned about advancing knowledge and technology, and not just seeking profits.

Starring Broadway star Al Jolson, *The Jazz Singer* not only revolutionized the industry by forcing studios to commit to the production of films with sound but also revived interest in the film industry, which had been on the wane for several years. Despite the fact that silent film art had reached its peak in the mid-1920s, movie attendance had started to decline, especially among those who could afford other forms of entertainment, such as live performances and home radio sets. To combat this decline, the large movie palaces increased the appeal of their screenings by adding live performances to the bill. Most large metropolitan theaters employed full orchestras and sometimes choirs to accompany the films, as well as using composers, arrangers, and extensive score libraries as resources. Silent films seldom had original scores composed for them by the studios; rather, they employed score sheets that gave theater composers and arrangers (and organists at theaters without orchestras) performance suggestions ranging from what moods to set (love, rage, sadness) to what musical sound effects to use (battles), and even suggestions of classical or popular songs to use. The most accomplished of the theater composers might have their scores adapted for general-release versions of films that had extended runs in New York and Los Angeles and that toured the larger theaters across the country. Road-show pictures, as these big-budget films were called, were treated more like Broadway plays than motion pictures. Most road shows toured for about a year before general release, but some, like *The Big Parade* (1925), toured for two years before its general release in 1927. In 1928 the over-two-and-a-half-hour road-show version of *The King of Kings* was cut to under two hours, and the score written by Hugo Riesenfeld for the Gaiety Theater was adapted and transferred to a synchronized soundtrack for the full release of the film, extending the run of the silent film into the era of sound. Many of the late silent films became synchronized sound films simply by transferring a musical score either to disk or film. The musicians employed at the movie palaces would also accompany live perform-ances as well as offer musical selections ranging from popular vaude-ville tunes to classical works. To attract audiences large enough to fill their theaters (from 2,000 to 6,000 seats), owners offered a variety of entertainments, with the motion picture being the headlining act.

With the introduction of sound, speakers and sound equipment re-placed live musicians, in part because films could now give audiences something they could not before, musical performances. Silent film had always had a problem with showing musicians and singers on film because the type of musical accompaniment varied widely from the-ater to theater. While major houses could reproduce almost any style of music, smaller theaters relied on a single organist or pianist, or had nothing at all. This meant that the need for diagetic music (music whose performance is being portrayed on the screen from musicians, a radio, or the like) could not always be met in a manner supportive of the story. Telling the story of *The Jazz Singer* would not have been possible in a silent film since the story is dependent on the way the songs are sung. Without the comparison between the sacredness of "Kol Nidre" sung on the Day of Atonement and the frivolity of "Blue Skies" sung by Jolson, the film could not musically express the major conflict in the story, between the Cantor Rabinowitz and his jazz-singing son, Jack Robin.

Jolson plays Jackie Rabinowitz, son of the cantor and next in a long line of cantors. While his immigrant father expects him to follow the family line, Jackie only wants to sing jazz. When the father learns of his son's inclination, he punishes Jackie, leading him to run away and seek his fortune as a vaudeville performer. In his struggle to make it as a jazz singer, Jackie (now Jack Robin) meets and falls in love with Mary Dale, a *shiksa*. By embracing jazz, as well as Mary, Jack has assimilated into American society, but at the cost of losing his traditions and religion. As Jack arrives back in New York on the verge of becoming a Broadway star, he visits his mother and sings her a couple of songs from his show, including "Blue Skies," an optimistic song that belies the trouble ahead: "Blue skies smiling at me, nothing but blue skies do I see." His father, hearing the music coming from his house, kicks Jack out and declares his son dead, but Jack is pulled back into the family when, on the eve of his big Broadway debut, his mother comes to the dress rehearsal to ask Jack to fill in as cantor for his ill father at the Day of Atonement services, which coincide with the opening. Jack is torn between his love of family and his devotion to his career, a career that his mother realizes is his calling once she hears him sing at the dress rehearsal. Yet Jack cannot completely reject his family and traditions, and, postponing his Broadway debut, he sings "Kol Nidre" on the Day of Atonement as his father listens from his bedroom across the street. His father then dies, content with his Jackie and the world. But Jackie does not stay with the synagogue; instead, the film ends with Jack Robin, a big star, singing "My Mammy" on Broadway with his overjoyed mother sitting in the front row.

Unlike *The King of Kings, The Jazz Singer* treats religion not in a detached, reverential, historical setting but in a contemporary setting. The film aimed not to resolve the problems of modern life through religion, as DeMille had sought to do, but rather to address the problem of fitting a religious life into a modern industrial society. While in the end Jack chooses American success over religious tradition, he does not abandon religion altogether, and the film shows the impact his faith has on his life. Much of the difference between the two films has to do with the religions in question, Christianity and Judaism, but the main conflict in *The Jazz Singer* is not between Jewish traditions and Christian ones, but between Old World, family traditions and New World, American values of success and assimilation. Likewise, DeMille sought to ensure that *The King of Kings* was not an indictment of Jews in the crucifixion of Jesus Christ but, rather, an indictment of Roman power. The film is more representative of anti-imperialist sentiment shaped by Great War experiences and American beliefs in democracy. "The difficult thing of course is to tell the story so as not to offend any religion or sect," DeMille stated, "to attack certain usages of Ancient Rome, and show the crucifixion of Christ, His persecution, not by the Jewish people, but by a group of Roman politicians who saw that the ideals of Jesus, accepted by the people, would sweep away the power of Rome."[16] In both films, religion lends a necessary balance to modern life.[17]

While the story of *The Jazz Singer* appealed to audiences conflicted about modern life, it would not have had the impact it did if people did not hear the voice of Al Jolson but instead heard a member of a choir or a solo pianist perform his songs. Part of the novelty of the film was not only its synchronized sound but the fact that people were able to hear a famous Broadway performer. Unlike earlier experiments with sound film, *The Jazz Singer* combined all the elements that a sound film could contain in a way no other medium could. A consistent musical performance by a popular performer presented along with a melodramatic story line that addressed the concerns of the audience made the film the huge success it became. Sound films increased the talent pool available to Hollywood with the inclusion of singers and musicians. The introduction of sound was good not only for sagging Hollywood receipts but also for the emerging genre of jazz, which *The Jazz Singer* exploited in its title, if not in the musical offerings. The title illustrates the broad definition given to jazz in the 1920s and the ability of the idea of jazz to represent the struggle between new and old. While jazz music in the 1920s spread throughout the country from its southern origins, most jazz on film revealed only traces of the innovative music. Authentic jazz could be heard to varying degrees in clubs, on records, and on the radio, but rarely in films of the 1920s.

F. Scott Fitzgerald and others used the term "jazz," and all it evoked, to represent the new and modern—as well as the superficial and decadent—but for many others jazz was not so simply defined. Some saw in the music a deep connection to an African American past, whether the recent past of slavery or the more distant past of Africa. Others saw jazz as a way to modernize and Americanize classical western music, much in the same way that Harlem Renaissance writers and artists sought to modernize and Americanize literature and art through the use of African American folk idioms and primitivism. Jazz was simultaneously seen as a cultural achievement to be celebrated, an aberration to be denounced, a means of self- and/or group expression, or a commodity to be packaged and sold. For many, jazz was all these things, and regardless of definition or intention, jazz permeated American culture in the 1920s, on the radio and stage, in ballrooms and nightclubs, in films and in literature. Historian Kathy Ogren argues that "for many Americans, to argue about jazz was to argue about the nature of change itself."[18] Dealing with jazz, in many respects, meant not only dealing with race but also dealing with the very ambiguity of modern American life.

The Jazz Singer's significance in the history of the motion picture industry, as well as its content, illustrates the way Hollywood entertainment sought to deal with issues of cultural modernization, but the film is also significant in its use of jazz and white perceptions of African American culture. While not what most jazz musicians of the day would have considered jazz music, the songs used in The Jazz Singer represented white interpretations of African American music, mainly inspired by the minstrel show. Even though the film does not promote the actual music of jazz musicians, it does promote the idea of jazz, a musical form based on the experiences of slaves and unique to the United States. Jack Robin does not become an American just by changing his name and shedding his Jewish heritage. He becomes an American by singing American music and through his realization that jazz music expresses the suffering of his people and his uniquely American situation. In relating his own experience to the experience of African Americans through the use of blackface performance, Jack Robin not only sheds his Jewish identity but also, as Michael Rogin argues, disempowers both Jews and African Americans. More than assimilation, the film promotes the silencing and marginalization of authentic minority voices for homogenized "American" ones.[19]

The film used the term "jazz" to represent modern America. For the Cantor Rabinowitz, a jazz singer and his music were the furthest thing from his Jewish religion and Old World tradition, not only because of its sound but also because of its commercialization. Indeed, the film makes the case that the intent and sound of jazz music is similar to religious music when Yudelson comments that Jack sings his Broadway song "with the cry in the voice, just like in the temple,"[20] and later, when Jack performs "Kol Nidre" at the temple, the Broadway producer remarks, "a jazz singer—singing to his God."[21] The Jazz Singer illustrates the broad definition of jazz familiar to American audiences, one that is only partially about the music. This expansive definition allows for the inclusion of a wide array of musicians within the world of jazz and eliminates the distinction between jazz as a black form of music and the appropriation of it by white musicians. For many Americans, both black and white musicians performed jazz music, and jazz distinguished more the difference between modernity and tradition, or the difference between artistic and commercial, than the difference between black and white. While this distinction brought respectability to jazz as a commercial product, it did not bring about an increase in respect for African American culture.

JAZZ AND AFRICAN AMERICAN CULTURE

Jazz began in turn-of-the-century New Orleans, the result of that city's unique racial mix of ethnic whites, African Americans, and Creoles, but it did not gain a national following since New Orleans at the turn of the century did not have the means to disseminate the music beyond live performances. What had started as a black folk music drawing on spirituals and blues had become, with the introduction of ragtime syncopation and European musical instruments such as those in a brass band, a new musical style, uniquely American. By 1927, "jazz," as a popular term, was about ten years old. In 1917, the white New Orleanians making up the Original Dixieland Jazz Band recorded the first jazz records in New York and became a phenomenon, mostly among white college students. The year 1917 also marked the entrance of the United States into the Great War and the attendant migration of rural southerners, mainly black, to the urban industrial centers of the North. The new commercial possibilities of jazz music, along with the dispersion of jazz musicians from New Orleans to Chicago, New York, and elsewhere, created a jazz craze throughout the 1920s.[22] Jazz in 1927 was still considered not mainstream music but, rather, a music of the younger generation that represented modernity in a home-grown musical form. Chicago-style jazz retained the closest ties to New Orleans–style jazz, with most major Chicago musicians being transplanted New Orleanians playing mainly in small bands for a midwestern regional audience. New York jazz favored a more mainstream version of the music played in larger bands and orchestras and catered to a more national audience of record buyers and radio listeners. Both styles of jazz represented the modern age to its listeners, since they took advantage of the latest technology and attracted a younger, less traditionally minded audience. "Jazz" as an idea reflected all that was new in the culture, as evidenced by its rhetorical, though not musical, use in *The Jazz Singer*.

New Orleans native Louis Armstrong "personified the jazz scene in Chicago" during the 1920s. Armstrong had been schooled in the New Orleans style by King Oliver while he was playing with Oliver's Creole Jazz Band, and he "combined New Orleans rhythm with Chicago elegance and invented a new approach to jazz."[23] According to one biographer, Armstrong "was in the process of developing the vocabulary of modern jazz,"[24] combining many different musical experiences into his playing and writing. Armstrong was influenced not only by his New Orleans musical upbringing but also by his exposure to classical and other popular music through his second wife, Lil Hardin, and by a year playing in New York with the dance-oriented Fletcher Henderson Orchestra. These influences created in Armstrong a style of playing unlike any other, with a definite focus on Armstrong as soloist and star. "Hot" jazz, as played in New Orleans and Chicago, featured multiple soloists. The democratic nature of solo breaks and improvisation prevented any one musician in a group from dominating completely since the character of the music came primarily from the interplay among the group's members. New York–style jazz, on the other hand, favored arranged orchestrations that centered attention on the bandleader (or conductor) rather than on soloists, who were allowed limited opportunity for improvisation. Armstrong excelled in both settings and by 1927 was playing regularly in a small "hot" band at the Sunset Café and in a large orchestra (first the Erskine Tate Orchestra at the Vendome Theater, then with Clarence Jones's Orchestra at the Metropolitan Theater), not to mention in recording gigs as sideman to such blues singers as Bessie Smith, Alberta Hunter, and Ma Rainey.

Armstrong's sense of experimentation and style appear most prominently in recordings he made from 1925 to 1928 under various names (Louis Armstrong's Hot Fives, Louis Armstrong and His Hot Fives, and Louis Armstrong and His Hot Sevens) with banjo player Johnny St.

Cyr, saxophonist Johnny Dodds, trombonist Kid Ory (all New Orleanians), and pianist Lil Hardin Armstrong, among others. While these recordings were popular among "hot" jazz enthusiasts and black urban populations, they were not at the time seen as the watershed recordings they are today considered. These recordings, made for Okeh Records, fit into Okeh's agenda of supplying records of New Orleans–style jazz music for a black population recently relocated from the South. As such, they targeted a specific audience and were not meant for mainstream (mainly white) audiences. Armstrong's Stompers, playing at the Sunset Café, likewise played for primarily black audiences, with a sprinkling of white musicians coming around to listen in, while his orchestra work reached the widest audience playing between, and even during, silent films. Even though Armstrong's repertoire included everything from classical pieces to popular songs, he is best remembered for his innovations in soloing with his "hot" jazz groups. Improvisation was Armstrong's strong suit, as it was for most New Orleans musicians who were "ear" players rather than more traditionally trained "sight" players, who could read music. One reason Armstrong left Fletcher Henderson's very successful dance orchestra in New York was the lack of improvisation and experimentation allotted to Armstrong, or to anyone else in the orchestra. Henderson's jazz was "light, polite music for dancing and socializing . . . and not intended as a means of self-expression."[25]

"Wild Man Blues" (1927) illustrates what made Armstrong unique. While it begins with a traditional polyphonic chorus in which Armstrong on coronet, Johnny Dodds on clarinet, and John Thomas on trombone all play counterpoised melodies, it quickly becomes a vehicle for an extended Armstrong solo that takes up almost two minutes of the just-over-three-minute-long song. The solo demonstrates Armstrong's ability to elaborate on the melody and to use his coronet in a manner that mimics a blues singer. It is followed by a shorter, similar solo by Dodds and ends with a reprise of the opening chorus. The record is remarkable not for the composition itself but, rather, for the individualistic characteristics of the musicians, especially Armstrong. His uniqueness would be reinforced in the songs in which he sang as well as played, since his gravelly voice was unlike any other popular singer's, and since he would often sing a solo not of words but of nonsense syllables, as if it were an instrumental solo (a technique that would become known as scat singing).

Armstrong's music appealed to the black migrant community in Chicago since it echoed the idioms of southern black music. Drawing from the blues, Dixieland, and New Orleans music and combining them in new ways, Armstrong evoked both black musical tradition and musical modernism; it was both down-home and urban. While classical motifs may have influenced elements of the music, it was for the most part what jazz afficionados dubbed "authentic," in that it retained more folk elements than studied or commercial elements. This was jazz at its most frenetic and chaotic, and that frenzy and chaos were what made it attractive to its listeners. Many young, classically trained musicians could pick up several books of Louis Armstrong transcriptions, taken from his Okeh recordings, and try to imitate his improvised solos. Some, like Bix Beiderbecke, learned well the soloing techniques of Armstrong and launched careers of their own as "hot" jazz musicians. Like Armstrong, Beiderbecke was able to move between small bands and large orchestras and cover a wide range of musical styles.

Beiderbecke was a classically trained white musician who sought inspiration from untrained black musicians. He performed with the Paul Whiteman Orchestra, as well as recording on his own with small groups and his own trio. In one of his most celebrated works, "In a Mist" (also known as "Bixology"; 1927), the trumpeter Beiderbecke plays solo piano in a manner that recalls the stride and ragtime piano of jazz tradition while also exhibiting the complexity, in terms of key changes, tempo changes, and variation, that would characterize post–World War II styles of jazz playing. The piece's syncopation is derived from jazz sources, whereas its structure is more classically inspired. This melding of styles and influences was only one way that the definition of jazz expanded beyond the music of New Orleans. The fact that no clear line separated jazz musicians from other musicians is another.

While many "hot" musicians also played dance music in ballrooms as well as in theater orchestras for silent movies, those who could not read music were not hired by the dance bands and orchestras. There were many practical reasons for this—for example, the demands of a theater orchestra required versatile players able to perform both popular and classical music—but there was also a bias against unschooled musicians, who were seen as unprofessional and a detriment to the profession, and since most of these ear players were African American, this bias often fell along and was reinforced by racial lines. While the majority of this bias stemmed from white booking agents and theater and club owners, some of it had to do with the aspirations of the black middle class in Chicago, which can be seen in the highly influential black newspaper, the *Chicago Defender*. The paper and its musical columnist Dave Peyton were concerned not only with equality (in pay, opportunities, treatment, and the like) but also with social uplift and refinement, those elements of concern to the black elite who sought to show white America that African Americans could be as sophisticated, refined, and "civilized" as they were. Peyton's weekly column, The Musical Bunch, admonished black musicians to practice scales and study musical theory, as well as to dress properly and act professionally. While Peyton did acknowledge that race was the reason many black bands did not receive bookings, he felt it was up to the black musicians to prove themselves worthy of consideration and jobs.[26] Peyton believed that jazz was an African American cultural creation for which white musicians were taking credit, but he nevertheless favored a style of jazz that would appeal to the largest possible audience, meaning a white audience. Paul Whiteman's orchestra, often cited as the most blatant offender in usurping jazz from the black community, received Peyton's praise and admiration primarily because of Whiteman's success on records and radio, as well as on tour.

Whiteman's orchestra was a tightly run business and professional organization that throughout the early 1920s was one of the premier dance bands in the nation. By 1927, Whiteman had parlayed his fame in the ballroom into a musical empire encompassing recordings, live appearances, radio broadcasts, and appearances in Broadway reviews. He also exploited his celebrity to launch a short-lived nightclub in New York and a very successful music publishing company. In 1927 Whiteman's music ran the gamut of standard dance fare ("Cheerie Beerie Bee," a waltz), popular tunes from Broadway and Tin Pan Alley ("Manhattan Mary," the title song from the Broadway show), elaborate orchestrations that mimicked classical pieces ("Mississippi Suite," a tone poem in four movements), and interpretations of jazz tunes ("Whiteman Stomp," originally recorded by the Fletcher Henderson Orchestra). Much of this variety had to do with the roles that Whiteman saw himself playing. While popular dance tunes and songs were the practical necessities of a touring orchestra, both the classically inspired and jazz-inspired numbers expressed Whiteman's desire for an American form of music equal to, but not similar to, European concert music.

Whiteman loved jazz music as it was played by black musicians, though he did not think it proper for his orchestra to play it in the same manner. His love of jazz can be seen in the increasing number of white jazz musicians in his band, which in 1927 included Tommy and Jimmy Dorsey, Hoagy Carmichael, and Bix Beiderbecke, and in the increasingly important role soloists took improvising during breaks within the songs. "Whiteman Stomp" illustrates this: the breaks in melody make it difficult to dance to, while the up-tempo pace and lighthearted parody of serious music signal that the piece was meant to be listened to, not just used as background or for dancing. Both Dorsey brothers have solos (saxophonist Jimmy plays an extended solo that weaves in and out of the whole song), adding to the less-structured nature of the song, compared to most Whiteman tunes. The improvisation built into the song was characteristic of the style of jazz played by Armstrong and others playing for primarily black and young white audiences. It is the abilities of the soloists, whether technical or expressive, that make the song what it is, not the composition or harmony of instruments. The individualistic nature of jazz is one of the characteristics that separate it from traditional concert music as well as from popular and dance music, and it is what distinguishes music by Armstrong and other "hot" jazz artists from much of Whiteman's music and the music of others like him. That Whiteman included these elements is a testament to his desire to take jazz music out of the speakeasies and dance halls and place it on the concert stage.

This attempt to concertize the music is best seen in such symphonic pieces as George Gershwin's "Rhapsody in Blue," which Whiteman debuted in 1924 at Aeolian Hall in New York and recorded in 1927, and Ferde Grofé's four-part "Mississippi Suite" (1927). Grofé's intention in "Mississippi Suite" was to create a musical journey down the Mississippi River from its source to its end in New Orleans. The first movement, "Father of Waters," was not originally recorded in 1927, probably because of the lack of space on a 12-inch, 78-rpm disc, but the final three movements, "Huckleberry Finn," "Old Creole Days," and "Mardi Gras," illustrate the attempt to paint a musical portrait of a uniquely American feature using the uniquely American musical style of jazz. The piece uses multiple tempos, along with syncopation and blues-tinged playing, as well as a wider range of instruments than was common for Whiteman or most popular orchestras (the piece features a bassoon, a whistle, and banjo). In his 1926 book *Jazz*, cowritten by Mary Margaret McBride, Whiteman describes the history and future of jazz as he saw it. While he acknowledged the African American origins of jazz, stating that "jazz came to America three hundred years ago in chains,"[27] he does not see it becoming an art form until it is adapted to classical standards of concert music. "Mississippi Suite," along with Grofé's "Grand Canyon Suite" (1932), was part of Whiteman's vision for jazz, an American contribution to classical music. "I am ambitious for jazz to develop always in an American way. I want to see compositions written around the great natural and geographical features of American life—written in the jazz idiom. I believe it would help Americans to appreciate their own country."[28]

This desire for an American form of music equal to but different from European music paralleled the desire of writers and visual artists during the 1920s. Centered in the Harlem neighborhood of uptown New York and focused on fostering "the new Negro," the Harlem Renaissance sought to elevate African Americans by promoting the contributions to western civilization made by black writers and artists. Key to this undertaking was the determination of what made African American arts and letters different from other American arts and letters. Much of that difference was found in black folk culture, both African American and African. In accord with folklorists studying various world cultures, many black intellectuals believed that the essence of a people (especially an illiterate or nonwesternized people) could be found in such folk expressions as songs, stories, and crafts. James Weldon Johnson found inspiration for his 1927 collection of poems *God's Trombones: Seven Negro Sermons in Verse* in African American preachers who enraptured congregations with their magnetism, charisma, and showmanship rather than with their theological knowledge. The seven poems, each based on a sermon topic, sought to capture the essence of the black preacher before this style of ministering faded. "The old-time Negro preacher is rapidly passing," Johnson wrote in the preface. "I have here tried sincerely to fix something of him."[29] Johnson's attempt to record the essence of the old-time preacher did not include mimicking the way he spoke. Johnson felt that African American poets needed "to find a form that will express the racial spirit by symbols from within rather than by symbols from without—such as the mere mutilation of English spelling and pronunciation." Johnson sought "a form that is freer and larger than dialect, but which would still hold the racial flavor; a form expressing the imagery, the idioms, the peculiar turns of thought and distinctive humor and pathos, too, of the Negro, but which will also be capable of voicing the deepest and highest emotions and aspirations and allow of the widest range of subjects and the widest scope of treatment" (8). In *God's Trombones,* Johnson used the form of the "primitive" sermon, as he called it, but he also acknowledged that "in the writing of them [these poems] I have, naturally, felt the influence of the Spirituals" (10).

Music played an important role in the heritage that black intellectuals sought to internalize, but not jazz. Johnson's use of spirituals as inspiration was not unique among black intellectuals and artists. "The Spirituals are really the most characteristic product of the race genius as yet in America," proclaimed Alain Locke in his essay on spirituals in the 1925 anthology and manifesto of the Harlem Renaissance, *The New Negro.* "They have escaped the lapsing conditions and the fragile vehicle of folk art, and come firmly into the context of formal music."[30] The entry into formal music came primarily by way of the Fisk Jubilee Singers, founded at Fisk University in 1871. While these African American singers sought to make a name for themselves singing classical and contemporary choral arrangements, they became best known for singing spirituals in a concert, as opposed to a religious, setting. But Locke's hope for a truly American music did not lie with the spirituals themselves; rather, "behind the deceptive simplicity of Negro song lie the richest undeveloped musical resources anywhere available."[31] It was up to educated and "enlightened" composers and musicians to take the raw material provided by black folk music and turn it into music that met the western classical standard. Examples of this process include "From the Land of Dreams" by William Grant Still, the African American protégé of Edgar Varèse, and James Weldon Johnson's "The Creation: A Negro Sermon." Folklorist John Wesley Work, whose book *Folk Song of the American Negro* (1915) traced the development of black folk music, felt that collecting spirituals and folk songs and preserving them for posterity was necessary but said, "[It] can never be the last word in the development of our music. . . . They are the starting point, not our goal; the source, not the issue, of our musical tradition."[32]

The only real mention of jazz in *The New Negro* came in J. A. Rogers's essay "Jazz at Home," in which Rogers treats jazz in much the same way that Locke treated spirituals. He claims that in spite of its spread around the world, jazz "is one part American and three parts American Negro" and "is really at home in its humble native soil wherever the modern unsophisticated Negro feels happy and sings and dances to his mood."[33] While Locke saw spirituals feeding the souls of post–Great War Americans, Rogers saw jazz as "a safety valve for modern machine-ridden and convention-bound society. It is the revolt of the emotions against repression" (217). But instead of springing from religious feeling, as did the spiritual, jazz came from the "barbaric rhythm and exuberance" of "a wild, abandoned dance" of West Africa set into a modern context. "It is a thing of the jungles—modern man-made jungles" (217–218). Because of its primitive parentage, jazz was in greater need of "civilizing" than were spirituals, a process that was beyond the "humble troubadours knowing nothing of written music or composition" who performed jazz. The musical future of jazz was best left to such professionals (both black and white) as Will Marion Cook, Fletcher Henderson, Vincent Lopez, and Paul Whiteman, whose music contained "none of the vulgarities and crudities of the lowly origin or the only too prevalent cheap imitations." Lopez and Whiteman were singled out by Rogers as the leaders of two white orchestras "that are now demonstrating the finer possibilities of jazz music" (221). Like Whiteman himself, Rogers saw the potential of jazz to be an influence on concert music rather than a substitute for traditional classical music.

Langston Hughes countered Rogers's belief that jazz needed civilizing. "Jazz to me is one of the inherent expressions of Negro life in America," Hughes wrote, "the eternal tom-tom beating in the Negro soul—the tom-tom of revolt against weariness in a white world, a world of subway trains, and work, work, work; the tom-tom of joy and laughter, and pain swallowed in a smile." For Hughes jazz was more than an African American creation that had caught the world's fancy because it relieved people's anxiety about modern life; it was the very essence of black expression in America. He did not think it should be changed to make it more acceptable to a white audience; rather, he declared, "Let the blare of Negro jazz bands and the bellowing voice of Bessie Smith singing the Blues penetrate the closed ears of the colored near-intellectuals until they listen and perhaps understand."[34] What these "near-intellectuals" needed to understand was the role music played in the lives of modern African Americans. For most black, as well as white, Americans, music was not something to be admired and appreciated like a painting or sculpture, but a part of daily life, an expression. With the greater accessibility of music on records and radio, more people had the opportunity to hear more music. This was especially true in black communities, where entertainment choices were often limited. But for the intellectuals of the Harlem Renaissance, black music needed to aspire to being elite culture, not popular culture. In fact, popular culture was detrimental to the goals of the movement, as Rogers points out: "For the Negro himself, jazz is both more and less dangerous than for the white—less, in that he is nervously more in tune with it; more, in that at his average level of economic development his amusement life is more open to the forces of social vice" (223). What jazz did offer was its spirit. "The jazz spirit, being primitive, demands more frankness and sincerity," but, according to Rogers, that spirit needs to be tamed. "Where at present it vulgarizes, with more wholesome growth in the future, it may on the contrary truly democratize. At all events, jazz is a rejuvenation, a recharging of the batteries of civilization with primitive new vigor. It has come to stay, and they are wise, who instead of protesting against it, try to lift and divert it into nobler channels" (223–224).

Rather than lifting it into "nobler channels," Hughes used the blues and jazz to infuse his writing with the same spirit as the music, instead of just borrowing the form of the music. In "Song for a Dark Girl" (1927) Hughes presents a blues lament for a black woman whose lover has been lynched:

Way Down South in Dixie
(Break the heart of me)
They hung my black young lover
To a cross roads tree.[35]

Each of the stanzas in the poem begins with the same line, and each "call" is followed by a parenthetical "response," a device often used in blues and jazz music. While not a formal blues structure, the feeling is undeniably bluesy in its rhythm and use of repetition, and the subject is undeniably African American. This is not poetry removed from the blues; rather, this poem could be sung as a blues song without appearing pretentious.

This elitist attitude from black intellectuals reinforced to some degree the racist complaints of whites who believed that blacks, in person and in culture, were inferior. By admitting the primitive nature of contemporary black culture and calling for uplift and civilizing, these writers lost sight of the culture that was present in the black community. Just as Dave Peyton called for more professional attitudes and behavior among black musicians, Locke and Rogers called for elevating black culture "up" to the standards of white culture. Hughes lamented this goal, pointing out that a desire to live up to white standards was the result of years of feeling inferior because of white suppression. "I am ashamed," Hughes wrote, "for the black poet who says, 'I want to be a poet, not a Negro poet,' as though his world were not as interesting as any other world."[36]

However, for many white intellectuals and bohemians, the Harlem Renaissance was not about raising black culture to the same level of white culture; rather, it was about the experience of descending into black culture as one would embark on an African safari. What the Harlem Renaissance provided was a safe way for these cultural voyeurs to experience the primitive in galleries, salons, and clubs that catered to white audiences. By 1927 Harlem was no longer an exclusively black neighborhood but had become an area in which many businesses embodying black culture catered to white patrons. Writer and physician Rudolph Fisher, after a five-year absence from Harlem to attend medical school, returned to find all his old haunts "had changed their names and turned white." As he sat in one cabaret, he "suddenly became aware that, except for the waiters and members of the orchestra, I was the only Negro in the place."[37] Fisher contemplates the sudden vogue among white New Yorkers for black culture in his essay "The Caucasian Storms Harlem," but he does not really provide any significant explanations for the phenomenon other than suggesting a possible reaction to the Broadway success of *Shuffle Along* (1921) and its many imitators.[38] Even though *Shuffle Along* contained skits of the minstrel variety, what made it a sensation was the music and dancing. The play introduced white New Yorkers to the kind of music and dancing that could be found regularly in Harlem cabarets, and when the imitators failed to live up to the original, audiences sought out the authentic in Harlem. Catering to this white clientele was good business for club owners in Harlem, and since downtowners had to travel uptown to Harlem, the experience was more exotic than seeing a show on Broadway.

The best-known of these uptown hot spots was the Cotton Club, located on the corner of Lenox Avenue and 142nd Street. The club opened in 1923 when former heavyweight boxing champion Jack Johnson sold his Club Deluxe to New York gangster Owen "Owney" Madden, then in prison for manslaughter. Madden's wealth came from selling Madden's No. 1 (a beer) during Prohibition, and he also owned the Stork Club and the Silver Slipper. Broadway producer Florenz Ziegfeld's set and costume designer, Joseph Urban, designed the interior to reflect downtown attitudes about uptown inhabitants, creating what has been called "a brazen riot of African jungle motifs, Southern stereotypology, and lurid eroticism."[39] Adding to the African colonial/southern plantation atmosphere was the club's policy of white only patrons catered to by a black staff and black entertainers. Well-to-do patrons of the club were treated not only to an evening of illicit beverages and entertainment but also to an exotic experience in which black culture (or rather, white stereotypes of black culture) became an exciting, provocative, and safe diversion from everyday life. The club, and others like it, provided white patrons "the chance to act black and feel primitive personally without having to change their downtown, public lives."[40] Shows at the club rivaled the Broadway productions of Ziegfeld, and some, such as *The Blackbirds of 1928,* found their way to Broadway after their run at the club. In 1927 the Cotton Club received even more exposure when the newly created Columbia Broadcasting System (CBS) radio network began broadcasting live performances from the club, and in December of that year, Duke Ellington brought his Washington, D.C.–based band, the Washingtonians, for an extended run.

Duke Ellington was, in many respects, a cross between the "hot" jazz players like Louis Armstrong and the conductor-showmen like Paul Whiteman, and his career in 1927 represents a synthesis of the more "authentic" black culture of "hot" jazz musicians and Chicago black-belt nightclubs and the symphonic jazz of Paul Whiteman and dance orchestras playing and recording for primarily white audiences. Twenty-three-year-old Ellington came to New York from Washington, D.C., with his band the Washingtonians in 1923. The band played gigs at various clubs and in various revues around Harlem, as well as on summer tours of the New England states. During this time, Ellington's dance band began developing its unique style of playing, which included various percussion instruments and a heavy use of mutes on the brass instruments. By 1927 Ellington had begun recording and publishing as well as performing, primarily under the influence of manager Irving Mills, who entered into an agreement with Ellington in which each would own 45 percent of their joint corporation, with 10 percent going to Mills's lawyer.[41] Mills had started a music-publishing firm with his brother in 1919 and was known for finding and publishing such unknown but talented songwriters and composers as Hoagy Carmichael, Dorothy Fields, Jimmy McHugh, and Harold Arlen. Mills not only booked the Ellington band in New York and New England but also encouraged Ellington to record and publish original material, which not only would increase the profits on the sale of records and sheet music—since no royalties would need to be paid to someone else—but also would speed the development of Ellington as a composer, a role that is perhaps his greatest contribution to American music. In this sense, the relationship between Mills and Ellington, while primarily an economic one, was also artistically beneficial to Ellington. Mills did not dictate what Ellington wrote, but much of the material was directed at the type of audiences for which Ellington's band performed, mainly white. Understanding that much of the attraction of black music for white audiences was its exotic nature, Ellington focused on compositions that represented aspects of black culture. "East St. Louis Toodle-Oo" and "Birmingham Breakdown" were two of the first original songs recorded by Ellington and his band and were the first Ellington compositions to be published. Recorded in November 1926 and published in February 1927, "East St. Louis Toodle-Oo" illustrates Ellington's compositional philosophy as it sought to illustrate musically an experience out of black life. "Those old Negroes who work in the fields for year upon year, and are tired at the end of their day's labour, may be seen walking home at night with a broken, limping step locally known as the 'Toddle-O,' with the accent on the last syllable. I was able to get a new rhythm from this."[42] Ellington later remarked, "Practically everything we wrote back then was supposed to be a picture of something, or represent a character."[43] In attempting "not so much to reproduce 'hot' or 'jazz' music as to describe emotions, moods, and activities which have a wide range, leading from the very gay to the sombre," Ellington looked "to the everyday life and customs of the Negro to supply [his] inspiration."[44]

While Ellington's approach to music was very much in line with what Harlem Renaissance writers and artists sought to do, he was not attempting to use black culture as inspiration for elite art music or symphonies. Ellington was very aware of the fundamental economic reason for the songs, as dance music and as records, and therefore his songs had danceable rhythms and he paid close attention to creating compositions that not only fit the 78-rpm records (three minutes per record side) but also took full advantage of the recording process, especially the use of electric microphones (as opposed to the older style ear-trumpet-like recording devices). Ellington paid close attention to the placement of instruments around the microphone to achieve a balance on a record that was not always possible for a live audience to hear. His recordings are technically superior to those of other bands, such as Fletcher Henderson's and Paul Whiteman's. Ellington also sought to create compositions that would both cause a live audience to dance and keep a record listener engaged in the song from beginning to end over multiple listenings. He wrote many pieces with varied introductions, interludes, and codas to keep the listener interested. Again, the demands of commerce reinforced the artistic ambitions of Ellington and his band, since recordings of original music made it possible for Ellington to showcase his players to the fullest extent, and since many of his players stayed with him for years and even decades, he was able to take advantage of his knowledge of their abilities as he composed. Ellington showed the ability to increase both the marketability and aesthetics of jazz without compromising either.

"Black and Tan Fantasy" (1927) is a perfect example of a song that is interesting in its structure, as a formal composition based on the blues, and still spontaneous in its feeling, since it is constructed around a series of improvised solos. The dirgelike song begins with an introduction that presents the main melody played by trumpeter and cowriter Bubber Miley with harmony by trombonist Joe Nanton, accompanied by simple drums, banjo, and piano. The introduction of the first theme is followed by the introduction of a second theme, this time by alto saxophonist Otto Hardwick and featuring a more lively and unique melody because of the blues-tinged playing with sliding notes and glissandos. The bulk of the song consists of a basic twelve-bar blues structure in which the first two choruses are devoted to a solo by Miley, the third to one by Ellington on piano, and the fourth to one by Nanton. The last chorus consists of a call-and-response sequence between Miley and the rhythm section, with the rest of the band entering near the end. An added coda features a "quotation" of Frédéric Chopin's "Funeral March" from his Sonata no. 2. Structurally, the song is basic blues, and while the feeling is melancholy, the overall feel is impressionistic. Without lyrics, the song does not tell a specific story, but it does convey a feeling of fantasy. Different moods and characters are suggested by the individual soloists, who utilize such unique elements as the use of mutes, sound effects, and growls in their playing. The final quotation ends the fantasy, like life, with death. "Black and Tan Fantasy" evokes the feeling of a fantastic and surreal night at a black-and-tan club (a club with a racial mix of patrons), while expanding the structure of jazz music with elements of classical arrangement, all within a three-minute song with a continuous danceable beat. The piece served the demands of dance music, tone poem, and marketable record. While more economically motivated musicians like Paul Whiteman diluted, or "whitened," jazz for record buyers and concertgoers, and elite black artists like James Weldon Johnson and William Grant Still "elevated" authentic black music for a sophisticated audience, Ellington made music that elevated black music not by adapting it to white styles and forms but by evolving it into a viable commercial yet authentic product.

This product, along with Ellington's shows, reinforced the image of black culture maintained by Harlem Renaissance artists and writers and sought out by white New Yorkers. When Ellington debuted at the Cotton Club in December 1927, the African jungle/southern plantation style of the club influenced the music played. While the initial show did not feature any Ellington originals, the band did play dance music between the midnight and 2:00 a.m. shows. Every six months, the Cotton Club would produce an entirely new show, with Ellington supplying much of the music. While Ellington's band was featured in only a few of the fifteen numbers making up most shows, it did provide accompaniment for the singers, dancers, and actors who performed as part of the shows. Such acts as dancer-contortionist Earl "Snakehips" Tucker, bawdy singer Edith Wilson, and dancers Mildred Dixon and Henri Wessell fronted a line of light-skinned, young (all under twenty-one years old), and tall (at least 5 feet, 11 inches) chorus girls dressed in exotic and erotic costumes. For the Cotton Club gig, Ellington's band changed its name from the Washingtonians (also sometimes called the Kentucky Club Orchestra because they had several engagements there) to Duke Ellington's Jungle Band. Ellington's music also started reflecting the jungle motif with such titles as "Jungle Jamboree," "Jungle Blues," "Jungle Nights in Harlem," and "Echoes of the Jungle." While much of this music has little or no jungle derivation, the unusual rhythms and unique sounds produced by Ellington and his band led people to refer to his sound as "jungle music."

This emphasis on the primitive reinforced the stereotypes and ideas about African Americans and Harlem already held by most of the white audience, however benign, while the distinct color line separating the management, the production staff (show producers, choreographers, writers), and the audience from the wait staff and the performers reinforced notions of segregation and black inferiority. As a result, black culture was simultaneously desired and denigrated in the simple act of attending a nightclub. This ambiguity toward black culture was not unique to clubgoers but can be seen in the culture at large between the intellectual celebrations of the "new Negro," and the resurgence of the Ku Klux Klan, southern lynchings of black men, and the treatment accorded to African American flood victims in the Mississippi Delta. The ambiguity extended beyond issues of race to attitudes toward the changes in American society as a whole. African Americans, like movie stars, sports celebrities, women, and other famous and infamous people, bore the brunt of Americans' anxieties about modern life.

THE POSSIBILITIES AND PRACTICALITIES OF RADIO

Jazz music and the idea of a jazz culture (modern, yet primitive; technologically driven, but emotionally based) spoke to the ambiguities Americans felt about modern life and became the symbol of the age. However, a better, more pervasive symbol for the times is radio, since radio brought the events and trends of the era to individual Americans. In 1927 several developments occurred that ensured the widespread use and influence of radio in America. Radio for the home became more affordable and practical with the introduction of receivers that ran on AC power instead of bulky batteries. The need for organization in the industry, mainly to reduce interference among broadcast stations, prompted a series of radio conferences organized by Secretary of Commerce Herbert Hoover and resulted in the passage of the Radio Act of 1927, which created the Federal Radio Commission (FRC, later the Federal Communications Commission, FCC) and regulated the industry. Demand on the part of consumers, as well as the benefits of sharing broadcasting content, led to the creation of national networks of stations disseminating across the country programming that emanated from New York City. The National Broadcasting Company (NBC), formed in late 1926 by the Radio Corporation of America (RCA), was quickly followed by the creation of CBS in 1927. Networks enabled people around the country to engage in a shared culture alongside their own individual cultures.

But more than cheap radios, federal authorization, and access to networks, radio programming brought a national culture to Americans. While this national culture developed according to the sometimes conflicting needs and demands of an industry, its acceptance by the population proved the most crucial aspect of radio's development. Radio programming, in many ways, defined the parameters of discourse about modern America by shaping the way the public perceived events. Every major event in 1927, whether in politics, entertainment, or sports, whether natural disaster or human achievement, was broadcast over radio to more people than could have witnessed them in person. To a great degree, radio shaped what people knew about their society at large, but it did not present a modern or unified message. While radio technology symbolized the modernity of the nation, program content reinforced traditional notions of society, especially about race. Radio, like almost everything else in 1927, expressed the ambiguity Americans experienced in their search for modern America.[45]

In September 1927, RCA introduced a new line of radio receivers ranging in price from $69.50 to $895. The Radiola 17 model sold for around $150, was compact and easy to operate, ran on house current (AC), and could be used with an attachable loudspeaker to allow more than a single listener with headphones. Demand for these sets outpaced production throughout the late 1920s, and radios such as the Radiola 17 enabled many Americans, both urban and rural, minority and majority, rich and not so rich, to experience what radio had to offer. "With the completion of the changeover to A.C. operation, the whole radio industry experienced the same kind of explosive release that follows removal of the key log in a jam, and into discard along with headphones and batteries went the last barrier between radio reception and a mass market."[46] One of the main suppliers of radio batteries was the Philadelphia Storage Battery Company, known as Philco, which developed a "socket-power" unit allowing radio operators to supply power to their radio sets by plugging into a light socket instead of hooking up to a large battery. Sales of "socket-power" units brought Philco over $15 million in 1927. Philco had also become very involved in advertising on the radio, sponsoring the weekly *Philco Hour* every Friday evening over twenty-six stations nationwide in

1927. Once AC power for radios became cheap and accessible, Philco found itself without a market, and in early 1928 it turned to the manufacturing of radio sets. By 1930 Philco was the number one producer of radios.[47]

While the spread of radio technology helped increase the number of radio listeners across the country, it also multiplied the number of problems experienced by radio operators and listeners, mainly problems of interference caused when different radio stations transmitted on the same or similar frequencies and when stations changed frequencies in order to produce a clear transmission. The Radio Act of 1912, which had been put in place as part of U.S. participation in the first international radio treaty, signed in April 1912, loosely regulated radio broadcasters and amateurs. Early radio was used primarily for marine and ship-to-shore communications, and regulations became necessary to control interference from amateur radio operators, especially after the *Titanic* disaster, which occurred the same month the treaty was enacted. The Radio Act of 1912 specified the operating requirements for a license, which was to be issued by the secretary of commerce, but the act did not grant the secretary any discretion in granting licenses. No attempts were made to specify in the licenses at which frequency an operator might broadcast, and no enforcement was provided to stop unlicensed operators from broadcasting. Both these deficiencies created the potential for interference. With the beginning of commercial broadcasting in the early 1920s, interference became an even bigger problem as owners of radio receivers sought regular programming at predictable frequencies.

With interference growing and with complaints from listeners increasing, Herbert Hoover, as secretary of commerce, in 1921 refused to renew the license of the Intercity Radio Company, citing its inability to broadcast on a frequency that did not interfere with other stations' transmissions. Intercity sued the Department of Commerce, and the courts ruled in *Hoover v. Intercity Radio Company* that the secretary did not have any discretion in granting licenses. Any and all who applied should be granted licenses, according to the ruling. As a result of this attack on the ability of the Commerce Department to regulate the industry and the ever-growing problems of interference, Hoover convened a series of conferences on radio annually from 1922 to 1925.

While Hoover directed these conferences, much of the agenda was controlled by the corporations that had the largest stake in the radio industry, such as RCA, Westinghouse, General Electric (GE), and American Telephone and Telegraph (AT&T). Participants in the conferences included officials from the Commerce Department and the Department of the Navy, a few politicians (most importantly Representative Wallace White and Senator Frank Kellogg, both vital in introducing radio legislation in Congress), radio inventors, and hobbyists. Participants agreed on the need for order in the industry but disagreed on how to achieve it. Attempts at legislation following each of the conferences failed to produce any results. In 1926 the courts struck down the Department of Commerce's ability to specify wavelengths and hours of operation in *U.S. v. Zenith Radio Corporation,* in which Zenith argued that the Commerce Department had created regulations that exceeded its authority as specified in the 1912 Radio Act. As a result of this decision, anarchy ensued in the industry, with stations broadcasting at any frequency and power they wanted, leading Congress finally to pass legislation regulating radio.[48]

The result was the Radio Act of 1927, which gave the federal government the ability to grant or deny radio operating licenses and to specify broadcast frequencies, broadcasting power, and hours of operation. This power, however, was not granted to the Commerce Department but, rather, fell to the newly created FRC, made up of industry experts who were assigned the task of creating order in the radio industry. The act divided the nation into five radio zones. Each zone was represented on the commission by a commissioner, and the zones were allotted equal numbers of licenses. The intent of the act was to create a commission of radio experts without financial attachment to the radio industry to sort out the industry; after a year, most of its functions would return to the secretary of commerce, and the FRC would act in an advisory capacity when necessary. The federal Radio Act of 1927 did provide order to the industry, and it avoided what industry leaders did not want, government control or ownership over radio. The act is a prime illustration of Hoover's belief that government and industry should work together to create prosperity. This was especially true in an industry that all believed would have benefits to society far beyond the economic ones. Most saw the potential for radio's role in the public interest, to inform and educate the public as well as to bring unity to the wide geographic expanse of the nation. Radio was seen as a way to reduce the differences in regions, between rural and urban, and between wealthy and poor; but to do so would require vigilance on the part of the federal government and cooperation on the part of the industry. The radio conferences illustrated the fact that the concerns of the major corporations involved in radio did not fundamentally conflict with Hoover's desire for order, and as a result the radio industry was able to grow at a much more rapid pace, and more evenly around the country, than it would have without government regulation.[49]

Adding to the rapid development of radio across the nation was the growth of national networks, pioneered by RCA with the formation of NBC in July 1926. While NBC was not the first network—it had in fact been created through the merging of two separate networks, AT&T's Red Network and the Radio Group Network formed by a group of stations owned by RCA—it pioneered the idea of national radio, that is, programming designed to appeal to a national audience instead of to a local or regional audience. Newspaper companies were owners of many radio stations, such as Chicago's WGN (which stood for "World's Greatest Newspaper"), which was owned by the *Chicago Tribune,* and therefore duplicated the local and regional interests of their parent companies. But others were created by businesses looking either to boost sales of their radio-related products (Westinghouse and General Electric both made radio receivers and owned stations) or to generate publicity on behalf of their non–radio-related products or services. By owning a string of stations, a single company could advertise its products in multiple markets while reducing the cost of each station by creating shared programming for broadcasts. Therefore, a network could reach a national audience and potential customers more efficiently and effectively than such traditional advertising methods as newspapers and magazines. AT&T's network consisted of six stations, with WEAF of New York responsible for most of the programming, and RCA owned four stations. AT&T, as the company most responsible for telephone service in the United States, used its own lines to share radio programming between stations, but the Radio Group was not able to secure favorable telephone circuits for its stations, nor did it have the same ability to draw advertising dollars as AT&T. In 1926,

RCA formed NBC in an agreement with AT&T in which the telephone company sold its radio stations to NBC in return for a contract to supply telephone circuits to NBC. AT&T's Red Network became NBC Red in November 1926, while the Radio Group Network became NBC Blue on January 1, 1927. By July 1927, NBC had also acquired a chain of western stations that became known as NBC Orange (also known as the Pacific Network), which allowed for coast-to-coast broadcasts by a single company and helped provide programming for an ever-increasing radio audience listening in on receivers made by RCA.

In September 1927 a competitor to NBC appeared in the form of the Columbia Broadcasting System (CBS), named after the Columbia Phonograph Corporation, which had made an agreement with the Judson Radio Program Corporation and United Independent Broadcasters to buy $163,000 worth of airtime on the new network. They would in turn resell the airtime to other clients. The new entity was a bureaucratic mess, and its initial broadcast was marred by a thunderstorm in upstate New York that disrupted the broadcast everywhere west of Buffalo. While the main association of the network was Columbia Phonograph, the recording company quickly withdrew from the enterprise after losing $100,000 in the first month of operation because they were not able to convince companies to advertise on time that was owned by another company. Columbia did allow the network to keep its name, but the network failed to make a profit until it was reorganized and taken over by a twenty-seven-year-old millionaire, William Paley. By 1929, Paley had turned CBS into a profitable business network firmly entrenched in advertisement-supported programming.

An estimate of the numbers of 1927 radio listeners calculated that there were, on average, five listeners for each of the 6 million sets in the United States, for a total radio audience of 30 million people, or roughly a quarter of the population.[50] By 1927 radio had indeed become a mass medium. The rapid development of radio technology and its adoption by Americans led many industry watchers to speculate on the role radio could play in American society. Optimistically, many believed that radio had unlimited potential for social good, that it was the means by which Americans—and by extension the world—would develop world peace, extend democracy at home and abroad, educate and enlighten the masses with refined culture, and save countless souls through religious programming. Guglielmo Marconi, the inventor of wireless technology, wrote in 1927 that "the most precious of all human privileges" was "the free and unrestricted exchange of ideas. And that [radio], I maintain, is the only force to which we can look with any degree of hope for the ultimate establishment of permanent world peace."[51] Various writers, both inside and outside the radio industry, believed that radio would serve to equalize and democratize the American people. "It has found a way to dispense with the political middlemen," proclaimed the *New Republic*. "In a fashion it has restored the demos upon which republican government is founded. No one will capture the radio vote unless he faces the microphones squarely and speaks his mind fully, candidly, and in extenso."[52]

Educators saw in radio the possibility of reaching thousands of students outside of the traditional classroom. As early as 1923, Harren High School in New York City broadcast an accounting class over the air, and in the mid-1920s Kansas State University offered a special diploma for completing radio courses that had listeners and students in thirty states, Mexico, and Canada. Many educators, like Virgil E. Dickson, deputy superintendent of schools in Oakland, California, believed that "the lid of the classroom has been blown off" by radio's ability to reach the masses.[53] Not only could radio bring education to the vast public, but it would also raise the general cultural appreciation of classical music among those who now had access to the concert hall and symphonic orchestras. According to the conductor of the Cincinnati Symphony, Fritz Reiner, "one of the beautiful possibilities of radio, as I see it, is to teach the fundamentals of music to the people. . . . Teach them the fundamentals of music and the genius of the nation will assert itself."[54]

In addition to enlightening minds, radio, some believed, could enlighten souls as well. Michael I. Pupin, a professor at Columbia University, believed that radio had the ability to spread inspirational words to a desperate public. "Think of what it would have meant to St. Paul if he had had such a method of communication," he was quoted as saying. "We need St. Pauls in our universities today—men who will rise up and preach the doctrine of truth and democracy." Pupin assumed that what was broadcast over the radio would be taken as the truth since people would receive information directly from the speaker rather than through the suspect mediation of newspapers. These writers and leaders who spoke for the potential of radio all assumed that the increased availability of news, educational, cultural, and religious programming would inherently aid democracy by creating a better-informed and more involved public.[55] And while technological progress made radio listening available to a greater number of Americans, the way the radio industry developed proved the optimistic predictions of these men false.

THE CONSEQUENCES OF NATIONAL RADIO

While national marketing was one reason for the creation of networks, a separate group of radio broadcasters sought national radio for different reasons. In 1927 approximately one-third of the radio stations in the United States had been created by such nonprofit organizations as universities, churches, and civic organizations. These stations often sought a different type of national radio, one not dominated by large corporations but, rather, controlled by the federal government in the public interest or funded through private donations or listener support mainly for educational and cultural purposes. In 1927, this type of radio industry was still a possibility until the FRC redistributed radio licenses in 1928 with the power granted it in the Radio Act of 1927. The FRC was made up primarily of persons connected to commercial radio, though not directly at the time of their service on the committee. The 1928 reallocation created forty clear channels, on each of which only one high-powered station would broadcast nationally. Thirty-seven of the forty clear channels went to network-affiliated stations, while the number of nonprofit stations dropped from a 1927 high of over a hundred to fewer than thirty by the early 1930s.[56] Not only did the networks get most of the licenses, including the most favorable ones, but the amount of capital needed to run a network (creating programming, leasing phone lines, and so on) ensured the dominance of commercial broadcasting paid for by advertisements over government-subsidized or listener-funded broadcasting. According to radio historian Susan Smulyan, "Before the advent of the networks, advertising stood out among the financing options only because it elicited the loudest protests and had the fewest supporters. The network system's need for large amounts of cash in order to rent wire lines suddenly gave broadcast advertising a privileged position."[57] As a result, broadcast radio solidified its foundation as a private, for-profit enterprise.

This emphasis on commercial broadcasting affected the content of radio programs by forcing broadcasters to focus on programs that would attract listeners, and therefore advertisers. But changes in program content also had to do with the fact that the nature of radio stations changed in the wake of the Radio Act of 1927. Independent radio stations serving smaller ethnic and religious communities lost out to network-affiliated stations in the contest for licenses and for favorable frequencies, power, and hours of operation. This was especially true for a city like Chicago, which had a very vibrant independent radio culture in the early 1920s. Many of these independent stations served white ethnic, working-class communities, broadcasting information and entertainment programming to immigrants in their native languages and religious programs for nonmainstream religions. The Chicago Federation of Labor ran its own station, WCFL, "the Voice of Labor," to reach the working class over the airwaves.[58] When the FRC reallocated frequencies in 1928, many of these smaller stations lost their licenses or had their broadcasting capability reduced (either in power or in hours). They were basically run off the dial by the corporate-based stations (either national networks or stations belonging to large established corporations, such as newspapers). In making its decisions, the FRC relied on a phrase in Section 4f of the Radio Act that claimed broadcasting stations must "promote public convenience or interest" or "serve public necessity." In the minds of the commissioners, powerful networks were more capable of serving the public interest than small, niche stations because they conceived of the public in the broadest, most homogeneous sense (specifically, as white and nonethnic). And by contrast, small ethnic-based stations were seen as not serving the broader public and therefore not as deserving of consideration. This bias favored the white middle class over other groups, and resulted in such decisions as the FRC's denial of WCFL's request to extend its working-class programming to evening hours when most of its audience would be home from work.[59]

Many supporters of network radio believed that not only would large national networks benefit the largest number of listeners, but networks' financial stake in radio would ensure the highest-quality programming. RCA argued that because of its role in the manufacture of radio sets by Westinghouse and General Electric, "it is more largely interested, more selfishly interested, if you please, in the best possible broadcasting in the United States than any one else."[60] In addition, a national network could "do much to bring order in the radio field," according to the *Brooklyn Eagle*. "The entire [radio] business has been developed in haphazard fashion and the multiplication of local stations, with all manner of programs being cast upon the ether, has brought about a situation that is injurious and a grave hardship in the development of this new form of communication."[61] While the *Washington Star* wondered "whether the newly formed organization can offer a wider variety and a more attractive series of programs remains to be seen—or heard," the writer still believed that NBC would have "a distinct value" in the "national distribution of important programs, not merely entertainment."[62] Despite these hopes for the future of the medium, the incorporation of the airwaves meant that there would be less diversity in who created programming and that ethnic and racial portrayals on the air more often than not were based on stereotypes from such existing forms of entertainment as vaudeville and minstrel shows.

The best example of this kind of programming was WGN's 1926 hit show *Sam 'n' Henry*, which became the NBC ratings winner *Amos 'n' Andy*. Created by white vaudeville singers Freeman Gosden and Charles Correll, *Sam 'n' Henry* was a ten-minute serial program that followed the exploits of two African American southerners who had recently migrated to Chicago and depicted the situations they got into as a result of their lack of big-city knowledge. This kind of characterization had been a staple of minstrel shows as far back as the antebellum era as a way to make light of the perceived ignorance of African Americans, especially free blacks. While radio had enabled white audiences to hear such black performers as Paul Robeson, Bert Williams, Duke Ellington, and others, it did not provide for many programs created by African Americans that would provide an avenue for black expression. Instead, mainstream radio, in seeking to attract the largest possible audience, sought programming that had a track record of appealing to large audiences. Vaudeville, minstrel shows, Broadway revues, and other theatrical entertainment provided most of the early programming, along with symphony orchestras, opera performances, and dance and jazz bands. As a result, radio did not provide new avenues of expression for African Americans (or any other ethnic group); rather, it mimicked and reinforced existing forms of entertainment, complete with negative stereotypes.

Sam 'n' Henry quickly caught on with listeners, many of whom became addicted to the ongoing story line. The *Chicago Tribune,* WGN's parent company, promoted the show through news stories highlighting the enthusiastic reactions of fans and through billboards asking the public to "Follow the Radio Comic Strip."[63] By 1927 WGN received fan letters about the show from as far away as New York State, and in both 1926 and 1927, *Sam 'n' Henry* was the only show from west of the Appalachians to perform at the annual Radio Industries Banquet in New York. The show received some of its first national exposure when around eighty stations carried the broadcast of the banquet around the country. In 1927 the characters of Sam and Henry could be heard over WGN not only on their daily show but in remote broadcasts from such major sporting events as the Jack Dempsey–Gene Tunney rematch from Chicago's Soldier Field, the Kentucky Derby, and the Indianapolis 500 auto race. Victor Records released over a dozen *Sam 'n' Henry* dialogues along with vaudeville songs by Gosden and Correll, many of which featured blackface dialogue along with the musical numbers. While WGN was based in Chicago, its signal could sometimes be heard as far away as the East Coast and the Deep South; record stores in Philadelphia and New Orleans sold copies of Gosden and Correll's musical and dialogue records. Through most of 1927, the *Tribune* capitalized on the popularity of *Sam 'n' Henry* by publishing the scripts of current episodes in the Sunday Metropolitan Section, written in "dialect," and a Chicago book publisher offered a book of twenty-four *Sam 'n' Henry* episodes for sale in stores and in the Montgomery Ward catalog. Avid listeners could buy a *Sam 'n' Henry* toy featuring the pair on a little metal wagon or a *Sam 'n' Henry* candy bar, or they could attend a performance of Gosden and Correll as Sam and Henry. The duo performed for private parties as well as at theater and movie houses, earning $800 or more per performance. When the performers asked WGN to allow the recording of episodes for lease to other stations nationwide, WGN refused, and Gosden and Correll quit, performing their last show on WGN in February 1928. The duo reappeared in March on WMAQ, owned by *Tribune* rival the *Chicago Daily News*, as *Amos 'n' Andy* before moving to NBC in 1929.[64]

Amos 'n' Andy demonstrated the potential for radio programming on a national scale and the benefits of network programming to advertisers; it also illustrated the dangerous spread, on a much larger scale, of stereotypes of African Americans. The dying art form of minstrel shows, although lingering in vaudeville shows and film, made a dramatic comeback on radio, which not only brought these stereotypes to a larger audience than any other medium but also reinforced them daily in the comfort of listeners' homes. *Amos 'n' Andy* and other blackface radio shows, as well as musical shows featuring jazz, created a "sound of whiteness" over the airwaves by marginalizing African Americans and presenting limited and distorted views of black culture to a primarily white audience. These programs "encoded the airwaves as a domain of white pleasure and power produced at the literal and figurative expense of racialized African-Americans."[65] In addition, broadcasting by African Americans faced severe limitations in most markets. The first show produced by and announced by African Americans did not debut until 1928 with WSBC's *The Negro Hour*, produced by Jack L. Cooper of the *Chicago Defender*. This foray into broadcasting coincided with the decline of independent stations and the loss of local control over much radio programming due to the Radio Act of 1927. As a result, both the network expansion of radio to national markets and the nationalization of the industry under the auspices of the Federal Radio Commission solidified the marginal and stereotypical portrayal of African Americans on the radio. In this sense, radio as a modernizing force did not bring new ideas about race to the public but, rather, made traditional prejudices and stereotypes available to more people. It was a modern invention used for traditional ends.

Advertising goods and services was another traditional goal of the modern medium. In the United States, unlike in Great Britain, radio's development was influenced by the fact that capital raising and program financing depended on selling airtime to advertisers. This meant that advertisers exercised control over program content and, at times, even over program creation. In his 1927 book *Using Radio in Sales Promotion*, Edgar H. Felix, a broadcasting and merchandising consultant as well as a contributing editor to *Radio Broadcast*, provides a manual for advertisers, station managers, and broadcasting artists on exactly how radio can benefit business. Calling radio broadcasting "the new goodwill medium," Felix recounts the early optimism of advertisers, who were "quick to recognize it as a means of gaining goodwill. Here was a countless audience, sympathetic, pleasure seeking, enthusiastic, curious, interested, approachable in the privacy of their own homes. What a glorious opportunity for the advertising man to spread his sales propaganda."[66]

But, Felix is quick to point out, this opportunity must be used wisely and must not be squandered by the old methods of sales promotion. He describes the earliest attempts at advertising on the air, which came in the form of informational lectures about a product, such as the Queensboro Corporation's ten-minute presentation on WEAF about the benefits of cooperative apartment ownership. While in its day the advertisement was successful ($27,000 worth of sales were directly attributable to the presentation, which cost the company $50), Felix notes that if the same talk were to be given in 1927, "there would be an outcry of indignation on the part of the radio audience" because "commercial broadcasting has become a specialized art; the radio audience has become discriminative; it does not tolerate educational lectures, however well delivered and authoritative, if their sole purpose is to promote sales" (3). The sophisticated radio audience should not be sold products on the radio; rather, advertisers should focus on "pleasing the listener, upon bringing him features he wants to hear, for the sake of winning his goodwill" (5). Advertisers need to consider not only the programs they present or sponsor but also the overall reputation of the radio station. Stations that recognize that "broadcasting is not an advertising medium" will best serve the needs of advertisers. Broadcasters are invited into the homes of thousands of listeners, and the commercial broadcaster should realize that he is "nothing less than a guest and he should conduct himself as a guest." Therefore, he no more has "the right to inflict selling propaganda in the midst of a broadcasting entertainment" than "an agreeable week-end guest may suddenly launch into an insurance solicitation at Sunday dinner." But, thinking like a guest, the right sales promotion "at the proper time, is assured preferred consideration and attention" (9).

Not only should a company carefully identify the proper station with which to associate itself and its product, but it should exercise great care in selecting the programs it sponsors. Felix outlines seven qualities a radio program should have to be effective for a sponsor: attention-compelling power, continuity, distinctiveness, fitness in relation to the concern presenting it, adaptability to the station's general character, degree and manner to which it directs attention to the sponsor, and acceptability to the radio audience.[67] He notes that mere popularity with an audience is not sufficient reason to associate a product with a program, and he uses the most popular of radio programs, the dance music broadcast, as his example. While many people listen to dance music on the radio, the way they listen to it, without serious attention, means that its effectiveness as a provider of goodwill to its sponsor is limited.

The most effective programs for advertisers, according to Felix, are those that involve the radio audience. He gives as examples shows presented by *Time* magazine and the U.S. Playing Card Company. *The Pop Question Game,* sponsored by *Time,* was a quiz show in which an announcer asked ten questions about current events based on articles in the magazine. Thirty seconds of silence followed in which the listeners attempted to answer the questions before the announcer provided the correct responses. "Thus a very subtle and successful selling message was put over because the listener was made conscious of his lack of knowledge of the events of the day as an argument for subscribing to *Time.*" The U.S. Playing Card Company involved its audience by having expert bridge players teach the radio audience the nuances of playing bridge. The show required a group of four listeners to deal hands identical to the ones held by the on-air experts and to play along as the experts provided rationales for each and every move. "Listeners are thus taught the fine points of bridge and sold the desirability and fascination of the game at the same time." These programs excelled in Felix's eyes since they were subtle and involved the listeners rather than beating them over the head with a sales pitch. These programs used "the broadcast medium to the greatest advantage" (133).

Radio programs could also be used in even more subtle ways by bringing good associations to a product. Fansteel Products Company, the sponsors of Walter Damrosch and the New York Symphony Orchestra, received the benefits of association with a program whose subject was highly regarded and which, thanks to Damrosch's explanations of the music performed, was informational as well as entertaining. "That a concern which does broadcasting with such thoroughness, undoubtedly makes a good product, is the inference carried to the listener" (134). The benefit for the advertiser is not primarily in associating a product with a highly regarded institution or genre of music but, rather, in addressing the audience on its own level, which for Felix means uneducated and uncultured. He explains that the *Atwater Kent Hour* program, even though it presents some of the world's greatest musical artists, "well appreciated by the concert-hall audience," does not explain the works to the public, nor does it employ any "radio showmanship" to make the program acceptable to radio audiences, and therefore the effectiveness to the advertiser is limited (134). Felix sees the uses of radio advertising in traditional terms, as dependent on goodwill and reputation, instead of in modern terms, valuing quantity, audience figures, cost, and other statistics. For Felix, the modernity of radio is in its ability to reach audiences, not necessarily in its effect on the audience.

Throughout his book, Felix takes seriously the subject of radio's use to advertisers by looking at every aspect of radio, from such general topics as which businesses should use or not use radio, how to select an appropriate station and program, how to determine the possible audience for a program, and what kinds of radio programs are the most effective for advertisers, to more specific topics such as how to prepare a script for a program or advertisement and what should be included in opening and closing announcements. What the book illustrates are the facts that by 1927 radio was firmly committed to commercial broadcasting and that the ever-increasing sophistication of the advertising industry was developing new techniques for use on the new medium. While Felix discusses every aspect of broadcasting that he deems important to advertisers, he never discusses radio broadcasting as an art form. He recognizes the entertainment value that listeners gave to radio, but he does not see radio as the conduit through which the world will achieve peace, the nation will become more democratic, the masses will be educated and cultured, or their spirits will be uplifted.

By 1927, due mainly to the Federal Radio Act, radio practitioners focused more on the practicalities of paying for radio than on the idealistic possibilities of the medium. While many hoped for a bright new world brought about by radio, what radio gave Americans was greater access to more of the same. News, entertainment, and even advertising were not significantly altered by radio but simply made more accessible. Radio technology may have revolutionized the way Americans received their news, entertainment, and information, but it was not revolutionary in its content or purpose. Like the respectable content of motion pictures, the goals of the Harlem Renaissance, and popular performers like Paul Whiteman, radio both propelled the country forward into a modern, mass-mediated, consumer society and at the same time reinforced older, traditional notions of race and class. The ambiguity created by transmitting traditional values through modern media allowed each of these industries a measure of respectability. The degree to which each individual accepted and participated in these industries illustrates the various ways Americans sought to reconcile the past with the present. While no one solution worked for all, what Americans did find in their search for modern America was an identifiable American culture.

Charles Demuth (1883–1935), *My Egypt,* 1927. Oil and graphite pencil on fiberboard, 35³/₄ × 30 in. (90.81 × 76.2 cm) (Whitney Museum of American Art, New York; Purchase, with funds from Gertrude Vanderbilt Whitney, 31.172)

The Search for American Culture

THE AMBIVALENCE OF AMERICAN CULTURE: *Charles Demuth's painting* My Egypt *illustrates the ambivalence many felt toward modern America. While it celebrates the achievements of American industry, it also calls into question the costs of industrial modernization. Even as the practical materialism of American consumer culture drew the disdain of many artists, it also served as their foundation and inspiration. Like many Americans, Demuth had a love/hate relationship with modernity.*

In 1927, with the publication of *America Comes of Age: A French Analysis,* economist André Siegfried presented his take on life in the United States after a six-month tour of the country "talking to people of every class, creed, and colour, and measuring . . . the subtle influences that are today shaping the destiny of the American nation."[1] While the book's focus is on the ethnic, economic, and political situations in the United States, it presents these issues in a way that exposes the character of American culture. Americans, Siegfried argues, have been thrust upon the world stage in a position of economic and military leadership. While generally reluctant to accept the responsibilities of this position, they nonetheless have accepted and forwarded an attitude of moral superiority over the world. As a result, Americans wish the rest of the world to follow their lead while they themselves focus on national issues of production and economic growth rather than on international leadership. The conflict between this moralistic attitude in world affairs and self-serving pragmatism in domestic matters is, according to Siegfried, not a conflict at all in American minds since the economic successes of American industry justify the sense of superiority. Success has made possible "luxury in every-day consumption and the extension to the many living conditions previously reserved for the few," resulting in the belief that Americans have reached the height of civilization. "To the American, Europe is a land of paupers, and Asia a continent of starving wretches."[2] But more important than the economic triumph of the United States over the world is the sense that economic prosperity is an expression of moral superiority.

Not only did the economic success of the United States make Americans feel superior, but the role of U.S. forces in the Great War and the country's newfound position as a creditor nation reinforced such feelings. "In this lies the danger that America may feel she can do as she likes without consideration for anyone else," Siegfried warns.

> She can act as arbitrarily as she pleases. She can strangle whole peoples and governments, or she can assist them on her own terms. She can control them and indulge in the pleasant sensation of judging them from her superior moral height, and then impose her verdict. This is bad not only for Europeans, who are humiliated, but also for Americans; for their sovereign independence makes them less and less willing to accept international obligations. Always being sought after as the rich are by the poor, and always giving without receiving, tends to destroy any consideration for the borrower, such as arises from free exchange on an equal footing. They are gradually and surreptitiously assuming the *rôle* of a missionary bailiff or of an ambitious man in search of power, and from this may arise a new and subtle imperialism unlike anything we have known before. (227)

Siegfried understood the dangers involved in well-meaning but controlling intrusions into the affairs of other nations, especially when those intrusions were indirectly or unconsciously expressed.

Siegfried was not the only observer to worry about the role of the United States in the world. Walter Lippmann, in his 1927 essay "Empire: The Days of Our Nonage Are Over," discusses the danger that arises from Americans' reluctant encroachment on the world. "All the world thinks of the United States today as an empire, except the people of the United States." Americans, he writes, "shrink from the word 'empire,' and insist that it should not be used to describe the dominion we exercise from Alaska to the Philippines, from Cuba to Panama, and beyond."[3] This feeling among Americans, Lippmann insists, is not intentionally hypocritical in that Americans genuinely believe that the United States is not an empire. Yet the nation's role in the world, especially in Latin America "is what the world at large calls an empire, or at least an empire in the making" (218). Lippmann suggests that

Americans must come to terms with the American empire, or else the nation "shall merely acquire a reputation for hypocrisy while we stumble unconsciously into the cares and perils of empire. Now an unconscious empire has dangers that may be even greater than a conscious one," primarily "this refusal to admit that we are assuming imperial responsibilities is to turn over the management of our empire to business men with a personal share in it" (219). For Lippmann, the real danger is not American imperialism but American *economic* imperialism, an empire based on the interests of American business and not the interests and ideals of the American people. The solution for Lippmann is simple: "There can be no remedy for this until Americans make up their minds to recognize the fact that they are no longer a virginal republic in a wicked world, but they are themselves a world power, and one of the most portentous which has appeared in the history of mankind" (222). If Americans realized this fact, he believed, they would willingly accept their role in the world. But while Lippmann sees Americans eventually stepping up to the plate of international power, Siegfried is not so optimistic.

Siegfried felt that not only are Americans in danger of imposing their ideals on the rest of the world, but American ideals have negative ramifications domestically as well. "Many of the most magnificent material achievements of the United States have been made possible only by sacrificing certain rights of the individual, rights which we in the Old World regard as among the most precious victories of civilization" (*America Comes of Age*, 347). Americans, according to Siegfried, willingly give up aspects of their individuality in order to increase efficiency and production, and this runs counter to the course of western civilization, which has sought out greater and greater freedoms for the individual. "But what is absolutely new about this society which is accomplishing such marvels is that in all aspects—even including idealism and religion—it is working towards the single goal of production. It is a materialistic society, organized to produce things rather than people, with output set up as a god" (348). This singular goal of production means Americans are constantly concerned about being ever more efficient and productive, and therefore they are always active as opposed to contemplative. "The American is entirely at ease only in practical matters, for he is completely out of his element when he is not active," writes Siegfried. "Simply to exist is not enough; he must always express himself in some tangible way" (40).

Reinforcing this idea, Edith Wharton's 1927 novel, *Twilight Sleep*, revolves around the lives of the extended family of Pauline and Dexter Manford, a new-money, New York couple whose every hour of every day is consumed with activity. While Dexter spends most of his waking hours working at his law firm, Pauline fills her day with scheduled social visits, fund-raisers, organizational meetings, exercise, and meditation and with learning about the newest and latest trends and fads in religion, social reform, and disaster relief. She unexpectedly experiences a free hour when her facial-massage artist cancels at the last minute, and Wharton describes her as "painfully oppressed by an hour of unexpected leisure." Pauline contemplates what to do with the time:

> To be sure, she had skipped her "Silent Meditation" that morning; but she did not feel in the mood for it now. And besides, an hour is too long for meditation—an hour is too long for anything. Now that she had one to herself, for the first time in years, she didn't in the least know what to do with it. That was something which no one had ever thought of teaching her; and the sense of being surrounded by a sudden void, into which she could reach out on all sides without touching an engagement or an obligation, produced in her a sort of mental dizziness. She had taken plenty of rest-cures, of course, all one's friends did. But during a rest-cure one was always busy resting; every minute was crammed with passive activities; one never had this queer sense of inoccupation, never had to face an absolutely featureless expanse of time. It made her feel as if the world had rushed by and forgotten her.[4]

Wharton's portrayal of Pauline Manford illustrates Siegfried's idea of constant activity as an American trait. If one is not engaged in gainful employment, then one needs to fill one's days with other occupations. To not do anything goes against the grain of society, against the task of production and the goal of consumption. But in describing the inability of a woman of leisure to be leisurely, Wharton also alludes to the contradictions inherent in American society. This contradiction is reinforced by such phrases as "busy resting" and "passive activities."

Those contradictions alluded to by Wharton include Pauline's efforts to uphold traditional society by scheming to keep her daughter-in-law from leaving and divorcing her son Jim, while she herself challenged traditional society by divorcing Jim's father to marry Dexter. Much like Lippmann's Americans who do not believe the United States is an empire yet engage in imperial policies, Wharton's characters communicate one set of ideals while living up to another set. In 1927, although not all Americans behaved hypocritically, what Americans did collectively did appear hypocritical and contradictory, since the range of experiences did not reflect a shared sense of what it meant to be an American; rather, it was the result of individuals' engaging in individual or group activities that each fit into different ideas about American society in different ways. And in 1927, Americans found many ways to express themselves both individually and collectively, from the unifying yet diverse responses to Charles Lindbergh's flight, to the similarly unifying but also divisive responses to the flooding of the Mississippi River. Both events brought Americans together in common celebration and common cause, but each event also illustrated the deep divides within American society, between older, traditional ideas about American values and newer, modern ideas, and between white landowners with the power incumbent in their position and the black tenant farmers and laborers with few rights in practice.

As Americans expressed themselves in art, literature, religion, sex, and consumerism, they also expressed the nature of American culture, a culture that is vague and general enough to encompass many ideals, many ambiguities, and many conflicts, while in its broadest sense still speaking for almost all Americans. What makes this flexibility possible is the fact that it is a culture based on consumerism in which everyone can individually express themselves through consumption while participating collectively in a shared cultural practice. This culture was made possible by the growth of mass production, which enabled larger numbers of people to participate in consumption, even with the homogenizing effect of mass culture. "To standardize the individual in order to standardize things it is intended that he should buy," claims Siegfried, "is to lose sight of the fact that goods were made for man and not man for goods" (*America Comes of Age*, 169). And although it is true that mass-produced goods do lack individual-

ity in design and craftsmanship, that conformity is somewhat countered by the fact that while 15 million people bought Ford's Model T,
they all used the product in the ways best suited to their own needs
and desires. The Model T made some feel as if they were a part of the
great mass of American consumers entering the bright future; others
saw their Model Ts as a means to remain independent, as in the case of
small farmers.

The individuality that Americans sought was not necessarily in the
products they selected but in the combination of products consumed
and the uses to which they were put, a concept only vaguely understood by Siegfried when he proclaims that "a democracy of capitalists
is being built up among the people, a democracy that will be conservative because it is satisfied" (165). His concern is for political, religious, and economic equality and not for cultural expression, and in
this sense he is correct in pointing out the limits placed on personal
freedom by mass consumerism. But Siegfried sees Americans making a
Devil's bargain by choosing efficiency and quantity over individuality
and social justice, all in the name of "service." "In the end," he writes,
"'service' is the doctrine of an optimistic Pharisee trying to reconcile
success with justice" (179). "Service" is the justification newspapers
offered for devoting more print space to violent crimes and sporting
events than to international events and domestic politics. Giving readers what they wanted to read instead of deciding what was important
for them to know marked a significant shift in journalism, emphasized
by the appearance of tabloid newspapers like the *New York Illustrated
Daily News,* the *New York Daily Mirror,* and the *New York Evening
Graphic,* which all specialized in image-driven content. Consumers
saw these tabloids as an efficient way to get the news, since they could
be read faster than a standard newspaper. The owners of the papers
made substantial profits from these ventures, which still provided the
basic service of informing the public, even though they were more focused on such events as the Snyder/Gray trial than on important issues of the day. "Service" is also what justified distributing radio licenses to large networks rather than to smaller independent, often
ethnic, radio stations after the Radio Act of 1927. Since large networks
served more people than did niche stations, the FRC saw fit to grant
them the most licenses at the best frequencies, despite the fact that

service to a small minority could also benefit not just that particular group but society in general. Again, in the name of service to the masses, the content of radio programming, like that of newspapers, became homogenized, leaving fewer choices for individual expression.

Yet people did express their preferences through consumption as consumer goods and services came more and more to dominate the definition of American culture. While novelists, playwrights, musicians, and artists sought to define a uniquely American culture with such works as Rolvaag's *Giants in the Earth,* Kern and Hammerstein's *Show Boat,* Whiteman's recording of Ferde Grofé's "Mississippi Suite," and Sheeler's *Criss-Crossed Conveyors,* most Americans expressed their culture by attending professional and college sporting events and motion pictures, listening to network radio programs, following the exploits of famous and infamous people, and celebrating national heroes such as Charles Lindbergh. They were able to share these experiences with each other yet not necessarily to interpret their experiences in the same way and according to the same values.

While some lamented the damaging impact a radio minstrel show could have on perceptions of African Americans, others (including many African Americans) celebrated the progress that they believed the inclusion of African American characters on a popular radio program represented. Likewise, the successes of Harlem Renaissance artists can be seen as a celebration and appreciation of black culture, a selling of black stereotypes to an eager white audience while selling out authentic African American culture, or a combination of the two. For every comment about the negative influence of movies portraying immoral behavior, there were positive comments about the benefits of easy access to entertainment. Clara Bow's films and life represented both the liberating effects of feminism and the dangers that the loss of traditional roles presented for the stability of society; the more economically successful businesswoman, Mary Pickford, represented traditional female subservience and infantilization in the roles she played. While onscreen they portrayed very different types of women, their lives represent the opportunities available to the "new woman." Ultimately, Pickford was the more modern woman, with her three marriages and business empire, as opposed to Bow's marriage and retirement from the screen, but each engaged in both traditional and modern practices. Bruce Barton believed that religion, modernized according to business methods, could save the world; Sinclair Lewis saw the same process as a danger to American society. Hollywood used religion to bring respectability to the film industry, while fundamentalism and religious intolerance continued. In a variety of ways, the uses and abuses of religion reveal the ambiguities of American culture.

Visually representing the ambiguities of American culture, Charles Demuth's 1927 painting of a Lancaster, Pennsylvania, grain silo is titled *My Egypt*. The title plays not only on the craze for everything Egyptian in the wake of the discovery of King Tutankhamen's tomb in 1922 but also on the many references, such as Le Corbusier's 1923 book *Towards a New Architecture*, that likened American grain elevators to the Egyptian pyramids. The comparison is meaningful on a number of levels; as a celebration of American industry and technology, as well as in sheer size, grain elevators illustrated the ingenuity of American business and efficiency. Also, the idea that American industrial and agricultural workers were similar to the slaves of ancient Egypt, building monuments to other men's glory, alluded to the negative aspects of American society. But Demuth's painting is more than an ambiguous look at modernization. Barbara Haskell argues that the "my" in *My Egypt* refers to the role industrial modernization plays in American society. Just as the bondage of slavery in Egypt helped create the religion and identity of the Jews, American industry serves as a source of inspiration as well as imprisonment for creative endeavors. "*My Egypt* was Demuth's radical assertion of the dilemma of the American artist as well as his acknowledgment that the very difficulties America posed were also the ultimate source of his aesthetic invention and creative freedom."[5] Or as Demuth himself put it, "America doesn't really care—still, if one is really an artist and at the same time an American, just this not caring, even though it drives one mad, can be artistic material."[6] The ideas Demuth felt about America and sought to convey were too complex for words alone and needed to be spoken through his art. "Words, Demuth now felt," Haskell argues, "could not generate sufficient ambiguity or force one to internalize the levels of meaning in a work of art."[7] The stately, monumental, and overwhelming structure in the painting both inspires and intimidates; the beams of light celebrate and cast shadows. Ambiguity abounds in both the painting and in the nation that inspired it.

Every event in American history contains clues to the way Americans felt about their nation and the world, and the events of 1927 illustrate a society deeply conflicted about the direction of American culture. This was more than a carefree age of flappers, bathtub gin, and ballyhoo. It was an age of anxiety, hope, caution, and fear. Anxiety about what the future would bring and what was being lost of the past, hope for economic prosperity and a rising standard of living, caution about changing too many things and ideas too quickly, and fear that the America that many people remembered and cherished was disappearing all created tension in American life. The contradictions expressed in American culture underscored the inherent differences in values held by individual Americans. These differences created an air of ambiguity that pervaded every moral crusade, every raucous speakeasy celebration, every celebrity's image, and every artistic expression.

While Siegfried does not address the cultural expressions of Americans, his analysis of the economic, political, and ethnic situation in the United States is fully reinforced by it. What Americans did, consumed, and experienced expressed their feelings about their world. The successes of Charles Lindbergh, Henry Ford, Clara Bow, Herbert Hoover, Jack Dempsey, Babe Ruth, Mary Pickford, Douglas Fairbanks, Duke Ellington, and others helped Americans reinforce their belief in the American superiority ushered in by the Great War. For most Americans, the culture reflected the economic and political triumph of American values as expressed in the military triumph of the war. But as Siegfried points out, these things also give warning to the dangers of American ideals. Would America's new leadership role bring about greater harmony, peace, and prosperity, or would it mark a turn in the progress of individual freedom? Is modern America good for individual Americans?

In 1927, that question was yet to be answered, but investigating the ways people dealt with these issues and expressed them in their everyday lives not only can help us understand how the past dealt with these issues but can also inform current debates over similar issues. Gay marriage and abortion now occupy the same ground where prohibition and antievolutionism stood in the 1920s, a basic argument over which values and morals should represent the nation as a whole. Illegal immigration, citizenship, and English-only debates mimic debates over immigration reform and nativism by arguing over who has a right to the American dream. While the subjects of such concerns have changed, the issues are consistent. Optimistic predictions about radio's democratizing effect mirrors current predictions concerning the "new media" of cyberspace, illustrating Americans' firm belief in the ability of progress and technology to ameliorate problems. The consequences of Hurricane Katrina, much like those of the Mississippi flood of 1927, revived concerns about racial inequality in the South and the nation and about whose vision of American society should be used to reconstruct devastated regions. In the end, it is a matter of dealing with inevitable change that some see as progress and others see as decline.

While some fear changes occurring in American society, others look to the future for a better world. Yet still, the conflict between the demands of the majority and the rights of individuals and minorities continues and is still expressed in the culture of everyday life. The main difference between the early twentieth century and the start of the twenty-first is that instead of dealing with an America on the rise in the world, we are dealing with one in decline, as a unified Europe and the growing economies of India and China seek to displace American economic strength and with it the political influence that the United States held during the American century. In many ways, the search for modern America that engaged Americans in 1927 is still going on today.

Notes

INTRODUCTION. THE SEARCH FOR MODERN AMERICA

1. John W. Ward, "The Meaning of Lindbergh's Flight," *American Quarterly* 10, no. 1 (Spring 1958), 15.

2. Allen Churchill, *The Year the World Went Mad* (New York: Thomas Y. Crowell, 1960), vii; Gerald Leinwald, *1927: High Tide of the Twenties* (New York: Four Walls Eight Windows, 2001), x; Frederick Lewis Allen, *Only Yesterday: An Informal History of the 1920s* (New York: Harper & Row, 1931); Nathan Miller, *New World Coming: The 1920s and the Making of Modern America* (New York: Scribner, 2003).

3. Lynn Dumenil, *The Modern Temper: American Culture and Society in the 1920s* (New York: Hill & Wang, 1995). Other useful works include Ellis W. Hawley, *The Great War and the Search for a Modern Order: A History of the American People and Their Institutions, 1917–1933* (Prospect Heights, Ill.: Waveland Press, 1992); David J. Goldberg, *Discontented America: The United States in the 1920s* (Baltimore: Johns Hopkins University Press, 1999); Elizabeth Stevenson, *Babbitts and Bohemians: From the Great War to the Great Depression* (Edison, N.J.: Transaction Books, 1997).

4. Roderick Nash, *The Nervous Generation: American Thought, 1917–1930* (Chicago: Ivan R. Dee, 1990), 2.

5. Paul A. Carter, *The Twenties in America* (New York: Thomas Y. Crowell, 1968), 8. My thanks to Paul Boyer for pointing out the particularly appropriate quotation here.

6. Lawrence W. Levine, "Progress and Nostalgia: The Self Image of the Nineteen Twenties," in *The Unpredictable Past: Explorations in American Cultural History* (New York: Oxford University Press, 1993), 189–205; Warren I. Susman, "Culture and Civilization: The Nineteen-Twenties," and "Culture Heroes: Ford, Barton, Ruth," both in *Culture as History: The Transformation of American Society in the Twentieth Century* (Washington, D.C.: Smithsonian Books, 2003), 105–121, 122–149.

7. Roland Marchand, *Advertising the American Dream: Making Way for Modernity, 1920–1940* (Berkeley and Los Angeles: University of California Press, 1985); Lewis A. Erenberg, *Steppin' Out: New York Nightlife and the*

Transformation of American Culture, 1890–1930 (Chicago: University of Chicago Press, 1981); Elaine Tyler May, *Great Expectations: Marriage and Divorce in Post-Victorian America* (Chicago: University of Chicago Press, 1980); Charles L. Ponce de Leon, *Self-Exposure: Human-Interest Journalism and the Emergence of Celebrity in America, 1890–1940* (Chapel Hill: University of North Carolina Press, 2002); Nathan Irvin Huggins, *Harlem Renaissance* (New York: Oxford University Press, 1971); Lary May, *Screening Out the Past: The Birth of Mass Culture and the Motion Picture Industry* (Chicago: University of Chicago Press, 1980).

CHAPTER ONE. SEEKING MASTERY:

THE MACHINE AGE AND THE IDEALIZED PAST

1. Charles Sorenson, quoted in David A. Hounshell, *From the American System to Mass Production, 1800–1932: The Development of Manufacturing Technology in the United States* (Baltimore: Johns Hopkins University Press, 1984), 222.

2. Keith Sward, *The Legend of Henry Ford* (New York: Atheneum, 1972), 44–45.

3. Ray Batchelor, *Henry Ford: Mass Production, Modernism and Design* (Manchester, England: Manchester University Press, 1994), 55–56.

4. Sward, *Legend of Henry Ford*, 199–201.

5. Mary Jane Jacob and Linda Downs, *The Rouge: The Image of Industry in the Art of Charles Sheeler and Diego Rivera* (Detroit: Detroit Institute of Arts, 1978), 7.

6. Robert Lacey, *Ford: The Men and the Machine* (Boston: Little, Brown, 1986), 298–299. See also Richard S. Tedlow, "Putting America on Wheels: Ford vs. General Motors," in his *New and Improved: The Story of Mass Marketing in America* (New York: Basic Books, 1990), 112–181.

7. There is an extensive literature describing the effects of the economic shift from production to consumption. Most important are T. J. Jackson Lears, *No Place of Grace: Antimodernism and the Transformation of American Culture, 1880–1920* (Chicago: University of Chicago Press, 1994); Roland Marchand, *Advertising the American Dream: Making Way for Modernity, 1920–1940* (Berkeley and Los Angeles: University of California Press, 1985); Warren I. Susman, *Culture as History: The Transformation of American Society in the Twentieth Century* (Washington, D.C.: Smithsonian Books, 2003); Lewis Erenberg, *Steppin' Out: New York Nightlife and the Transformation of Ameri-*

can Culture, 1890–1930 (Chicago: University of Chicago Press, 1981); Susan Strasser, *Satisfaction Guaranteed: The Making of the American Mass Market* (Washington, D.C.: Smithsonian Institution Press, 2004); Hal Barron, *Mixed Harvest: The Second Great Transformation in the Rural North, 1870–1930* (Chapel Hill: University of North Carolina Press, 1997); Lizabeth Cohen, *Making a New Deal: Industrial Workers in Chicago, 1919–1939* (Cambridge: Cambridge University Press, 1991); William R. Leach, *Land of Desire: Merchants, Power, and the Rise of a New American Culture* (New York: Knopf Doubleday, 1994); Charles F. McGovern, *Sold American: Consumption and Citizenship, 1890–1945* (Chapel Hill: University of North Carolina Press, 2006); Tedlow, *New and Improved;* and Richard Wrightman Fox and T. J. Jackson Lears, eds., *The Culture of Consumption: Critical Essays in American History, 1880–1980* (New York: Pantheon Books, 1983).

8. William Knudsen, quoted in Hounshell, *From the American System to Mass Production,* 265.

9. Henry Ford, quoted in Batchelor, *Henry Ford,* 40. Batchelor believes that Ford made the statement not in 1909, as he claimed, but only later in his ghostwritten autobiography, *My Life and Work* (New York: Doubleday, Page, 1923). Regardless, it did become part of the myth of Henry Ford and the Model T.

10. Batchelor, *Henry Ford,* 60.

11. Sward, *Legend of Henry Ford,* 204.

12. Terry Smith, *Making the Modern: Industry, Art, and Design in America* (Chicago: University of Chicago Press, 1993), 100–101.

13. Smith, *Making the Modern,* 101.

14. Susan Fillin Yeh, "Charles Sheeler: Industry, Fashion, and the Vanguard," *Arts Magazine,* February 1980, 156.

15. For a more detailed account of this argument, see Smith, *Making the Modern.*

16. Yeh, "Charles Sheeler," 158.

17. Quoted in Yeh, "Charles Sheeler," 156.

18. Karen Tsujimoto, *Images of America: Precisionist Painting and Modern Photography* (Seattle: University of Washington Press, 1982), 22.

19. Reyner Banham, quoted in Tsujimoto, *Images of America,* 22.

20. Louis Lozowick, "The Americanization of Art," in *The Machine-Age Exposition Exhibit Catalogue* (New York: Little Review, 1927), 18–19.

21. Miles Orvell, "Inspired by Science and the Modern: Precisionism and

American Culture," in *Precisionism in America, 1915–1941: Reordering Reality* (New York: Harry N. Abrams, 1994), 54.

22. Jane Heap, "Machine-Age Exposition," in *Machine-Age Exposition Exhibit Catalogue,* 36.

23. *Machine-Age Exposition Exhibit Catalogue,* 37.

24. Hounshell, *From the American System to Mass Production,* 263.

25. George Antheil, *Bad Boy of Music* (Hollywood, Calif.: Samuel French, 1990), 193.

26. Ibid., 140.

27. The precision necessary for a complete, as-written performance of *Ballet Mécanique* could not be achieved until computers became available, decades after Antheil wrote it. For more on the use of computers to perform *Ballet Mécanique,* see the documentary film *Bad Boy Made Good: The Revival of the Ballet Mécanique* (directed by Ron Frank, 2006) and Paul Lehrman, "Reconstructing *Ballet Mécanique:* An Interview with Paul Lehrman," by Preston Wright, American Public Media, January 2003, available at http://musicmavericks.publicradio.org/features/interview_lehrman.html.

28. Josephine Herbst, "A Year of Disgrace," in *The Starched Blue Sky of Spain, and Other Memoirs* (Boston: Northeastern University Press, 1999), 84.

29. Ibid., 84–85.

30. Ibid., 85.

31. G. Louis Joughin and Edmund M. Morgan, *The Legacy of Sacco and Vanzetti* (New York: Harcourt, Brace, 1948), 197.

32. Felix Frankfurter, "The Case of Sacco and Vanzetti," *Atlantic Monthly,* March 1927, 409–432.

33. Joughin and Morgan, *Legacy of Sacco and Vanzetti,* 271.

34. Ibid., 297.

35. Ibid.

36. Ibid., 513.

37. Herbst, "Year of Disgrace," 97.

38. Walter Lippmann, "The Causes of Political Indifference Today," in *Men of Destiny* (New York: Macmillan, 1927), 28–30.

39. Bruce Barton, "Creed of an Advertising Man," quoted in Susman, *Culture as History,* 128.

40. Bruce Barton, *What Can a Man Believe?* (Indianapolis, Ind.: Bobbs-Merrill, 1927), 5. Henceforth cited in text.

41. Calvin Coolidge, "Remarks to Amherst College Alumni Association, February 4, 1916," in *Have Faith in Massachusetts: A Collection of Speeches and Messages* (New York: Houghton Mifflin, 1919), 14.

42. For an extended discussion of Lewis's depiction of modern society, see Stephen S. Conroy, "Sinclair Lewis's Sociological Imagination," *American Literature* 42, no. 3 (November 1970): 348–362.

43. Nicholas Birns, "Building the Cathedral: Imagination, Christianity, and Progress in Willa Cather's *Death Comes for the Archbishop*," *Religion and the Arts: A Journal from Boston College* 3, no. 1 (1999): 10.

44. Willa Cather, *Death Comes for the Archbishop* (New York: Alfred A. Knopf, 1927; repr., New York: Vintage Classics, 1990), 290. Citations are to the Vintage Classics edition. Henceforth cited in text.

45. Richard Hofstadter, *The Progressive Historians: Turner, Beard, Parrington* (New York: Alfred A. Knopf, 1968), 299.

46. Dorothy Ross, "Grand Narrative in American Historical Writing: From Romance to Uncertainty," *American Historical Review* 100, no. 3 (June 1995): 657, 656.

47. Charles A. Beard and Mary R. Beard, *The Rise of American Civilization* (New York: Macmillan, 1927, rev. and enlarged, two volumes in one, 1933), x. Citations are to the 1933 edition.

48. David W. Marcell, "Charles Beard: Civilization and the Revolt against Empiricism," *American Quarterly* 21, no. 1 (Spring 1969): 68.

49. Ross, "Grand Narrative," 658.

50. April Schultz, "'The Pride of the Race Had Been Touched': The 1925 Norse-American Immigration Centennial and Ethnic Identity," *Journal of American History* 77, no. 4 (March 1991): 1294.

51. O. E. Rolvaag, quoted in April Schultz, *Ethnicity on Parade: Inventing the Norwegian American through Celebration* (Amherst: University of Massachusetts Press, 1994), 58.

52. Glenway Wescott, *The Grandmothers: A Family Portrait* (New York: Harper & Brothers, 1927; repr. Madison: University of Wisconsin Press, 1996), 33. Citations are to the University of Wisconsin Press edition. Henceforth cited in text.

53. Jonathan Zimmerman, "'Each "Race" Could Have Its Heroes Sung': Ethnicity and the History Wars in the 1920s," *Journal of American History* 87, no. 1 (June 2000): 110.

CHAPTER TWO. SEEKING EQUALITY: FEMINISM AND FLOOD WATERS

1. Dorothy Dunbar Bromley, "Feminist—New Style," *Harper's Monthly,* October 1927, 552. Henceforth cited in text.

2. For more on the transformation of feminism after suffrage, see Nancy F. Cott, *The Grounding of Modern Feminism* (New Haven: Yale University Press, 1987), 158.

3. For a more elaborate discussion of the ascendance of personality over character, see Warren I. Susman, *Culture as History: The Transformation of American Society in the Twentieth Century* (Washington, D.C.: Smithsonian Books, 2003).

4. F. Scott Fitzgerald, quoted in Margaret Reid, "Has the Flapper Changed?" *Motion Picture,* July 1927, 28–29, 104.

5. Ibid.

6. Elinor Glyn, quoted in Meredith Etherington-Smith and Jeremy Pilcher, *The "It" Girls: Lucy, Lady Duff Gordon, the Couturiere "Lucile," and Elinor Glyn, Romantic Novelist* (London: Hamish House, 1986), 240–241.

7. For a fuller discussion of marriage rates and sexual practices, see Cott, *Grounding of Modern Feminism,* 147–151.

8. Budd Schulberg, *Moving Pictures: Memories of a Hollywood Prince* (New York: Stein & Day, 1981), 172.

9. Ben B. Lindsey and Wainwright Evans, *The Companionate Marriage* (New York: Boni & Liveright, 1927), 17. Henceforth cited in text.

10. Charles Larsen, *The Good Fight: The Life and Times of Judge Ben B. Lindsey* (Chicago: Quadrangle Books, 1972), 173.

11. Ibid., 174.

12. Quoted in Larsen, *The Good Fight,* 175.

13. Quoted in Larsen, *The Good Fight,* 176.

14. Virginia Dale, "The Season in Chicago," in *The Best Plays of 1927–1928,* ed. Burns Mantle (New York: Dodd, Mead, 1928), 17.

15. *Her First Affaire,* a comedy in three acts; by Merrill Rogers. Produced by Gustav Blum at the Bayes Theatre, New York, August 22, 1927.

16. Mantle, *Best Plays of 1927–1928,* 394–395.

17. *Five O'Clock Girl,* a musical comedy in two acts; book by Guy Bolton and Fred Thompson; music and lyrics by Bert Kalmar and Harry Ruby. Produced by Philip Goodman at the 44th Street Theatre, New York, October 10, 1927.

18. Mantle, *Best Plays of 1927–1928,* 427.

19. *Padlocks of 1927,* a musical review in two acts. Sketches by Paul Gerard Smith and Ballard Macdonald; lyrics by Billy Rose; music by Lee David, Jesse Greer, and Henry H. Tobias. Produced by Duo Art Productions at the Shubert Theatre, New York, July 5, 1927.

20. *New York Evening Post,* February 19, 1927, quoted in Louise Berliner, *Texas Guinan: Queen of the Night Clubs* (Austin: University of Texas Press, 1993), 121–123.

21. Lewis A. Erenberg, *Steppin' Out: New York Nightlife and the Transformation of American Culture, 1890–1930* (Chicago: University of Chicago Press, 1981), 248.

22. Quoted in Larsen, *The Good Fight,* 177.

23. *Coquette,* a play in three acts by George Abbott and Ann Preston Bridgers. Produced by Jed Harris at the Maxine Elliott Theatre, New York, November 8, 1927.

24. Abbott and Bridgers, *Coquette,* in Mantle, *Best Plays of 1927–1928,* 146–147.

25. *Show Boat,* a musical comedy adapted from Edna Ferber's novel of the same name; book and lyrics by Oscar Hammerstein II; music by Jerome Kern. Produced by Florenz Ziegfeld at the Ziegfeld Theatre, New York, December 27, 1927.

26. Oscar Hammerstein II, "Ol' Man River," from *Show Boat.*

27. Edna Ferber, *Show Boat* (New York: Book League of America, 1926), 111. Henceforth cited in text.

28. Hammerstein, "Ol' Man River."

29. Statistical information concerning the flood and relief measures comes from *The Mississippi Valley Flood Disaster of 1927: Official Report of the Relief Operations* (Washington, D.C.: American National Red Cross, 1928), 4–10.

30. For a full account of the flood, see John M. Barry, *Rising Tide: The Great Mississippi Flood of 1927 and How It Changed America* (New York: Simon & Schuster, 1997).

31. Ibid., 408–411.

32. Ibid., 133.

33. Pete Daniel, *The Shadow of Slavery: Peonage in the South, 1901–1969* (Urbana: University of Illinois Press, 1972), 151.

34. Ibid., 149. See also Pete Daniel, *Deep'n as It Come: The 1927 Mississippi River Flood* (Fayetteville: University of Arkansas Press, 1996).

35. Barry, *Rising Tide,* 183.

36. E. C. Sanders, "Report of Activities at Camp Rex," in *Report of Flood Relief Expedition,* Mississippi National Guard, Office of the Adjunct General, quoted in Barry, *Rising Tide,* 200.

37. A. G. Paxton, "National Guard Activities in Connection with Levee Fight and Flood Relief Expedition, Greenville, Mississippi," in *Report of Flood Relief Expedition,* quoted in Barry, *Rising Tide,* 202.

38. Barry, *Rising Tide,* 202.

39. *Mississippi Valley Flood Disaster of 1927,* 7–8.

40. "The Flood, the Red Cross, and the National Guard," *Crisis,* January 1928, 5.

41. *The Final Report of the Colored Advisory Commission Appointed to Cooperate with the American National Red Cross and the President's Committee on Relief Work in the Mississippi Valley Flood Disaster of 1927* (Washington, D.C.: American National Red Cross, 1929), available online at www.pbs.org/wgbh/amex/flood/filmmore/ps_cac.html.

42. *Mississippi Valley Flood Disaster of 1927,* 11.

43. Sidney Redmond to Calvin Coolidge, April 30, 1927, quoted in Daniel, *Shadow of Slavery,* 153–154.

44. Daniel, *Shadow of Slavery,* 154.

45. Ibid., 156.

46. Quoted in ibid., 159.

47. Robert Moton to Herbert Hoover, June 13, 1927, available online at www.pbs.org/wgbh/amex/flood/filmmore/ps_moton1.html.

48. Ibid.

49. Ibid.

50. Robert Moton, "Memorandum for the Committee," quoted in Daniel, *Shadow of Slavery,* 161.

51. Walter White, "The Negro and the Flood," *Nation,* June 22, 1927, 688. Henceforth cited in text.

52. Pete Daniel, *Breaking the Land: The Transformation of Cotton, Tobacco, and Rice Cultures since 1880* (Urbana: University of Illinois Press, 1985), 66.

53. *Mississippi Valley Flood Disaster of 1927,* 11.

54. Ibid., 16.

55. Calvin Coolidge, quoted in *Mississippi Valley Flood Disaster of 1927,* 13.

56. John Crowe Ransom to Allen Tate, quoted in Mark G. Malvasi, *The Unregenerate South: The Agrarian Thought of John Crowe Ransom, Allen Tate, and Donald Davidson* (Baton Rouge: Louisiana State University Press, 1997), 44.

57. Quoted in Kendrick A. Clements, *Hoover, Conservation, and Consumerism: Engineering the Good Life* (Lawrence: University Press of Kansas, 2000), 114.

58. Bruce Lohof, "Herbert Hoover, Spokesman of Humane Efficiency: The Mississippi Flood of 1927," *American Quarterly* 22, no. 3 (Autumn 1970): 693.

59. Quoted in ibid., 695.

60. For a full description of how these state credit corporations worked, see Lohof, "Herbert Hoover, Spokesman of Humane Efficiency," 695–696.

61. U.S. House of Representatives, *Eleventh Annual Report of the Federal Farm Loan Board, 1927,* 70th Cong., 1st sess., 1928, House Doc. 324, quoted in Lohof, "Herbert Hoover, Spokesman of Humane Efficiency," 696.

62. Lohof, "Herbert Hoover, Spokesman of Humane Efficiency," 696.

63. Ibid., 692.

64. Herbert Hoover, memorandum, May 12, 1927, Hoover Papers, Herbert Hoover Presidential Library, West Branch, Iowa, as quoted in Lohof, "Herbert Hoover, Spokesman of Humane Efficiency," 697.

65. Lohof, "Herbert Hoover, Spokesman of Humane Efficiency," 697.

66. Barry, *Rising Tide,* 395. Barry provides a detailed discussion of the interactions between Hoover and Moton; see especially chaps. 31–33, and 34.

CHAPTER THREE. SEEKING NOTORIETY:

THE INFAMOUS AND THE FAMOUS

1. Joan Hoff Wilson, *Herbert Hoover: Forgotten Progressive* (Boston: Little, Brown, 1975), 80.

2. Ibid., 81–82.

3. Arthur Capper, editorial, *Topeka (Kansas) Daily Capital,* July 19, 1927, quoted in Craig Lloyd, *Aggressive Introvert: A Study of Herbert Hoover and Public Relations Management, 1912–1932* (Columbus: Ohio State University Press, 1972), 120.

4. Wilson, *Herbert Hoover,* 118.

5. Quoted in Richard M. Fried, *The Man Everybody Knew: Bruce Barton and the Making of Modern America* (Chicago: Ivan R. Dee, 2005), 128–129.

6. Nan Britton, *The President's Daughter* (New York: Elizabeth Ann Guild, 1927), i.

7. Ibid., iii–iv.

8. Robert H. Ferrell, *The Strange Deaths of President Harding* (Columbia: University of Missouri Press, 1996), 68.

9. Britton, *President's Daughter,* 385.

10. Paul Sann, *The Lawless Decade: A Pictorial History of a Great American Transition; From the World War I Armistice and Prohibition to Repeal and the New Deal* (New York: Crown, 1957), 165.

11. Nan Britton, *Honesty or Politics* (New York: Elizabeth Ann Guild, 1932), ix–x.

12. For a full discussion of Harding's reputation as president, see Ferrell, *Strange Deaths of President Harding.*

13. Most of the accounts of the trial, including newspaper and later book-length accounts, tended to side with Gray for several reasons, some valid, some not so much. The most convincing argument lies in the fact that Gray's account of the murder in no way seeks to absolve him of wrongdoing, nor did it work to his advantage in any way, whereas Snyder's testimony sought to place the blame fully on Gray.

14. Ruth Snyder, quoted in John Kobler, *The Trial of Ruth Snyder and Judd Gray* (New York: Doubleday, Doran, 1938), 53. Kobler does not provide citations in his work.

15. Kobler, *Trial of Ruth Snyder and Judd Gray,* 4.

16. Judd Gray, *Doomed Ship: The Autobiography of Judd Gray, Prepared for Publication by His Sister Margaret Gray* (New York: Horace Liveright, 1928), 154–155. Henceforth cited in text.

17. Aimee Semple McPherson, quoted in Sann, *Lawless Decade,* 139.

18. *Chicago,* a satirical comedy in three acts; by Maurine Watkins. Produced by Sam H. Harris at the Music Box Theatre, New York, December 30, 1926; in *The Best Plays of 1926–1927,* ed. Burns Mantle (New York: Dodd, Mead, 1927), 104.

19. Kobler, *Trial of Ruth Snyder and Judd Gray,* 51. The case would later inspire another writer, James M. Cain, to write *Double Indemnity* (1943, first published in *Liberty Magazine* in 1936), which became a classic film noir in 1944.

20. Townsend Scudder, quoted in Kobler, *Trial of Ruth Snyder and Judd Gray,* 56.

21. Quoted in Kobler, *Trial of Ruth Snyder and Judd Gray,* 58.

22. Ruth Snyder, quoted in Kobler, *Trial of Ruth Snyder and Judd Gray,* 60.

23. *New York Times,* January 15, 1927, quoted in Kobler, *Trial of Ruth Snyder and Judd Gray,* 64–65.

24. Damon Runyon, "A Chilly-Looking Blonde and Her Paramour," in *These Were Our Years: A Panoramic and Nostalgic Look at American Life between the Two World Wars,* ed. Frank Brookhouser (Garden City, N.Y.: Doubleday, 1959), 208.

25. Charles Merz, "Bigger and Better Murders," *Harper's Monthly,* August 1927, 341.

26. John R. Brazil, "Murder Trials, Murder, and Twenties America," *American Quarterly* 33, no. 2 (Summer 1981): 163–164.

27. Bernard McFadden, quoted in Brazil, "Murder Trials, Murder, and Twenties America," 164.

28. According to John R. Brazil, the trial was a media circus in which "a special switchboard manned by 28 operators, 60 specially leased telegraph wires, 200 correspondents (including 16 from the staid *New York Times*), and more than 50 photographers kept the newspapers supplied with material. In the 24 days of the trial 12,000,000 words went out over the telegraph wires, 'enough, if put into one newspaper,' said the Associated Press, 'to fill 960 pages. . . . Words enough if put into book form to make a shelf of novels 22' long.'" Brazil, "Murder Trials, Murder, and Twenties America," 164.

29. Brazil, "Murder Trials, Murder, and Twenties America," 164.

30. Silas Bent, "The Art of Ballyhoo," *Harper's Monthly,* September 1927, 492–493.

31. Brazil, "Murder Trials, Murder, and Twenties America," 170–171.

32. Alexander Woolcott, *Long, Long Ago* (New York: Viking, 1943), 122, cited in Brazil, "Murder Trials, Murder, and Twenties America," 167.

33. Brazil, "Murder Trials, Murder, and Twenties America," 168.

34. Maurine Watkins, "Mrs. Gaertner Has 'Class' as She Faces Jury," *Chicago Tribune,* June 4, 1924, reprinted in Maurine Watkins, *"Chicago": With the Chicago Tribune Articles That Inspired It,* edited and with an introduction by Thomas H. Pauly (Carbondale: Southern Illinois University Press, 1997), 149.

35. Maurine Watkins, "Select Jury to Pronounce Fate of Beulah Annan," *Chicago Tribune,* May 23, 1924, reprinted in Watkins, *"Chicago,"* 137.

36. Maurine Watkins, "Mystery Victim Is Robert Law; Hold Divorcee," *Chicago Tribune,* March 12, 1924, reprinted in Watkins, *"Chicago,"* 116.

37. Maurine Watkins, "Woman Plays Jazz Air as Victim Dies," *Chicago Tribune,* April 4, 1924, reprinted in Watkins, *"Chicago,"* 122–123.

38. Maurine Watkins, "Beulah Annan Awaits Stork, Murder Trial: Jail Women Wonder 'What Jurors Think About,'" *Chicago Tribune,* May 9, 1924, reprinted in Watkins, *"Chicago,"* 134.

39. Thomas H. Pauly, introduction to Watkins, *"Chicago,"* xxvii.

40. *Chicago Post,* September 12, 1927, quoted in Watkins, *"Chicago,"* xxvii.

41. *Chicago Herald Examiner,* September 19, 1927, quoted in Watkins, *"Chicago,"* xxvi–xxvii.

42. Walter Lippmann, "Blazing Publicity: Why We Know So Much about 'Peaches' Browning, Valentino, Lindbergh and Queen Marie" (1927), in *Vanity Fair: Selections from America's Most Memorable Magazine; A Cavalcade of the 1920s and 1930s,* ed. Cleveland Amory and Frederic Bradlee (New York: Viking, 1960), 121.

43. Ibid., 122.

44. Walter Lippmann, "The Causes of Political Indifference Today," in *Men of Destiny* (New York: Macmillan, 1927), 20. Henceforth cited in text.

45. Grantland Rice, "The Golden Panorama," in *Sport's Golden Age: A Close-Up of the Fabulous Twenties,* ed. Allison Danzig and Peter Brandwein (New York: Harper & Brothers, 1948), 1.

46. Ibid., 7.

47. Robert Lipsyte, *SportsWorld: An American Dreamland* (New York: Quadrangle/New York Times Book Company, 1975), 170.

48. Ibid., 170–171.

49. Ibid., 172.

50. Ibid., 173.

51. Paul Gallico, *The Golden People* (New York: Doubleday, 1965), 25.

52. Ibid., 77.

53. Ibid., 186.

54. Ibid., 191.

55. James P. Dawson, "Boxing," in Danzig and Brandwein, *Sport's Golden Age,* 40.

56. Gallico, *Golden People,* 78.

57. James Crusinberry, quoted in Mark Inabinett, *Grantland Rice and His Heroes: The Sportswriter as Mythmaker in the 1920s* (Knoxville: University of Tennessee Press, 1994), 29.

58. Gene Tunney, "My Fights with Jack Dempsey," in *The Aspirin Age, 1919–1941,* edited by Isabel Leighton (New York: Simon & Schuster, 1949), 154. Henceforth cited in text.

59. Jack Dempsey, quoted in Randy Roberts, *Jack Dempsey: The Manassa Mauler* (Baton Rouge: Louisiana State University Press, 1979), 232.

60. Roberts, *Jack Dempsey,* 237.

61. Tex Richard, quoted in Roberts, *Jack Dempsey,* 250.

62. Roberts, *Jack Dempsey,* 255–256.

63. Jack Dempsey to Dan Daniel, quoted in Roberts, *Jack Dempsey,* 259.

64. John Kieran, quoted in Roberts, *Jack Dempsey,* 262.

65. Quoted in Mel Heimer, *The Long Count* (New York: Atheneum, 1969), 233.

66. Elliott J. Gorn, "The Manassa Mauler and the Fighting Marine: An Interpretation of the Dempsey-Tunney Fights," *Journal of American Studies* 19 (1985): 32.

67. Ibid., 35.

68. Ibid., 37.

69. Ibid., 39.

70. Ibid., 43.

71. Michael Oriard, *King Football: Sport and Spectacle in the Golden Age of Radio and Newsreels, Movies and Magazines, the Weekly and the Daily Press* (Chapel Hill: University of North Carolina Press, 2001), 68–69.

72. Grantland Rice, "Notre Dame's Cyclone Beats Army," *New York Herald Tribune,* October 19, 1924, quoted in Lipsyte, *SportsWorld,* 171.

73. Estimates of attendance vary between 115,000 to 120,000, but no accurate account exists.

74. The first clause in Knute Rockne's contract with the Wilson Athletic Equipment Company, 1927, quoted in Murray Sperber, *Shake Down the Thunder: The Creation of Notre Dame Football* (New York: Henry Holt, 1993), 232.

75. "Annual Report of the Carnegie Foundation for the Advancement of Teaching," 1924, quoted in Sperber, *Shake Down the Thunder,* 183.

76. G. Edward White, *Creating the National Pastime: Baseball Transforms Itself, 1903–1953* (Princeton, Princeton University Press, 1996), 117–118.

77. H. I. Phillips, quoted in Leo Trachtenberg, *The Wonder Team: The True Story of the Incomparable 1927 New York Yankees* (Bowling Green, Ohio: Bowling Green State University Popular Press, 1995), 2.

78. Background information on Babe Ruth comes from Robert W. Creamer, *Babe: The Legend Comes to Life* (New York: Simon & Schuster, 1974); John G. Robertson, *The Babe Chases 60: That Fabulous 1927 Season, Home Run by Home Run* (Jefferson, N.C.: McFarland, 1999); and Ken Sobol, *Babe Ruth and the American Dream* (New York: Ballantine Books, 1974).

79. David Quentin Voigt, *America through Baseball* (Chicago: Nelson-Hall, 1976), 112.

80. Patrick Trimble, "Babe Ruth: The Media Construction of a 1920's Sports Personality," *Colby Quarterly* 32, no. 1 (Spring 1996): 46.

81. No copy of this film exists. The description is from Kenneth W. Munden, executive ed., *The American Film Institute Catalog of Motion Pictures Produced in the United States: Feature Films, 1921–1930* (New York: R. R. Bowker, 1971), 31.

82. Grantland Rice, *The Tumult and the Shouting: My Life in Sport* (New York: A. S. Barnes, 1954), 112–113.

CHAPTER FOUR. SEEKING RESPECTABILITY:
MODERN MEDIA AND TRADITIONAL VALUES

1. Allene Talmey, *Doug and Mary and Others* (New York: Macy-Masius, 1927), 33.

2. Booton Herndon, *Mary Pickford and Douglas Fairbanks: The Most Popular Couple the World Has Ever Known* (New York: W. W. Norton, 1977), 1.

3. Herndon, *Mary Pickford and Douglas Fairbanks,* 228.

4. Cecil B. DeMille, "The Screen as a Religious Teacher: How the Much-Discussed Filming of *The King of Kings,* the New Religious Drama, Was Produced with Reverence and Accuracy," *Theatre,* June 1927; reprinted in notes to *The King of Kings,* directed by Cecile B. DeMille, Criterion Collection DVD (2004), booklet included with the DVD, 31.

5. W. C. DeMille and Cecil B. DeMille, quoted in Robert S. Birchard, *The King of Kings,* in notes to *The King of Kings,* Criterion Collection DVD, booklet included with the DVD, 17.

6. Cecil B. DeMille, radio broadcast, Los Angeles, KNX, July 11, 1927, quoted in Birchard, *King of Kings,* 20.

7. DeMille, "The Screen as a Religious Teacher," 33.

8. Advertisements, included on *The King of Kings,* Criterion Collection DVD.

9. "Hundreds of Police Battle to Keep Crowds in Check," *Los Angeles Examiner,* May 19, 1927.

10. *Los Angeles Times,* May 15, 1927, quoted in David Karnes, "The Glamorous Crowd: Hollywood Movie Premieres between the Wars," *American Quarterly* 38, no. 4 (Autumn 1986): 560.

11. Grauman's advertisement, *Los Angeles Times,* May 19, 1927.

12. Cecil B. DeMille, quoted in Welford Beaton, "Industry Fashioning Weapon of Defense," *Film Spectator* 3, no. 7 (May 28, 1927), 3.

13. "Invitation to the Organizational Banquet of the Academy of Motion Picture Arts and Sciences, May 11, 1927," quoted in Pierre Norman Sands, *A Historical Study of the Academy of Motion Picture Arts and Sciences (1927–1947)* (New York: Arno Press, 1973), 38–39.

14. Academy of Motion Picture Arts and Sciences, *Annual Report,* 1929, 49, quoted in Sands, *Historical Study,* 85.

15. Sands, *Historical Study,* 86.

16. Cecil B. DeMille, as quoted in Birchard, *King of Kings,* 16.

17. For a much more complex interpretation of *The Jazz Singer,* see Michael Rogin, "Blackface, White Noise: The Jewish Jazz Singer Finds His Voice," *Critical Inquiry* 18 (Spring 1992): 417–453.

18. Kathy J. Ogren, *The Jazz Revolution: Twenties America and the Meaning of Jazz* (New York: Oxford University Press, 1989), 7.

19. For a fuller discussion of these ideas, see Rogin, "Blackface, White Noise."

20. Sampson Raphaelson, *The Jazz Singer,* ed. Robert L. Carringer (Madison: University of Wisconsin Press, 1979), 122.

21. *The Jazz Singer,* directed by Alan Crosland (Warner Brothers, 1927).

22. For a full discussion of this process, see Court Carney, *Cuttin' Up: How Early Jazz Got America's Ear* (Lawrence: University Press of Kansas, 2009).

23. Ibid., 73.

24. Laurence Bergreen, *Louis Armstrong: An Extravagant Life* (New York: Broadway Books, 1997), 200.

25. Ibid., 258.

26. For a fuller discussion of Peyton's writings and attitudes, see Carney, *Cuttin' Up,* 64–68.

27. Paul Whiteman and Mary Margaret McBride, *Jazz* (New York: J. H. Sears, 1926), 3.

28. Ibid., 257.

29. James Weldon Johnson, *God's Trombones: Seven Negro Sermons in Verse* (New York: Viking Penguin, 1927; repr., 1990), 11. Citations are to the 1990 edition and are henceforth given in the text.

30. Alain Locke, "The Negro Spirituals," in *The New Negro,* ed. Alain Locke (New York: Albert & Charles Boni, 1925; repr., New York: Touchstone, 1997), 199. Citations are to the Touchstone edition.

31. Ibid., 200.

32. John Wesley Work, *Folk Song of the American Negro* (Nashville, Tenn.: Fisk University Press, 1915), 93.

33. J. A. Rogers, "Jazz at Home," in Locke, *The New Negro,* 216. Henceforth cited in text.

34. Langston Hughes, "The Negro Artist and the Racial Mountain," *Nation,* June 23, 1926, reprinted in *The Harlem Renaissance: A History and an Anthology,* ed. Cary D. Wintz (Maplecrest, N.Y.: Brandywine Press, 2003), 151.

35. Langston Hughes, "Song for a Dark Girl," in *Fine Clothes to the Jew* (New York: Knopf, 1927), reprinted in Wintz, *Harlem Renaissance,* 162.

36. Hughes, "Negro Artist," 151.

37. Rudolph Fisher, "The Caucasian Storms Harlem," *American Mercury,* August 1927, reprinted in *Double-Take: A Revisionist Harlem Renaissance Anthology,* ed. Venetria K. Patton and Maureen Honey (New Brunswick, N.J.: Rutgers University Press, 2001), 96.

38. *Shuffle Along,* a musical in two acts; book by Flournoy Miller and Aubrey Lyles; music by Eubie Blake; lyrics by Noble Sissle. Produced by Nikko Production Co. at the 63rd Street Music Hall, May 23, 1921.

39. Barry Singer, *Black and Blue: The Life and Lyrics of Andy Razaf* (New York: Schirmer, 1992), 100.

40. Lewis A. Erenberg, *Steppin' Out: New York Nightlife and the Transformation of American Culture, 1890–1930* (Chicago: University of Chicago Press, 1981), 257.

41. Mark Tucker, *Ellington: The Early Years* (Urbana: University of Illinois Press, 1991), 198.

42. Duke Ellington, "My Hunt for Song Titles," *Rhythm,* August 1933, quoted in John Edward Hasse, *Beyond Category: The Life and Genius of Duke Ellington* (New York: Simon & Schuster, 1993), 90–91.

43. Duke Ellington, quoted in Robert Levi, booklet notes to the Duke Ellington recording *Reminiscing in Tempo,* Columbia Legacy CK 48654 (1991), 6, quoted in Hasse, *Beyond Category,* 90.

44. Ellington, "My Hunt for Song Titles," 92.

45. The historiography on radio is vast, with many studies focusing on a single aspect, such as the development of radio technology, the radio industry, or radio programming. See Erik Barnouw, *A Tower in Babel: A History of Radio Broadcasting in the United States to 1933* (New York: Oxford University Press, 1966); Tom Lewis, *Empire of the Air: The Men Who Made Radio* (New York: Edward Burlingame Books/HarperCollins, 1991); Susan Douglas, *The Invention of American Broadcasting, 1899–1922* (Baltimore: Johns Hopkins University Press, 1987); Robert W. McChesney, *Telecommunications, Mass Media,*

and Democracy: The Battle for the Control of U.S. Broadcasting, 1928–1935 (New York: Oxford University Press, 1993); Michele Hilmes, *Radio Voices: American Broadcasting, 1922–1952* (Minneapolis: University of Minnesota Press, 1977); J. Fred MacDonald, *Don't Touch That Dial! Radio Programming in American Life from 1920 to 1960* (Chicago: Nelson-Hall, 1979); Susan Smulyan, *Selling Radio: The Commercialization of American Broadcasting, 1920–1934* (Washington, D.C.: Smithsonian Institution Press, 1994); and Daniel J. Czitrom, *Media and the American Mind: From Morse to McLuhan* (Chapel Hill: University of North Carolina Press, 1982).

46. Frederick V. Hunt, *Electroacoustics: The Analysis of Transduction, and Its Historical Background* (New York: American Institute of Physics, for the Acoustical Society of America, 1982), 81.

47. John P. Wolkonowicz, "The Philco Corporation: Historical Review and Strategic Analysis, 1892–1961" (master's thesis, Massachusetts Institute of Technology, 1981), 10.

48. For a fuller explanation of the court cases and their consequences, see Jora R. Minasian, "The Political Economy of Broadcasting in the 1920s," *Journal of Law and Economics* 12, no. 2 (October 1969): 391–403.

49. For more on the Radio Act of 1927, see Louise Benjamin, "Working It Out Together: Radio Policy from Hoover to the Radio Act of 1927," *Journal of Broadcasting and Electronic Media* 42, no. 2 (1998): 221–236; and Mark Goodman and Mark Gring, "The Ideological Fight over Creation of the Federal Radio Commission in 1927," *Journalism History* 26, no. 3 (2000): 117–124.

50. Lewis, *Empire of the Air,* 181.

51. Guglielmo Marconi, "Where Is Radio Going?" *Saturday Evening Post,* December 3, 1927, 48.

52. "Electioneering on the Air," *New Republic,* September 3, 1924, 9.

53. Virgil E. Dickson, quoted in Clayton R. Koppes, "The Social Destiny of Radio: Hope and Disillusionment in the 1920s," *South Atlantic Quarterly* 68 (1969): 367.

54. Fritz Reiner, quoted in Koppes, "Social Destiny of Radio," 367.

55. For a fuller discussion of the perceived potential of radio in the early 1920s, see Koppes, "Social Destiny of Radio," 363–376.

56. Robert W. McChesney, "Media and Democracy: The Emergence of Commercial Broadcasting in the United States, 1927–1935," *OAH Magazine of History,* Spring 1992, 34–40.

57. Smulyan, *Selling Radio,* 68.

58. For more on independent radio in Chicago in the early 1920s, see Lizabeth Cohen, "Encountering Mass Culture at the Grassroots: The Experience of Chicago Workers in the 1920s," *American Quarterly* 41, no. 1 (March 1989): 6–33; and Derek W. Vaillant, "Sounds of Whiteness: Local Radio, Racial Formation, and Public Culture in Chicago, 1921–1935," *American Quarterly* 54, no. 1 (March 2002): 25–66.

59. Vaillant, "Sounds of Whiteness," 52.

60. "Radiocasting on a National Scale," *Literary Digest,* October 2, 1926, 13.

61. Quoted in *Literary Digest,* October 2, 1926, 13.

62. Quoted in *Literary Digest,* October 2, 1926, 13.

63. Melvin Ely, *The Adventures of Amos 'n' Andy: A Social History of an American Phenomenon* (Charlottesville: University Press of Virginia, 1991), 55.

64. For more detail on the creation and marketing of *Sam 'n' Henry,* see Ely, *Adventures of Amos 'n' Andy.*

65. Vaillant, "Sounds of Whiteness," 38.

66. Edgar H. Felix, *Using Radio in Sales Promotion: A Book for Advertisers, Station Managers, and Broadcasting Artists* (New York: McGraw-Hill, 1927), 1. Henceforth cited in text.

67. For a fuller discussion of these seven characteristics, see Felix, *Using Radio in Sales Promotion,* 98–105.

CONCLUSION. THE SEARCH FOR AMERICAN CULTURE

1. H. H. Hemming and Doris Hemming, translator's introduction to André Siegfried, *America Comes of Age: A French Analysis,* trans. H. H. Hemming and Doris Hemming (New York: Harcourt, Brace, 1927), vi.

2. Siegfried, *America Comes of Age,* 348. Henceforth cited in text.

3. Walter Lippmann, "Empire: The Days of Our Nonage Are Over," in *Men of Destiny* (New York: Macmillan, 1927), 215. Henceforth cited in text.

4. Edith Wharton, *Twilight Sleep* (New York: Scribner, 1927; repr., 1997), 116–117. Citations are to the 1997 edition.

5. Barbara Haskell, *Charles Demuth* (New York: Whitney Museum of American Art, in association with Harry N. Abrams, 1987), 195.

6. Charles Demuth to Alfred Stieglitz, August 15, 1927, quoted in Haskell, *Charles Demuth,* 195.

7. Haskell, *Charles Demuth,* 198.

Bibliography

Allen, Frederick Lewis. *Only Yesterday: An Informal History of the 1920s.*
New York: Harper & Row, 1931.

Antheil, George. *Bad Boy of Music.* Hollywood, Calif.: Samuel French, 1990.

Armstrong, Louis. *Louis Armstrong: In His Own Words.* Edited by Thomas
Brothers. New York: Oxford University Press, 1999.

Baker, Houston A., Jr. *Modernism and the Harlem Renaissance.* Chicago:
University of Chicago Press, 1987.

Barnouw, Erik. *A Tower in Babel: A History of Radio Broadcasting in the
United States to 1933.* New York: Oxford University Press, 1966.

Barron, Hal. *Mixed Harvest: The Second Great Transformation in the Rural
North, 1870–1930.* Chapel Hill: University of North Carolina Press, 1997.

Barry, John M. *Rising Tide: The Great Mississippi Flood of 1927 and How It
Changed America.* New York: Simon & Schuster, 1997.

Barton, Bruce. *What Can a Man Believe?* Indianapolis, Ind.: Bobbs-Merrill,
1927.

Batchelor, Ray. *Henry Ford: Mass Production, Modernism and Design.*
Manchester, England: Manchester University Press, 1994.

Beard, Charles A., and Mary R. Beard. *The Rise of American Civilization.*
New York: Macmillan, 1927; rev. and enlarged edition, two volumes in
one, 1933.

Beaton, Welford. "Industry Fashioning Weapon of Defense." *Film Spectator*
3, no. 7 (May 28, 1927): 3.

Benjamin, Louise. "Working It Out Together: Radio Policy from Hoover to
the Radio Act of 1927." *Journal of Broadcasting and Electronic Media* 42,
no. 2 (1998): 221–236.

Bent, Silas. "The Art of Ballyhoo." *Harper's Monthly,* September 1927, 485–
494.

Berg, A. Scott. *Lindbergh.* New York: G. P. Putnam's Sons, 1998.

Bergreen, Laurence. *Look Now, Pay Later: The Rise of Network Broadcasting.*
Garden City, N.Y.: Doubleday, 1980.

———. *Louis Armstrong: An Extravagant Life.* New York: Broadway Books,
1997.

Berliner, Louise. *Texas Guinan: Queen of the Night Clubs.* Austin: University of Texas Press, 1993.

Berrett, Joshua. *Louis Armstrong and Paul Whiteman: Two Kings of Jazz.* New Haven: Yale University Press, 2004.

Birns, Nicholas. "Building the Cathedral: Imagination, Christianity, and Progress in Willa Cather's *Death Comes for the Archbishop.*" *Religion and the Arts: A Journal from Boston College* 3, no. 1 (1999): 1–19.

Brazil, John R. "Murder Trials, Murder, and Twenties America." *American Quarterly* 33, no. 2 (Summer 1981): 163–184.

Britton, Nan. *Honesty or Politics.* New York: Elizabeth Ann Guild, 1932.

———. *The President's Daughter.* New York: Elizabeth Ann Guild, 1927.

Bromley, Dorothy Dunbar. "Feminist—New Style." *Harper's Monthly,* October 1927, 552–560.

Brownlow, Kevin. *The Parade's Gone By . . . .* New York: Alfred A. Knopf, 1968.

Carney, Court. *Cuttin' Up: How Early Jazz Got America's Ear.* Lawrence: University Press of Kansas, 2009.

Carter, Paul A. *The Twenties in America.* New York: Thomas Y. Crowell, 1968.

Cather, Willa. *Death Comes for the Archbishop.* New York: Alfred A. Knopf, 1927. Reprint, New York: Vintage Classics, 1990.

———. *On Writing.* New York: Alfred A. Knopf, 1949.

Chase, Stuart, and F. J. Schlink. *Your Money's Worth: A Study in the Waste of the Consumer's Dollar.* New York: Macmillan, 1927.

Churchill, Allen. *The Year the World Went Mad.* New York: Thomas Y. Crowell, 1960.

Clements, Kendrick A. *Hoover, Conservation, and Consumerism: Engineering the Good Life.* Lawrence: University Press of Kansas, 2000.

Cohen, Lizabeth. "Encountering Mass Culture at the Grassroots: The Experience of Chicago Workers in the 1920s." *American Quarterly* 41, no. 1 (March 1989): 6–33.

———. *Making a New Deal: Industrial Workers in Chicago, 1919–1939.* Cambridge: Cambridge University Press, 1991.

Conroy, Stephen S. "Sinclair Lewis's Sociological Imagination." *American Literature* 42, no. 3 (November 1970): 348–362.

Cook, Alistair. *Douglas Fairbanks: The Making of a Screen Character.* New York: Museum of Modern Art, 1940.

Coolidge, Calvin. *Have Faith in Massachusetts: A Collection of Speeches and Messages.* New York: Houghton Mifflin, 1919.

Cott, Nancy F. *The Grounding of Modern Feminism.* New Haven: Yale University Press, 1987.

Cowley, Malcolm. *Exile's Return: A Literary Odyssey of the 1920s.* New York: Viking Penguin, 1951.

———. *A Second Flowering: Works and Days of the Lost Generation.* New York: Viking Penguin, 1973.

Creamer, Robert W. *Babe: The Legend Comes to Life.* New York: Simon & Schuster, 1974.

Czitrom, Daniel J. *Media and the American Mind: From Morse to McLuhan.* Chapel Hill: University of North Carolina Press, 1982.

Daniel, Pete. *Breaking the Land: The Transformation of Cotton, Tobacco, and Rice Cultures since 1880.* Urbana: University of Illinois Press, 1985.

———. *Deep'n as It Come: The 1927 Mississippi River Flood.* Fayetteville: University of Arkansas Press, 1996.

———. *The Shadow of Slavery: Peonage in the South, 1901–1969.* Urbana: University of Illinois Press, 1972.

———. *Standing at the Crossroads: Southern Life in the Twentieth Century.* New York: Hill & Wang, 1986.

Danzig, Allison, and Peter Brandwein, eds. *Sport's Golden Age: A Close-Up of the Fabulous Twenties.* New York: Harper & Brothers, 1948.

Dawson, James P. "Boxing." In *Sport's Golden Age: A Close-Up of the Fabulous Twenties,* ed. Allison Danzig and Peter Brandwein, 38–85. New York: Harper & Brothers, 1948.

Douglas, Susan. *The Invention of American Broadcasting, 1899–1922.* Baltimore: Johns Hopkins University Press, 1987.

Dumenil, Lynn. *The Modern Temper: American Culture and Society in the 1920s.* New York: Hill & Wang, 1995.

"Electioneering on the Air." *New Republic,* September 3, 1924, 9.

Ellington, Duke. *Music Is My Mistress.* New York: Da Capo Press, 1973.

Ely, Melvin. *The Adventures of Amos 'n' Andy: A Social History of an American Phenomenon.* Charlottesville: University Press of Virginia, 1991.

Erenberg, Lewis A. *Steppin' Out: New York Nightlife and the Transformation of American Culture, 1890–1930.* Chicago: University of Chicago Press, 1981.

Etherington-Smith, Meredith, and Jeremy Pilcher. *The "It" Girls: Lucy, Lady Duff Gordon, the Couturiere "Lucille," and Elinor Glyn, Romantic Novelist.* London: Hamish House, 1986.

Everson, William K. *American Silent Film.* New York: Oxford University Press, 1978.

Fass, Paula S. *The Damned and the Beautiful: American Youth in the 1920s.* New York: Oxford University Press, 1977.

Fearon, Peter. *War, Prosperity and Depression: The U.S. Economy, 1917–1945.* Lawrence: University Press of Kansas, 1987.

Felix, David. *Protest: Sacco-Vanzetti and the Intellectuals.* Bloomington: Indiana University Press, 1965.

Felix, Edgar H. *Using Radio in Sales Promotion: A Book for Advertisers, Station Managers, and Broadcasting Artists.* New York: McGraw-Hill, 1927.

Ferber, Edna. *Show Boat.* New York: Book League of America, 1926.

Ferrell, Robert H. *The Strange Deaths of President Harding.* Columbia: University of Missouri Press, 1996.

The Final Report of the Colored Advisory Commission Appointed to Cooperate with the American National Red Cross and the President's Committee on Relief Work in the Mississippi Valley Flood Disaster of 1927. Washington, D.C.: American National Red Cross, 1929.

"The Flood, the Red Cross, and the National Guard." *Crisis,* January 1928, 5–7, 26, 28.

Floyd, Samuel A., Jr., ed. *Black Music in the Harlem Renaissance: A Collection of Essays.* New York: Greenwood Press, 1990.

Ford, Henry. *My Life and Work.* New York: Doubleday, Page, 1923.

Fox, Richard Wrightman, and T. J. Jackson Lears, eds. *The Culture of Consumption: Critical Essays in American History, 1880–1980.* New York: Pantheon Books, 1983.

Frankfurter, Felix. "The Case of Sacco and Vanzetti." *Atlantic Monthly,* March 1927, 409–432.

Fried, Richard M. *The Man Everybody Knew: Bruce Barton and the Making of Modern America.* Chicago: Ivan R. Dee, 2005.

Gallico, Paul. *The Golden People.* New York: Doubleday, 1965.

Glyn, Elinor. *It.* New York: Bantam, 1978.

Goldberg, David J. *Discontented America: The United States in the 1920s.* Baltimore: Johns Hopkins University Press, 1999.

Goodman, Mark, and Mark Gring. "The Ideological Fight over Creation of the Federal Radio Commission in 1927." *Journalism History* 26, no. 3 (2000): 117–124.

Gorn, Elliott J. "The Manassa Mauler and the Fighting Marine: An Interpretation of the Dempsy-Tunney Fights." *Journal of American Studies* 19 (1985): 27–47.

Gray, Judd. *Doomed Ship: The Autobiography of Judd Gray, Prepared for Publication by His Sister Margaret Gray*. New York: Horace Liveright, 1928.

Griffith, Jean C. "'Lita Is—Jazz': The Harlem Renaissance, Cabaret Culture, and Racial Amalgamation in Edith Wharton's *Twilight Sleep*." *Studies in the Novel* 38, no. 1 (Spring 2006): 74–94.

Grossman, James R. *Land of Hope: Chicago, Black Southerners, and the Great Migration*. Chicago: University of Chicago Press, 1989.

Hamilton, J. G. de Roulhac. *Henry Ford: The Man, the Worker, the Citizen*. New York: Henry Holt, 1927.

Haskell, Barbara. *Charles Demuth*. New York: Whitney Museum of American Art, in association with Harry N. Abrams, 1987.

Haskins, Jim. *The Cotton Club*. New York: Random House, 1977.

Hasse, John Edward. *Beyond Category: The Life and Genius of Duke Ellington*. New York: Simon & Schuster, 1993.

Haugen, Einar. *Ole Edvart Rolvaag*. Boston: Twayne, 1983.

Hawley, Ellis W. *The Great War and the Search for a Modern Order: A History of the American People and Their Institutions, 1917–1933*. Prospect Heights, Ill.: Waveland Press, 1992.

———. *Herbert Hoover as Secretary of Commerce: Studies in New Era Thought and Practice*. Iowa City: University of Iowa Press, 1981.

Haytock, Jennifer. "Marriage and Modernism in Edith Wharton's *Twilight Sleep*." *Legacy* 19, no. 2 (2002): 216–229.

Heap, Jane. "Machine-Age Exposition." In *The Machine-Age Exposition Exhibit Catalogue*, 36–37. New York: Little Review, 1927.

Heimer, Mel. *The Long Count*. New York: Atheneum, 1969.

Herbst, Josephine. "A Year of Disgrace." In *The Starched Blue Sky of Spain, and Other Memoirs*, 53–98. Boston: Northeastern University Press, 1999.

Herndon, Booton. *Mary Pickford and Douglas Fairbanks: The Most Popular Couple the World Has Ever Known*. New York: W. W. Norton, 1977.

Hilmes, Michele. *Radio Voices: American Broadcasting, 1922–1952*. Minneapolis: University of Minnesota Press, 1997.

Hofstadter, Richard. *The Progressive Historians: Turner, Beard, Parrington*. New York: Alfred A. Knopf, 1968.

Holley, Donald. *The Second Great Emancipation: The Mechanical Cotton Picker, Black Migration, and How They Shaped the Modern South*. Fayetteville: University of Arkansas Press, 2000.

Hoover, Herbert. *The Memoirs of Herbert Hoover: The Cabinet and the Presidency, 1920–1933*. New York: Macmillan, 1952.

Hounshell, David A. *From the American System to Mass Production, 1800–1932: The Development of Manufacturing Technology in the United States*. Baltimore: Johns Hopkins University Press, 1984.

Huggins, Nathan Irvin. *Harlem Renaissance*. New York: Oxford University Press, 1971.

———, ed. *Voices from the Harlem Renaissance*. New York: Oxford University Press, 1976.

Hunt, Frederick V. *Electroacoustics: The Analysis of Transduction, and Its Historical Background*. New York: American Institute of Physics, for the Acoustical Society of America, 1982.

Inabinett, Mark. *Grantland Rice and His Heroes: The Sportswriter as Mythmaker in the 1920s*. Knoxville: University of Tennessee Press, 1994.

Jacob, Mary Jane, and Linda Downs. *The Rouge: The Image of Industry in the Art of Charles Sheeler and Diego Rivera*. Detroit: Detroit Institute of Arts, 1978.

Johnson, Ira. *Glenway Wescott: The Paradox of Voice*. Port Washington, N.Y.: National University Publications, 1971.

Johnson, James Weldon. *God's Trombones: Seven Negro Sermons in Verse*. 1927. Reprint, New York: Viking Penguin, 1990.

Joughin, G. Louis, and Edmund M. Morgan. *The Legacy of Sacco and Vanzetti*. New York: Harcourt, Brace, 1948.

Kahn, Roger. *A Flame of Pure Fire: Jack Dempsey and the Roaring '20s*. New York: Harcourt Brace, 1999.

Karnes, David. "The Glamorous Crowd: Hollywood Movie Premieres between the Wars." *American Quarterly* 38, no. 4 (Autumn 1986): 553–572.

Kobler, John. *The Trial of Ruth Snyder and Judd Gray*. New York: Doubleday, Doran, 1938.

Koppes, Clayton R. "The Social Destiny of Radio: Hope and Disillusionment in the 1920s." *South Atlantic Quarterly* 68 (1969): 363–376.

Kreuger, Miles. *Show Boat: The Story of a Classic American Musical.* New York: Da Capo Press, 1977.

Lacey, Robert. *Ford: The Men and the Machine.* Boston: Little, Brown, 1986.

Larsen, Charles. *The Good Fight: The Life and Times of Judge Ben B. Lindsey.* Chicago: Quadrangle Books, 1972.

Leach, William R. *Land of Desire: Merchants, Power, and the Rise of a New American Culture.* New York: Knopf Doubleday, 1994.

Lears, T. J. Jackson. *No Place of Grace: Antimodernism and the Transformation of American Culture, 1880–1920.* Chicago: University of Chicago Press, 1994.

Leighton, Isabel, ed. *The Aspirin Age, 1919–1941.* New York: Simon & Schuster, 1949.

Leinwald, Gerald. *1927: High Tide of the Twenties.* New York: Four Walls Eight Windows, 2001.

Levine, Lawrence W. "Progress and Nostalgia: The Self Image of the Nineteen Twenties." In *The Unpredictable Past: Explorations in American Cultural History,* 189–205. New York: Oxford University Press, 1993.

Lewis, David Levering. *When Harlem Was in Vogue.* New York: Alfred A. Knopf, 1981.

Lewis, Sinclair. *Elmer Gantry.* New York: Harcourt, Brace, 1927.

Lewis, Tom. *Empire of the Air: The Men Who Made Radio.* New York: Edward Burlingame Books/HarperCollins, 1991.

Lindbergh, Charles A. *Autobiography of Values.* New York: Harcourt Brace Jovanovich, 1976.

———. *The Spirit of St. Louis.* New York: Charles Scribner's Sons, 1953.

———. *We.* New York: G. P. Putnam's Sons, 1927.

Lindsey, Ben B., and Wainwright Evans. *The Companionate Marriage.* New York: Boni & Liveright, 1927.

Lippmann, Walter. "Blazing Publicity: Why We Know So Much about 'Peaches' Browning, Valentino, Lindbergh and Queen Marie." 1927. In *Vanity Fair: Selections from America's Most Memorable Magazine; A Cavalcade of the 1920s and 1930s,* ed. Cleveland Armory and Frederic Bradlee, 121–122. New York: Viking, 1960.

———. *Men of Destiny.* New York: Macmillan, 1927.

Lipsyte, Robert. *SportsWorld: An American Dreamland*. New York: Quadrangle/New York Times Book Company, 1975.

Lisio, Donald J. *Hoover, Blacks, and Lily-Whites: A Study of Southern Strategies*. Chapel Hill: University of North Carolina Press, 1985.

Lloyd, Craig. *Aggressive Introvert: A Study of Herbert Hoover and Public Relations Management, 1912–1932*. Columbus: Ohio State University Press, 1972.

Locke, Alain, ed. *The New Negro*. New York: Albert & Charles Boni, 1925. Reprint, New York: Touchstone, 1997.

Lohof, Bruce. "Herbert Hoover, Spokesman of Humane Efficiency: The Mississippi Flood of 1927." *American Quarterly* 22, no. 3 (Autumn 1970): 690–700.

Lozowick, Louis. "The Americanization of Art." In *The Machine-Age Exposition Exhibit Catalogue*, 18–19. New York: Little Review, 1927.

Lucic, Karen. *Charles Sheeler and the Cult of the Machine*. London: Reaktion Books, 1991.

MacCann, Richard Dyer. *Films of the 1920s*. Lanham, Md.: Scarecrow Press, 1996.

MacDonald, J. Fred. *Don't Touch That Dial! Radio Programming in American Life from 1920 to 1960*. Chicago: Nelson-Hall, 1979.

The Machine Age Exposition Exhibit Catalogue. New York: Little Review, 1927.

Malvasi, Mark G. *The Unregenerate South: The Agrarian Thought of John Crowe Ransom, Allen Tate, and Donald Davidson*. Baton Rouge: Louisiana State University Press, 1997.

Mantle, Burns, ed. *The Best Plays of 1926–1927*. New York: Dodd, Mead, 1927.

———. *The Best Plays of 1927–1928*. New York: Dodd, Mead, 1928.

Marcell, David W. "Charles Beard: Civilization and the Revolt against Empiricism." *American Quarterly* 21, no. 1 (Spring 1969): 65–86.

Marchand, Roland. *Advertising the American Dream: Making Way for Modernity, 1920–1940*. Berkeley and Los Angeles: University of California Press, 1985.

Marconi, Guglielmo. "Where Is Radio Going?" *Saturday Evening Post*, December 3, 1927, 48.

May, Elaine Tyler. *Great Expectations: Marriage and Divorce in Post-Victorian America*. Chicago: University of Chicago Press, 1980.

May, Lary. *Screening Out the Past: The Birth of Mass Culture and the Motion Picture Industry.* Chicago: University of Chicago Press, 1980.

McChesney, Robert W. "Media and Democracy: The Emergence of Commercial Broadcasting in the United States, 1927–1935." *OAH Magazine of History,* Spring 1992, 34–40.

———. *Telecommunications, Mass Media, and Democracy: The Battle for the Control of U.S. Broadcasting, 1928–1935.* New York: Oxford University Press, 1993.

McGovern, Charles F. *Sold American: Consumption and Citizenship, 1890–1945.* Chapel Hill: University of North Carolina Press, 2006.

Merz, Charles. "Bigger and Better Murders." *Harper's Monthly,* August 1927, 338–343.

Metz, Robert. *CBS: Reflections in a Bloodshot Eye.* Chicago: Playboy Press, 1975.

Middleton, Jo Ann. *Willa Cather's Modernism: A Study of Style and Technique.* Cranbury, N.J.: Associated University Presses, 1990.

Miller, Nathan. *New World Coming: The 1920s and the Making of Modern America.* New York: Scribner, 2003.

Minasian, Jora R. "The Political Economy of Broadcasting in the 1920s." *Journal of Law and Economics* 12, no. 2 (October 1969): 391–403.

The Mississippi Valley Flood Disaster of 1927: Official Report of the Relief Operations. Washington, D.C.: American National Red Cross, 1928.

Moseley, Ann. *Ole Edvart Rolvaag.* Western Writer Series. Boise, Idaho: Boise State University, 1987.

Munden, Kenneth W., executive ed. *The American Film Institute Catalog of Motion Pictures Produced in the United States: Feature Films, 1921–1930.* New York: R. R. Bowker, 1971.

Nash, Roderick. *The Nervous Generations: American Thought, 1917–1930.* Chicago: Ivan R. Dee, 1990.

Nye, David E. *Henry Ford: "Ignorant Idealist."* Port Washington, N.Y.: National University Publications, 1979.

Ogren, Kathy J. *The Jazz Revolution: Twenties America and the Meaning of Jazz.* New York: Oxford University Press, 1989.

Oriard, Michael. *King Football: Sport and Spectacle in the Golden Age of Radio and Newsreels, Movies and Magazines, the Weekly and the Daily Press.* Chapel Hill: University of North Carolina Press, 2001.

Orvell, Miles. "Inspired by Science and the Modern: Precisionism and

American Culture." In *Precisionism in America, 1915–1941: Reordering Reality*. New York: Harry N. Abrams, 1994.

Osbourne, Robert. *50 Golden Years of Oscar: The Official History of the Academy of Motion Picture Arts and Sciences*. Beverly Hills, Calif.: Academy of Motion Picture Arts and Sciences, 1979.

Ostransky, Leroy. *Jazz City: The Impact of Our Cities on the Development of Jazz*. Englewood Cliffs, N.J.: Prentice-Hall, 1978.

Patton, Venetria K., and Maureen Honey, eds. *Double-Take: A Revisionist Harlem Renaissance Anthology*. New Brunswick, N.J.: Rutgers University Press, 2001.

Peretti, Burton W. *Jazz in American Culture*. Chicago: Ivan R. Dee, 1997.

Ponce de Leon, Charles L. *Self-Exposure: Human Interest Journalism and the Emergence of Celebrity in America, 1890–1940*. Chapel Hill: University of North Carolina Press, 2002.

The Precisionist View in American Art. Minneapolis, Minn.: Walker Art Center, 1960.

"Radiocasting on a National Scale." *Literary Digest,* October 2, 1926, 13.

Raphaelson, Sampson. *The Jazz Singer*. Edited by Robert L. Carringer. Madison: University of Wisconsin Press, 1979.

Rayno, Don. *Paul Whiteman: Pioneer in American Music*. Vol. 1, *1890–1930*. Lanham, Md.: Scarecrow Press, 2003.

Reid, Margaret. "Has the Flapper Changed?" *Motion Picture,* July 1927, 28–29, 104.

Rice, Grantland. "The Golden Panorama." In *Sport's Golden Age: A Close-Up of the Fabulous Twenties,* ed. Allison Danzig and Peter Brandwein, 1–7. New York: Harper & Brothers, 1948.

———. *The Tumult and the Shouting: My Life in Sport*. New York: A. S. Barnes, 1954.

Roberts, Randy. *Jack Dempsey: The Manassa Mauler*. Baton Rouge: Louisiana State University Press, 1979.

Robertson, John G. *The Babe Chases 60: That Fabulous 1927 Season, Home Run by Home Run*. Jefferson, N.C.: McFarland, 1999.

Rogers, J. A. "Jazz at Home." In *The New Negro,* ed. Alain Locke, 216–224. New York: Albert & Charles Boni, 1925. Reprint, New York: Touchstone, 1997.

Rogin, Michael. "Blackface, White Noise: The Jewish Jazz Singer Finds His Voice." *Critical Inquiry* 18 (Spring 1992): 417–453.

Rolvaag, O. E. *Giants in the Earth: A Saga of the Prairie*. New York: Harper & Brothers, 1927.

Ross, Dorothy. "Grand Narrative in American Historical Writing: From Romance to Uncertainty." *American Historical Review* 100, no. 3 (June 1995): 651–677.

Rourke, Constance. *Charles Sheeler: Artist in the American Tradition*. New York: Harcourt, Brace, 1938.

Rueckert, William H. *Glenway Wescott*. New York: Twayne, 1965.

Runyon, Damon. "A Chilly-Looking Blonde and Her Paramour." In *These Were Our Years: A Panoramic and Nostalgic Look at American Life between the Two World Wars*, ed. Frank Brookhouser, 208–213. Garden City, N.Y.: Doubleday, 1959.

Sacco, Nicola, and Bartolomeo Vanzetti. *The Letters of Sacco and Vanzetti*. New York: Viking, 1928.

Sands, Pierre Norman. *A Historical Study of the Academy of Motion Picture Arts and Sciences (1927–1947)*. New York: Arno Press, 1973.

Sann, Paul. *The Lawless Decade: A Pictorial History of a Great American Transition; From the World War I Armistice and Prohibition to Repeal and the New Deal*. New York: Crown, 1957.

Schickel, Richard. *His Picture in the Papers: A Speculation on Celebrity in America, Based on the Life of Douglas Fairbanks, Sr.* New York: Charterhouse, 1973.

Schulberg, Budd. *Moving Pictures: Memories of a Hollywood Prince*. New York: Stein & Day, 1981.

Schultz, April. *Ethnicity on Parade: Inventing the Norwegian American through Celebration*. Amherst: University of Massachusetts Press, 1994.

———. "'The Pride of the Race Had Been Touched': The 1925 Norse-American Immigration Centennial and Ethnic Identity." *Journal of American History* 77, no. 4 (March 1991): 1265–1295.

Siegfried, André. *America Comes of Age: A French Analysis*. Translated by H. H. Hemming and Doris Hemming. New York: Harcourt, Brace, 1927.

Simonson, Harold P. *Prairies Within: The Tragic Trilogy of Ole Rolvaag*. Seattle: University of Washington Press, 1987.

Singer, Barry. *Black and Blue: The Life and Lyrics of Andy Razaf*. New York: Schirmer, 1992.

Smith, Terry. *Making the Modern: Industry, Art, and Design in America*. Chicago: University of Chicago Press, 1993.

Smulyan, Susan. *Selling Radio: The Commercialization of American Broadcasting, 1920–1934*. Washington, D.C.: Smithsonian Institution Press, 1994.

Sobol, Ken. *Babe Ruth and the American Dream*. New York: Ballantine Books, 1974.

Sperber, Murray. *Onward to Victory: The Crisis That Shaped College Sports*. New York: Henry Holt, 1998.

————. *Shake Down the Thunder: The Creation of Notre Dame Football*. New York: Henry Holt, 1993.

Starr, Kevin. *Material Dreams: Southern California through the 1920s*. New York: Oxford University Press, 1990.

Stenn, David. *Clara Bow: Runnin' Wild*. New York: Cooper Square Press, 2000.

Stevenson, Elizabeth. *Babbitts and Bohemians: From the Great War to the Great Depression*. Edison, N.J.: Transaction Books, 1997.

Strasser, Susan. *Satisfaction Guaranteed: The Making of the American Mass Market*. Washington, D.C.: Smithsonian Institution Press, 2004.

Susman, Warren I. *Culture as History: The Transformation of American Society in the Twentieth Century*. Washington, D.C.: Smithsonian Books, 2003.

Sward, Keith. *The Legend of Henry Ford*. New York: Atheneum, 1972.

Talmey, Allene. *Doug and Mary and Others*. New York: Macy-Masius, 1927.

Tedlow, Richard S. *New and Improved: The Story of Mass Marketing in America*. New York: Basic Books, 1990.

Tibbetts, John C., and James M. Welsh. *His Majesty the American: The Cinema of Douglas Fairbanks, Sr*. New York: A. S. Barnes, 1977.

Topp, Michael M. *The Sacco and Vanzetti Case: A Brief History with Documents*. New York: Bedford/St. Martin's, 2005.

Townsend, Peter. *Jazz in American Culture*. Jackson: University Press of Mississippi, 2000.

Trachtenberg, Leo. *The Wonder Team: The True Story of the Incomparable 1927 New York Yankees*. Bowling Green, Ohio: Bowling Green State University Popular Press, 1995.

Trani, Eugene P., and David L. Wilson. *The Presidency of Warren G. Harding*. Lawrence: Regents Press of Kansas, 1977.

Trimble, Patrick. "Babe Ruth: The Media Construction of a 1920's Sports Personality." *Colby Quarterly* 32, no. 1 (Spring 1996): 45–57.

Tsujimoto, Karen. *Images of America: Precisionist Painting and Modern Photography*. Seattle: University of Washington Press, 1982.

Tucker, Mark, ed. *The Duke Ellington Reader*. New York: Oxford University Press, 1993.

————. *Ellington: The Early Years*. Urbana: University of Illinois Press, 1991.

Tunney, Gene. "My Fights with Jack Dempsey." In *The Aspirin Age, 1919–1941*, ed. Isabel Leighton, 152–168. New York: Simon & Schuster, 1949.

Tygiel, Jules. *Past Time: Baseball as History*. New York: Oxford University Press, 2000.

Vaillant, Derek W. "Sounds of Whiteness: Local Radio, Racial Formation, and Public Culture in Chicago, 1921–1935." *American Quarterly* 54, no. 1 (March 2002): 25–66.

Voigt, David Quentin. *America through Baseball*. Chicago: Nelson-Hall, 1976.

Ward, John W. "The Meaning of Lindbergh's Flight." *American Quarterly* 10, no. 1 (Spring 1958): 3–16.

Watkins, Maurine. *"Chicago": With the Chicago Tribune Articles That Inspired It*. Edited and with an introduction by Thomas H. Pauley. Carbondale: Southern Illinois University Press, 1997.

Watterson, John Sayle. *College Football: History, Spectacle, Controversy*. Baltimore: Johns Hopkins University Press, 2000.

Wescott, Glenway. *The Grandmothers: A Family Portrait*. New York: Harper & Brothers, 1927. Reprint, Madison: University of Wisconsin Press, 1996.

Wharton, Edith. *Twilight Sleep*. 1927. Reprint, New York: Scribner, 1997.

White, G. Edward. *Creating the National Pastime: Baseball Transforms Itself, 1903–1953*. Princeton: Princeton University Press, 1996.

White, Walter. "The Negro and the Flood." *Nation*, June 22, 1927, 688–689.

Whiteman, Paul, and Mary Margaret McBride. *Jazz*. New York: J. H. Sears, 1926.

Wik, Reynold M. *Henry Ford and Grass-Roots America*. Ann Arbor: University of Michigan Press, 1972.

Wilson, Joan Hoff. *Herbert Hoover: Forgotten Progressive*. Boston: Little, Brown, 1975.

Wintz, Cary D., ed. *The Harlem Renaissance: A History and an Anthology*. Maplecrest, N.Y.: Brandywine Press, 2003.

Wolkonowicz, John P. "The Philco Corporation: Historical Review and Strategic Analysis, 1892–1961." Master's thesis, Massachusetts Institute of Technology, 1981.

Work, John Wesley. *Folk Song of the American Negro.* Nashville, Tenn.: Fisk University Press, 1915.

Yeh, Susan Fillin. "Charles Sheeler: Industry, Fashion, and the Vanguard." *Arts Magazine,* February 1980, 154–158.

Zimmerman, Jonathan. "'Each "Race" Could Have Its Heroes Sung': Ethnicity and the History Wars in the 1920s." *Journal of American History* 87, no. 1 (June 2000): 92–111.

Index